COLLABORATION AND WRITING

Open University Press
English, Language, and Education series
General Editor: Anthony Adams
Lecturer in Education, University of Cambridge

This series is concerned with all aspects of language in education from the primary school to the tertiary sector. Its authors are experienced educators who examine both principles and practice of English subject teaching and language across the curriculum in the context of current educational and societal developments.

TITLES IN THE SERIES

Narrative and Argument
Richard Andrews

Time for Drama
Roma Burgess and Pamela Gaudry

Computers and Literacy
Daniel Chandler and Stephen Marcus (eds.)

Readers, Texts, Teachers
Bill Corcoran and Emrys Evans (eds.)

Developing Response to Poetry
Patrick Dias and Michael Hayhoe

The Primary Language Book
Peter Dougill and Richard Knott

Children Talk About Books: Seeing Themselves as Readers
Donald Fry

Literary Theory and English Teaching
Peter Griffith

Assessing English
Brian Johnston

Lipservice: The Story of Talk in Schools
Pat Jones

The English Department in a Changing World
Richard Knott

Oracy Matters
Margaret MacLure, Terry Phillips and Andrew Wilkinson (eds.)

Teaching Literature for Examinations
Robert Protherough

Developing Response to Fiction
Robert Protherough

Microcomputers and the Language Arts
Brent Robinson

English Teaching from A–Z
Wayne Sawyer, Anthony Adams and Ken Watson

Reconstructing 'A' Level English
Patrick Scott

Collaboration and Writing
Morag Styles (ed.)

English Teaching in Perspective
Ken Watson

The Quality of Writing
Andrew Wilkinson

The Writing of Writing
Andrew Wilkinson (ed.)

COLLABORATION AND WRITING

EDITED BY
Morag Styles

Open University Press
Milton Keynes • Philàdelphia

Open University Press
12 Cofferidge Close
Stony Stratford
Milton Keynes MK11 1BY

and
242 Cherry Street
Philadelphia, PA 19106, USA

First Published 1989

Copyright © The Editor and Contributors 1989

All rights reserved. No part of this publication may be
reproduced, stored in a retrieval system or transmitted in
any form or by any means, without written permission from the
publisher.

British Library Cataloguing in Publication Data

Styles, Morag
  Collaboration and writing. – (English, language
  and education)
  1. Schools. Curriculum subjects: Creative
  writing. Teaching
  I. Title II. Series
  808'.042

  ISBN 0–335–09574–7 (pbk)

Library of Congress Cataloging-in-Publication Data

Collaboration and writing/[edited] by Morag Styles.
    p.   cm. – (English, language, and education series)
  Bibliography: p.
  Includes index.
  ISBN 0–335–09574–7
  1. English language – Composition and exercises – Study and
teaching. 2. Authorship – Collaboration.   I. Styles, Morag.
II. Series.
PE1404.C613   1989   89–32395
808'.042'07 – dc20   CIP

Photoset and printed in Great Britain by
Redwood Burn Limited, Trowbridge, Wiltshire

Contents

Acknowledgements	vii
List of contributors	ix
General editor's introduction	xi
1 **Setting the agenda** Morag Styles	1
Part One Children as writers	7
2 **'Mission to Hell'** Morag Styles with Jennie Dunn	9
3 **Discovering a need to write:** **the role of the teacher as collaborator** Gareth Davies	16
4 **Listening to children's writing** David Somerville	30
5 **Profiling in English:** **the potential for real pupil–teacher collaboration** **in assessment** Nick Brown	42
Part Two Cross-phase writing exchanges	55
6 **Four examples of cross-phase collaboration**	57
I *'Seven Up'* Edited by Morag Styles	57
II *Mapping our world* Cathy Pompe	62
III *Heroes and Heroines* Gabrielle Cliff Hodges	70
IV *Animation across the divide* Cathy Pompe	73

7 Collaboration at transition 79
'By pupils, for pupils': an alternative information booklet for incoming first years
Frances D. Findlay

Part Three Strategies promoting collaboration 91

8 Writing without a pencil 93
Gareth Davies
9 'Which Way Now?' 106
A whole-class collaboration to write a novel
Jo Southon
10 Children as critics 120
Mary Martin
11 'Hotel Beck' 133
Cathy Pompe

Part Four A community of writers 151

12 The school as a community of writers 153
Jennie Dunn
13 Talking and writing with parents and grandparents 165
Gabrielle Cliff Hodges
14 Stories and remembering 178
Mary Hilton

Part Five Endpiece 193

15 Teachers as collaborators 195
Morag Styles

Bibliography 203
Author Index 207
Subject Index 209

Acknowledgements

The authors would like to thank the following for their help in the writing of this book:

Tony Adams, who had faith in our enterprise and who made this satisfying end product possible.

Kate Oswald, who was not only a member of the Writing Group from its inception, but who helped plan and organize meetings, discussed key issues, read and commented on the first draft of the manuscript and generally guided our endeavours in innumerable important ways. We owe a lot to Kate and were only sorry that her new, challenging post made it impossible for her to contribute a chapter.

Myra Barrs, who visited us in discontented mood during the worst part of teachers' action and who tactfully and generously shared her expertise with us.

John Richmond, whose visit during the early stages of the project helped to sharpen our thinking and encouraged us to further efforts.

Eve Bearne, whose wisdom and experience of children and writing was inspirational and who kindly provided the final collaboration of the project – a written contribution.

Cambridgeshire LEA, for allowing us to draw on local pupils' writing.

Homerton College, who provided rooms to meet in and a small grant towards costs.

The National Writing Project, whose writings influenced us.

Our pupils, past and present, who make our attempts at understanding worthwhile, and who continue to challenge and reward us in the fascinating, exhausting and wonderful job of teaching!

NOTE: the following terms are used regularly in the text
juniors – children aged 7–11
infants – children aged 4/5–7
secondary pupils – aged 11–16/18
first-year juniors – aged 7–8

second-year juniors – aged 8–9 and so on
first-year secondary – aged 11–12 and so on
top juniors – aged 10–11
top infants – aged 6–7

In many instances the names of pupils have been changed to ensure anonymity.

List of contributors

Nick Brown is currently Head of English at Comberton Village College, an 11–16 Community College.

Gabrielle Cliff Hodges is Head of English at Ernulf Community College. At the time of writing she taught at Longsands Community College.

Gareth Davies taught at Kings Hedges Junior School at the time of writing and is now an advisory teacher for information technology.

Jennie Dunn is Deputy Head Teacher at St Paul's Primary School where she holds the Language post and runs the school bookshop.

Frances D. Findlay was Head of English at Neale-Wade Community College at the time of writing.

Mary Hilton teaches at the Grove Primary School where she has special responsibility for Language. Some of her work was carried out while she taught at Arbury Primary School.

Mary Martin is the Language Co-ordinator at Comberton Community College.

Cathy Pompe was a teacher at St Paul's Primary School at the time of writing. She is now working freelance on Media Education.

David Somerville is Deputy Head Teacher at Stapleford Primary School. At the time of writing he taught at Little Paxton Primary School, St Neots.

Jo Southon teaches English at Bottisham Village College.

Morag Styles is Language Co-ordinator at Homerton College, Cambridge.

General editor's introduction

Morag Styles is likely to be best known to teachers of English as an excellent and well-established editor of poetry anthologies such as *I Like That Stuff*, published by Cambridge University Press. She has done much to bring new and exciting poetry, from many cultural traditions, into the classroom, and primary teachers, in particular, will be aware of how much they and their pupils owe her in this respect.

She is also Language Co-ordinator at Homerton College, Cambridge, where she has recently established a Language Centre and where she is engaged in both initial and in-service work with primary teachers. This book grew out of her work in that respect. A glance at the list of contributors will reveal that all of them are teachers working in a variety of schools in the Cambridge area. In that respect it is itself evidence of its major theme – the way in which writing may be effectively developed through collaborative work. As well as a worthy book in its own right, *Collaboration and Writing* may stand as a record of collaborative in-service work developed over a period of years in which mutual expertise and trust developed among a group of teachers who came to work with each other and in each other's classrooms.

We need many more models of work of this kind, especially those which (like the present volume) bridge the stages of transition between periods of schooling. *Collaboration and Writing* spans a wide range of collaborative patterns in its component articles, spreading from the world of the junior school to that of grandparents. As the title indicates, the theoretical focus throughout is on the collaborative process leading to a finished product which usually, by its very nature, could not have been produced in any other way. Important questions of 'ownership' are, therefore, involved. I have argued elsewhere (in Daniel Chandler and Stephen Marcus (eds), *Computers and Literacy*, Open University Press, 1985) for the importance of redefining the notion of individual ownership of writing in an age when more and more writing is the product of collaborative work with a word processor, a point developed further in Gareth Davies's contribution to the present volume. We may, given this facility, in work up to and including the General Certificate of Secondary Education, increasingly begin to look forward to more active collaborations among children and their teachers, to what in this volume is strikingly called 'the school as a community of writers'. Apart from anything else, it seems likely that eight-year-olds who have been taught in the ways indicated here are unlikely to wish to work in individual isolation when they reach secondary school.

The book will be found to contain many examples and explorations of good practice, material that the classroom teacher can immediately take and use in the writing class. Much of the theory on which it is based is well established and sound: the need to provide real purposes and real (and varied) audiences for all kinds of writing. Much of the most exciting writing will, of course, grow naturally out of the pupils' own interests and the purposes that they have defined for themselves.

In line with this, one of the most influential developments in writing theory in recent years, associated especially with the names of Frank Smith and Donald Graves, has been the concept of conferencing – getting pupils to comment upon each other's work and enabling the teacher to act as a writing consultant, intervening at a formative stage in the work rather than operating as an evaluator working on the product alone. The emphasis has shifted to 'process writing' and this shift has been highly instrumental in the production of better and more willing writers among pupils. In the same spirit, although this book is concerned mainly and formally with writing, it goes into and beyond the writing process to look at the holistic nature of language activity and at the fruitful interaction of school with school and schools with community, an appropriate emphasis in Cambridgeshire which is, after all, where modern community education began with the work of Henry Morris.

Writing, as such, has been centrally placed on the educational map in recent years by the exciting work generated by the National Writing Project, much of which is shortly to be published by Nelson. The present volume is itself, at least in part, as Morag makes clear in her acknowledgements, one of the first published outcomes of the Project and Eve Bearne, who was especially influential in this respect, is now one of Morag's colleagues at Homerton College. One of the National Writing Project's main achievements was that of getting teachers to think about the writing process through practising it themselves, leading them to discover through direct experience the power and excitement that flowed through writing. In so doing it led them to discover how empowerment might be transmitted also to their pupils. By the time the present volume is in print it is likely that the Working Party under the Chairmanship of Professor Cox will have delivered itself of the national curriculum guidelines for English. It is to be hoped (as the interim report dealing with the primary phase published in November 1988 suggests) that the recommendations of the final report will be conceived with sufficient breadth to allow a recognition of the importance of seeing language always as a reciprocal activity: reading and writing (as with talking and listening) are essentially interrelated activities, so that successful writing entails a process that puts the writer frequently in the role of reader, and therefore critic, of his or her own work. In many of the collaborations described here this is exactly what was happening and what had been formally established in the writing situation – the young writers were readers and critics of their own and each other's work. The examples of pupils' work which are included may make us wish to think carefully about the possibilities in language work about talking in terms of 'stages of development' at ages 7, 11, 14 and 16. Above all, if we are to engage in the business of assessing such development it seems most important to involve pupils in the business of setting and assessing their own goals and progress, as suggested in Nick Brown's article and in Brian Johnston's *Assessing English* in this series.

Over the last four years a common theme has begun to emerge in many of the books in the *English, Language, and Education* series. It has been concerned with the need to enable students to develop as autonomous learners, to help them move from dependency to self-sufficiency in the classroom. Morag and her contributors continue this theme admirably and make the point throughout that such self-sufficiency should not be confused with narrow individualism.

Good writing grows out of the need to communicate, the expression of a felt concern over something that matters deeply and needs to be told to others. It was out of the excitement of what they were engaged with that the collaborative team represented here felt the need to write this book. It breathes the air of that involvement and sends the reader away moved by some of the excitement that the authors obviously felt as a result of their enterprise.

Anthony Adams

1 Setting the agenda

MORAG STYLES

> Learning is first and foremost a *process* – a continuous making and remaking of meanings in the lifelong enterprise of constructing a progressively more and more effective mental model of the world in which one lives. Learning is never complete. Furthermore, since this process is essentially interactive, it is more helpful for the apprentice learner to work with teachers who are themselves actively engaged in learning and willing to engage with their pupils in doing so than it is to be instructed and evaluated by those who apparently no longer have the need to engage in such processes themselves.
>
> Gordon Wells[1]

In February 1986, I wrote to a group of teacher colleagues inviting them to form a writing group, to take part in an informal investigation into whether children could encourage other children to write. Our intention was to produce materials where different forms of writing by children were introduced by their authors, stimulating the readers to 'have a go' themselves. We called the enterprise 'By Kids, For Kids'. The National Writing Project had recently been set up and we thought we might draw on their expertise.

The group I had gathered together was made up of teachers all well known to me. Several of our number had recently been (mature) postgraduate students with whom I had worked closely. The others were primary or secondary English teachers, including three Heads of English and an advisory teacher. We met regularly for two years, only losing three members to other pressing concerns. Of the remaining 11, all have contributed at least one chapter to this book. The twelfth member, Kate Oswald (now English Inspector) has been closely involved in the entire project.

The project began when we asked our various pupils to write about themselves. We chose autobiography as it is a familiar and accessible mode of writing for all age groups. Nobody tackled the task by attempting the obvious diary- or journal-type writing. Each teacher found a different angle into autobiographical writing and the results were fascinating. We formed mini-groups (mixed phase) to compare notes and to start to explore how our pupils could help one another find inroads into various forms of writing.

As we continued to meet our original aims became less interesting to us than the new ideas generated by exchanges between members of the group. This did not worry me. I thought it likely that our concerns would shift as our 'research' developed and that we could not necessarily know at the beginning where we would end. It would be important, however, not to go down too many blind alleys and to retain a clear focus. Gradually, we became convinced that it would *not* be worthwhile to attempt to produce classroom materials to promote writing even 'by kids, for kids'. However worthy our intentions, packaged materials would inevitably become 'textbook fodder' and we were all cynical about the artificial and ineffectual nature of such ways of encouraging writing. Our trials had only served to reinforce our beliefs about the importance of real writing for real purposes *and* the crucial role of the teacher as facilitator, editor, typist, publisher and sympathetic critic. And as we experimented with children writing for others within and across schools, the notion of audience became a central concern.

Around that time, I took part in a conference where I talked to Myra Barrs, Director of the Centre for Language in Primary Education, ILEA. I told her what we were doing and how 'audience' was becoming our focus. Myra said something to the effect that we should not get too hooked on audience. Real writing clearly involves real readership, but having got that out of the way, it was other issues relating to writing that we should be concentrating on. Looking back, I cannot remember Myra's exact words (and may be misquoting her), but I know this discussion shaped my future thinking. When I shared these ideas with the group Nick Brown remarked casually that *collaboration* now seemed to be at the core of our concerns. He was right, of course. Someone had put into words what we had all been struggling to appreciate: that our collaborations together and the collaborative exchanges between pupils which we had set up were now the core of our investigations.

Before I go any further I had better define what I mean by 'collaboration'. John Richmond provides a useful definition in *About Writing*: collaboration

> doesn't usually mean a group of children writing the same piece at the same time, though sometimes that can work. It usually means one of two (overlapping) things. Children need to consult with each other about writing in progress, or just completed, to ask questions and offer advice, first about content and organisation of a piece, then about its control of conventions. And children need opportunities to write within the context of a group activity, whether that be the compilation of a display of research or a radio script, or a magazine or a brochure about the school – any activity which involves planning, allocation of tasks, mutual support and criticism, leading to a product where individuals can see their own contributions within a larger whole.[2]

Frank Smith offers further insights on the nature of collaborative learning in his booklet *Collaboration in the Classroom*.[3] Smith talks about the naturalness of collaborative learning in the world outside school where the more experienced (parents, grandparents, older siblings) spontaneously help the less experienced to talk, swim, walk, read, and so on. For example, experienced speakers help babies to talk by replying to them, often repeating what they say, elaborating on their utterances and providing a rich model of spoken language. Smith describes this process as 'continual, effortless and inconspicuous to learner and collaborator alike'. He also draws on George Miller's work on language[4] in which the author writes of a 'spontaneous apprenticeship' between the young learner and the more experienced collaborator. Smith goes on to suggest that most schools (and universities and colleges of education) are at present inhospitable places for promoting collaborative learning. Smith maintains that schools should become environments where individuals can help each other in a self-sustaining fashion, enjoy the companionship and gain confidence from working together.

To return to John Richmond for a moment; in the same issue of the National Writing Project Newsletter as mentioned above[5] he drew a simple model that reflected the aims and intentions of our project (Figure 1.1). Our writing group had been grappling with ways of working where pupils' endeavours were respected, writing tasks generated from meaningful contexts, teachers writing alongside pupils, parents and other members of their community drawn into writing ventures, pupils' writing published and read by a real audience; and, of course, all sorts of ways and means of pupils writing with and for each other. It was reassuring to find the intuitive, spontaneous direction we had taken given shape and definition in this way.

We began to make a rough list of what we wanted to find out:

- Who would collaborate with whom on writing, given a free choice?
- Would the age of the pupils make a difference in the choice of collaborative partners?
- At what age might differentiation occur in single-sex and mixed-sex collaboration?

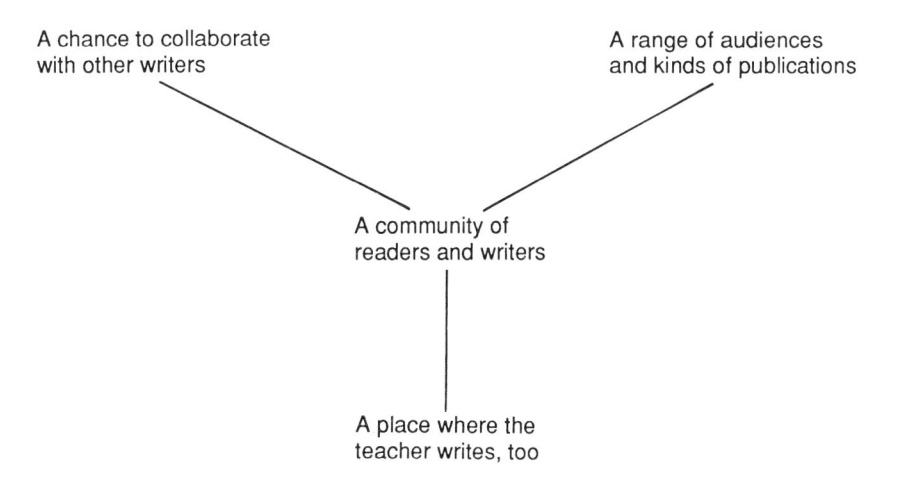

```
A chance to collaborate              A range of audiences
with other writers                   and kinds of publications
            \                       /
             \                     /
              \                   /
               A community of
               readers and writers
                      |
                      |
               A place where the
               teacher writes, too
```

Figure 1.1 Pupils' writing is ...

- What happened when pairs, small groups, or a whole class collaborated on writing?
- At which stage of the writing process was collaboration most useful? If we used Frank Smith's model of pre-writing, writing and re-writing,[6] would the first and last stages be more suitable for collaboration than the middle stage, the 'writing' itself?
- Might collaboration aid younger pupils to produce more successful transactional writing?
- Was there scope to involve parents, grandparents and, indeed, the wider community in writing?
- Would young children find it motivating to write for older pupils – and vice versa?
- Could the teacher–pupil relationship become more of a collaborative enterprise?
- What difference would collaboration make to the quality of writing compared to what pupils normally achieved?
- What would happen to the concept of ownership of a piece of writing in a collaboration between pupils?
- What implications did collaboration in writing have for other areas of the curriculum? (We decided to look at History and Media Studies because members of the group had expertise in these areas.)
- Would the use of word processors with groups of children lead to fruitful collaborative discussion during composition as well as drafting? Would the finished product show evidence of the benefits of collaboration?

Having raised some interesting questions the group went off to set up collaborative writing activities. These would take place within the classroom with pairs, groups, or even a whole class writing together; they would take place across classrooms and schools, with children writing with and for other children in the same school, of the same age in a different school, of a different age in a different school, even for a school in Sweden; we also wanted to draw parents, grandparents and the wider community into writing projects.

We agreed to undertake: meticulous record-keeping of collaborations, using observation, notes, tapes and occasionally video; interviews with pupils, where appropriate, to investigate their perceptions of the collaborative process; and we extended invitations to the two members of the group who were not teaching in schools to help scrutinize classrooms more thoroughly.

Our group had been set up shortly after the National Writing Project started work. We had been drawing on their resources – reading their newsletters, joining the Writing Network, going to talks by project officers, and examining articles generated by the project. Eventually, we invited John Richmond, a project officer, to come and speak to our group. Before his visit, I sent him our work in progress, which he took the trouble to read and offer feedback on. We found his comments most valuable. As well as encouraging us to continue our research, he asked searching questions: two in particular were taken up by the group. The first was: *What do we want children to use writing for?* The second was: *How can we make transactional writing more available to children?* Some of the chapters which follow go some way along those paths, but certainly not far enough. These questions will continue to concern us.

He also made insightful comments that served to shape our future course. John's concept of a 'community of writers' so influenced our concerns that Part Four of this book is devoted to that idea. And if any of us doubted centrality of writing in the language curriculum, John's emphasis on writing 'as a unique road to understanding' refuelled our interest and sparked off one or two members of the group to investigate writing and thinking.

Towards the end of our two-year project we asked Eve Bearne, another National Writing Project Officer, to discuss our findings with us. She also read samples of our material and was, therefore, able to offer us advice and stimulate us to further action. Eve posed some challenging questions which probed to the heart of our endeavours: *When do the moments of intervention by a teacher in a pupil's writing take place? What is said by whom? How does the pupil react? Does the intervention move learning on? What sort of critical judgements do pupils employ in assessing their own and their peer's work? Can a framework of evaluation be agreed between pupil and teacher? Can pupils learn to read their own writing as readers?* Eve's visit was an inspiration to us all. Her questions have been addressed in some of the chapters that follow, though by no means adequately answered yet.

Collaboration and Writing, then, documents teachers at different phases of schooling, examining their own practice, observing their pupils, experimenting with new ways of working and analysing their results. We do not have any 'theory' of collaboration and writing to offer readers. Nor can we unreservedly outline the many advantages which collaboration offers to young writers. In most cases, collaboration did seem to benefit the quality of the finished product; at other times, and for some pupils, it did not. We do feel able, however, to suggest some very definite gains from most collaborative ventures.

- Children write with more conviction for a *real audience* – and that audience can usefully be peers in the same class, older or younger children in the same school, pupils in another school or another phase of education, the pupils' own parents, grandparents and the local community.
- The sheer drudgery of writing for some pupils can be relieved by collaborative work. The lonely isolation of writing is necessary some of the time, but it is worthwhile to offer pupils the *companionship of collaborative writing* at least now and again.
- Collaboration inevitably leads to *talking about writing*. Children engaged on a joint activity will invariably discuss it with one another and the quality of these exchanges tends to be rich – lots of hypothetical and reflective discussion.
- Collaborative ventures lead quite naturally to consideration of the *style, content and technical features of writing*.
- Collaborations can sometimes offer teachers a window into the *actual writing processes of particular pupils*.

- Children tend to *enjoy* collaborating on writing.
- Our collaborative activities encouraged *pupil-initiated learning*.

A lot of the ideas and the processes undertaken were suggested and negotiated by the pupils themselves. It is useful here to cite Gordon Wells:

> ... we know that children are innately disposed to make sense of their experience, to pose problems for themselves, and actively search for and achieve solutions. There is every reason to believe, therefore, that given the opportunity, they will continue to bring these characteristics to bear inside the school as well, provided that the tasks that they engage in are ones that *they have been able to make their own*. All of us ... function most effectively when we are working on a task or problem to which we have a personal commitment ...
>
> For children to achieve this active involvement in their own learning, it is important to find ways of enabling them to share in the responsibility for deciding what tasks to undertake and how to set about them. This does not mean that the teacher should abnegate responsibility or tolerate a free-for-all in which children do exactly as they choose when they choose. Few children can work productively without the support of an understood framework and clear ideas about what is expected of them ... what is required, therefore, is some form of *negotiation in which both pupils' and teachers' suggestions are given serious consideration*.[7]

In the course of our project, we have been deeply involved in examining some of the key issues in writing – from the writing process itself to revision and editing in particular: from the role of the unconscious in writing to how writing aids thinking. Our pupils have engaged in writing of different forms with different functions: long and short stories, poems, autobiography, various types of transactional writing, film scripts, plays, letters, guides, profiles.

So we open the doors of our various classrooms to the reader and invite him or her in to meet our pupils, read their writings, sniff around the displays, share our insights into how our pupils tackle writing, listen to their views, note their discussions and observe them at work. In this way, we hope the reader will be able to share our meanings.

Notes

1. Gordon Wells, *The Meaning Makers*, Hodder and Stoughton, 1986.
2. John Richmond, 'Teachers of writing need a clearer view ... of the classroom', *About Writing*, no. 4. Newsletter of National Writing Project, SCDC, 1986.
3. Frank Smith, *Collaboration in the Classroom*, University of Reading, Centre for Reading/Abel Press, Canada, 1986.
4. George Miller, *Spontaneous Apprentices: Children and Language*. Seabury, 1977.
5. *About Writing*, no. 4.
6. Frank Smith, *Writing and the Writer*, Heinemann, 1982.
7. Wells, *The Meaning Makers* (emphasis added).

PART ONE
Children as writers

2 'Mission to Hell'

MORAG STYLES with JENNIE DUNN

PROLOGUE
Once, the land of Straven was peaceful until the Lord of Demons, Rothgar and his vast army of orcs cast their dark shadows over the land. The war council of Straven met in secret to deal with the problem. At the end of the meeting three champions were chosen. They were Annelise, a tall beautiful elven woman. However, her appearance did not change her skill with a longbow. Larmas, a human man, skilled highly with a two-handed sword and Orando, a powerful wizard. Next day they set off to find Mazereth, a magical sword. Mazereth was (supposedly) the only weapon strong enough to even harm Rothgar. Then they must find the key to hell, then find and defeat Rothgar. Hoping luck was on their side, they set off to find Mazereth.

CHAPTER 1 'TO ARMS!'
'To arms! To arms! The village is under attack!' yelled a soldier as an orc shot him in the chest. The village of Ambrile was being pillaged by orcs.

Thus began a short novel, 'Mission to Hell' by my son, Ross, then aged ten, and his friend, Kieran, 11, written while Jennie Dunn was their class teacher. We chose to begin the section on 'Children as Writers' with this piece for several reasons. First, it offered various interesting perspectives – that of the two pupils who collaborated on a long-term writing project, their teacher who initiated the work, and a parent who observed her child blossom in confidence as it progressed. Second, the children did take their writing seriously and, indeed, considered themselves real writers. In fact, they thought of trying to get their book published and went on to write a sequel. Third, it is a good example of two pupils with different talents and abilities collaborating happily together. They were both intelligent boys, but at this stage Ross was underachieving and rarely chose to write if he could avoid it. Kieran, by contrast, was a high-flying, strongly motivated pupil. Finally, it was an idea of Ross's that led to the writing project being set up – he had actually suggested I investigate whether kids could produce stories and poems to get other children writing. It seems fitting, therefore, to start with this modest, small-scale collaboration.

Ross: Ms Dunn was talking about us writing books in class. I asked Kieran if we could write a story together.
Kieran: No, you can't write or draw.
Ross: Yeah, but I've got brilliant ideas.
Kieran: OK Ross, you're on.

The pair of them were mad about fantasy, had gobbled up Tolkien, Lewis and Garner's early novels and were rapidly getting involved in the 'Dungeons and Dragons' craze. They often discussed fantasy scenarios together and were very much in tune with each other's interests. It was inevitable that their long story would be an adventure fantasy.

I asked the boys separately several questions about writing the story. I was interested in the followng issues:

- *The writing process*. How did they go about writing the story together? At what stage of the writing process were they working together and at what stage separately? How much talk was involved?
- *The collaboration*. Which aspects of the partnership improved the writing and were enjoyable? Conversely, what were the difficulties encountered in trying to write together? Who owned the writing in the end?
- *Teacher involvement*. Later in this chapter, Jennie Dunn describes the project from her point of view as the teacher who set up the work. I was interested in the boys' perceptions of how much their teacher influenced their work.

Handwriting

Kieran did all the actual writing of the story. Ross, a left-hander, felt that his handwriting was poor and found writing at any length laborious. It was this that often led him to feel discouraged about his writing – he would rather give up than struggle to produce something he knew would look mediocre:

> I hate writing. My hand goes much slower than my brain. I just get discouraged. The only bit I like is – it's my ideas. I like using my imagination.

Kieran, a fluent, effective writer and a boy who liked to be in control, did not mind being the one to wield the pencil and Ross was liberated from the painful limitations of his handwriting.

As a parent, I was delighted that Ross was involved and highly motivated in composing a story. Many teachers would not have allowed a ten-year-old to spend so much time not actually writing. Jennie Dunn knew better. She realized that it was important for Ross to create collaboratively a story he could be proud of. And she was convinced that he would be actively involved in the composition. But this was an act of faith on her part. And wouldn't this enlightened practice be so easy to criticize in today's educational climate? (Incidentally, by the end, even Kieran was exhausted with so much handwriting. He was highly motivated and saw the point in writing neatly, but it was still a chore to produce a long story. This is where word processors can be so liberating.)

Drafting

It always seems fruitful for writers to collaborate at the pre-writing and re-writing stages of the writing process, but I wondered whether this would be the case when it came to composition – the bit where the writing is fast and almost unconscious when it is going well. Could composition work in tandem? Apparently it could, as the boys talked casually of working together through the whole process.

Kieran: I used to say the next sentence or two aloud, and Ross would often change it.
Ross: Improve it, you mean.

So by the time Kieran wrote it down, the boys were happy with it. Thus the story was modified as it was being written. They discussed improvements as they went along. Sometimes, they would axe a chunk or fill in a bit more detail. Usually, the adjustments were minor and were to do with improvement of vocabulary or style. For example:

Larmas hit the dragon over the head

became

Larmas struck the dragon a mighty blow.

Ross was often the one suggesting modifications. Presumably being freed from the burden of handwriting enabled him to concentrate on the text in hand. There was also a fair amount of controversy about the storyline which might happen at any phase of the writing process. Some possible redrafting was avoided through the well-prepared preliminary stages. The boys had made a plan, decided on a basic plot line, worked out characters' names and attributes, talked through possible ideas and produced a flow chart. So although there was a continuous ebb and flow of ideas, they knew basically where they were heading and how to get there.

As for punctuation and spelling, the boys didn't worry about this until the final copy. (They only made one preliminary draft.) As Kieran is a competent writer, he did not make many mistakes anyway.

It must be useful for children to learn to identify some of the principal features of a successful story and plan accordingly before writing. Of course, on occasions, it is perfectly legitimate to let a story bubble out spontaneously without prior thought. But one of the reasons why so many children flounder in their story-writing is uncertainty as to how to go about the task. They get themselves into what Myra Barrs describes as 'narrative problems'[1] and do not have the inventiveness or stamina to work through them. It does not stifle creativity to teach children the tools of writing – it can be a great enabler.

Collaboration

As I've mentioned above, the boys worked together throughout the composition of their story. This brought its compensations, among them a considerable flow of good ideas. It also had its drawbacks: 'I didn't have overall say in what happened.' 'You couldn't work on it whenever just you wanted to.' But the good things outweighed the bad – both were satisfied with the outcome. 'It was the best of both of us.'

I am sure it was beneficial for the boys to learn to compromise, but in such a collaborative venture, restrictions on the individual's creativity are inevitable. Yet both boys felt that their story was better composed together than it would have been if either of the individuals had written it alone. It is important that children have both experiences – the more common one of writing one's own ideas in one's own way; and the possibility of a grander, more ambitious venture with others on occasion.

Collaboration also opened up rich possibilities for talk. Kieran and Ross were continuously holding *real* discussions – purposeful and meaningful debates about the next section of their novel. There was no need for their teacher to set up decontextualized talk activities for them: hypothetical talk was the norm. They both admitted they sometimes strayed from the work in hand and chatted about everyday matters. I do not find this surprising. Some of the most productive meetings I take part in also contain a great deal of inconsequential chit-chat. Pleasant conversation may be a useful preliminary to, or pause between, intense discussion – the kind that moves things forward.

Both the boys are strong characters but, in fact, they had no major disagreements. Both felt their story was based on equal input: despite the unequal workload (to an adult's eye) they felt they had equal power in the partnership and equally owned the end product.

The teacher's input

Later Jennie gives her own account of the collaboration, but the boys' point of view on teacher intervention is interesting. Both felt that she had very little to do with their story. This was not a criticism – they were pleased she had given them the freedom to get on and write as they wished. Both mentioned her interest and encouragement in writing the text, but if any specific help was offered, they had forgotten it. (After reading Jennie's account, it seems likely that she did offer more help than the boys realized – quiet, unobtrusive intervention.)

This is the teacher as enabler. By immersing the children in literature, highlighting features of stories, helping them become aware of structure, plan appropriately and *believe in themselves as writers* – Jennie enabled the boys to write happily and productively by themselves.

The end product

The boys knew they were writing for a real audience and with a real purpose. Their book would be read by their peers and would be placed on the library shelves. Both remarked that this was important to them. In the event Jennie took the book home and read it with genuine enjoyment. The next morning the whole class heard how she had not been able to put it down – how successful the boys had been in telling a story well. And the final accolade came from a teacher they knew to be literary person: 'It's better than many books published today sitting in bookshops.' And she meant it!

I will leave the boys the last word in their ending to 'Mission to Hell'. Their work is heavily influenced by Tolkien, science fiction, 'Choose Your Own Adventure' stories and current films. But they make their own vivid narrative out of derivative material. And what a lot they have learned about this genre.

THE ESCAPE
Suddenly a piece of debris fell. More and more fell until the roof began to cave in.
'The citadel is only in existence because of Rothgar's existence,' said Orando. 'His collapse is resulting in the collapse of hell itself. We must hurry if we are to escape.'
The three ran. All around them were falling rocks. Passages caved in behind them. They jumped through the gate into Straven just as the gate shattered into a thousand pieces. The three sent to destroy Rothgar had achieved their mission and lived to tell the tale.

EPILOGUE
Wedding bells rang out as the victorious (and newly wedded) Larmas and Annelise walked between the cheering rows of men and elves. The ceremony was over and all that remained was a huge feast. All were happy but when they sat down to eat, a huge voice boomed out like thunder. 'You have not won! Mere mortals do not triumph over me! In a century, I Rothgar will return to totally annihilate Straven.' And the voice died away as the warm sun shed light over the wedding group and they wondered which heroes would triumph or be triumphed over when Rothgar returned in a hundred years.

Taking responsibility for writing: the teacher's point of view

A small child starting school soon learns to attach importance to the name she writes under her first paintings. By listening to stories she learns that writers have power to communicate thoughts and feelings. Later, when she begins to read independently, she has direct access to that power. When she begins to write independently she wields that power herself. She is learning to create her own world and must be taught to communicate her own truth.

When I joined the staff of a small and caring primary school, I expected to find real engagement and honesty in the children's writing. However, I was disappointed. The writing of my top juniors was perfunctory; competent but dull. The children were detached from the content, revealed little of themselves and did not expect writing to be worthy of much attention or effort – before, during or after the physical act of putting pen to paper. One of my first tasks, therefore, was to try and change this attitude. I set about this in the only way I have found to be really effective – by using literature.

I decided to allocate as much time as possible to reading activities. During the course of each week the children were given opportunities to read independently, in small groups, to each other, in pairs and to me individually. They listened to tapes of wonderful stories read by a variety of skilled actors and actresses. I read to them from a novel at least once every day. They talked about books, exchanged books, bought books from the school bookshop and brought in books from home. Some of the children taped book reviews for other children, read to infant classes during wet lunchtimes and helped me to choose new titles for the classroom library.

At about this time there was a growing interest in the 'Choose Your Own Adventure' type of story and many of the books I sold in the school shop were of this genre. Although I think such texts are of limited value, they did encourage the more reluctant readers to get involved in a book.

Towards the end of this first term I borrowed a selection of dramatic posters from our local bookshop and used these as the stimulus for writing activities. I read a passage from the beginning of one of the most popular 'Fighting Fantasy' books and asked the children to continue the story. I told them they could write a rough first draft and that they could work in pairs if this appealed to them. Their work had been improving during the term, but in this session there was a different atmosphere in the room. The children were excited and there was a definite sense of purpose. After ten weeks' hard work, I was hoping their writing would reflect a new attitude, and, during that particular session, I remember being almost afraid of helping individuals for fear of breaking the spell.

When the session was over and I began to look at the writing, I was immensely relieved to discover that every child had been motivated to write with conviction. The community of writers within my classroom had, at last, taken the decision to write. They had begun to own their scripts in the same way that any creative artist owns his or her creation. My job had been to provide the supportive atmosphere in which such personal and important writing could flourish.

The children and I were pleased with this success in their writing, but I did sound a note of caution. I reminded the class that the hardest thing for them now was to be able to go on from that point. They had proved they were writers. Could they keep it up?

Round about this time some children began to talk about the problems of writing a whole book. Someone suggested that a group of people working on one story could help one another. From here it was easy for me to ask: 'Would any of you like to try that?' I had been cautious about such an invitation earlier in the term but now I felt that it was possible. The children were making decisions about their writing and were taking responsibility for those decisions. When this happens the teacher's role changes. If two children elect to write together then the teacher becomes a third member of that group, advising, supporting and guiding the writing process (and sometimes the relationship between the two writers!) but the teacher is *not* a writer. The new role is more that of an agent, which is demanding and requires real knowledge of the children involved.

In this way 'Mission to Hell' came to be written. Not all the books produced at this time were based on adventure stories, but 'Mission to Hell' most successfully demonstrates the value of collaborative ventures in that the two authors most obviously used the process to learn about how language works to produce powerful meaning through the medium of story. They learned about writing and about themselves.

Much of the planning was done before the writing really began. I can recall the boys perched on their desks earnestly discussing characters, locations, names, the plot and the artwork involved. Once various conventions had been established, it was interesting to note how well they understood them. They both knew that characters had to be uncomplicated, the plot reasonably simple and fast-moving. In such stories they knew that heroines are truly beautiful, heroes are handsome and that, eventually, good triumphs over evil. The description of people and places must be brief and easily identified by the reader. These two authors, Ross and Kieran, knew the stereotypes they were creating and understood what was acceptable and what was not. There were no complex moral issues and, though description enhanced the plot, there was not too much to slow the action. Drawings were appropriately placed and were given captions.

At times the relationship was strained and the arguments heated, each author wanting to dominate. Collaborative writing, like collaborative teaching, requires patience, compromise and a recognition of the skills and limitations of each collaborator. As Doris Lessing said in a BBC Radio 4 interview: 'The whole point of being a writer, it seems to me, is that you change as you write. You change yourself, you change the way you think.' It seems to me that is also the point of being a teacher. Teaching is a creative activity and, as such, it ought to change the teacher. Taking a collaborative role in the writing process alters the traditional role of the teacher. You must learn to move into the background. This alters your view of writing and of children. It can develop your skills as a teacher as much as it develops and changes the writers themselves.

Note

1. Myra Barrs, 'Knowing by Becoming' in Margaret Meek and Jane Miller (eds), *Changing English*, Heinemann, 1984.

3 Discovering a need to write: the role of the teacher as collaborator

GARETH DAVIES

Every teacher comes across suggestions for classroom activities which contain variations on the words 'If you do this the children will sit down and write with commitment'. Sometimes, miraculously, they do, but mainly they don't. With my class of third- and fourth-year juniors I reached the conclusion that even the most carefully planned, wildly stimulating writing session I could devise was for many of them going to fall into the 'mainly they don't' category. It was not that they were unwilling. They were happy to humour me by completing the task, but not to be positively enthusiastic. Despite the years of effort which had been put into teaching these children to write, many, perhaps most, did not find it a satisfying task. Of course, there were exceptions. In the class were children bursting with ideas and others who occasionally did something so exciting that they could scarcely wait to record it. But most claimed never to write outside school and, left to themselves, would rarely, if ever, have picked up a writing implement.

What was I doing wrong? After considering the obvious – that I was a rotten teacher, that I was not matching tasks to ability and interest – I began to search for answers in the writing process itself. Looking at my own practice, it was clear that I was putting most emphasis on the act of writing rather than the reasons for writing. Not just the physical act of making legible marks on paper but the whole process of pre-writing, writing and re-writing: that is, writing seen as a process which begins with thinking about what to write and finishes with consideration and redrafting of what has been written. But the answer to the lack of motivation did not seem to lie here. I began to consider why it was that I felt it important for the children to want to write. This brought me to the whole purpose of writing. What is it for? In considering that question I found it useful to draw on the work of Andrew Wilkinson[1] and in particular on his description of the models of communication. These three models seemed to give me a useful answer to the question of why children should want to write.

Models of communication

The first model identified by Wilkinson is *transmission*. This is the process whereby one person communicates information to another with no expectation of feedback. The relationship of published author and reader often falls into this category.

Reciprocity, the second model, carries this a stage further since it requires not only an initial transmission of information but a subsequent response. A dialogue is set up. Correspondence is a common form of reciprocity in the field of written communication.

The third model is *reflection*. Here a person writes to or for herself in order to reflect either immediately or later on what has been written. Such writing might be carried out in order to make sense of a mass of information or to release some pent-up emotion or to try and make sense of ourselves and our ideas. This is the sort of writing which John Richmond has called 'the unique road to understanding'. Personal journals fall under this heading.

Wilkinson's models comprehensively covered the reasons for writing and set a bench-mark against which I could judge the breadth of the writing tasks which I was setting my class. But still something was missing. Having covered types of writing and the process of writing I eventually reached the conclusion that the missing ingredient was the *need* to write. In adult life we perceive the need to achieve an objective before necessarily deciding how to achieve it. I know I need an overdraft before I decide that writing a letter is the best way to negotiate one. My need to obtain further qualifications precedes my realization that in order to do so I will have to write examination papers. Writing is a tool which we use to service our needs when it is appropriate. And this is true even where the writing is creative or personal rather than transactional. The person who has something to say about the world or who feels the need to change it will sooner or later use the written word as a tool.

But the needs of the adult world seem a long way off to third- and fourth-year juniors. Was it surprising that many of my class were unenthusiastic about writing if the only justification for it that they could see was that it might be a useful tool in the future? If I wanted their enthusiasm as well as their co-operation then they had to see that writing was a skill which was relevant to their existing needs; a tool which could serve their interests *now*. I had to give more emphasis to writing which was done for a purpose and which produced an end result beyond itself. At the same time that writing had to cover the different communication models since I had realized in examining Wilkinson's categories that I was by no means covering the whole range in my teaching. The outcome of these considerations was to make me reassess my role as teacher and ultimately extend it.

The transmission model in the classroom

How often in classrooms do the children get an opportunity to write something on which they get no feedback? The very nature of school dictates that their written work has some comment made on it. They are rarely if ever in a position to transmit information which receives no response. 'Home news' may be an example but even then there would usually be a response from the teacher, either in the form of corrections (the *marking* response) or in the form of comment (the *positive feedback* response).

The audience for writing under the transmission model is invariably known. Writing for an unseen audience, as a novelist does, is a rare occurrence. It certainly was in my classroom. Does that matter? Why do people feel the need to write in this way? What motivates somebody to write something to which they expect no direct or immediate response? Altruism perhaps. Desire to influence: the reader writing letters for publication in her newspaper. Money: an author who has to make a living. Satisfaction: the author who enjoys the process of setting down and manipulating words and for whom a readership is a secondary consideration. Social responsibility: the parent writing to school to say that Mary will be late back from holiday.

All of these involve having something to say that you believe will be unknown to the recipient but which you think might be of value to him though you expect no reply. It involves being able to consider the needs of others as well as yourself. How does this fit in with a child's world? First, all these types of writing spring from a need to take action. That need cannot be imparted by somebody else. So if children are to write in the transmission model – which, as Wilkinson points out, is how we define ourselves in relationship to the world around us: this is *me*! – it has far-reaching consequences for the sorts of opportunity they are given in school. The overriding need is for children to have confidence in themselves, irrespective of other people's views. They should be helped to develop standards of their own so that in their writing they can gain satisfaction from their work, whether or not they get positive feedback. Second, children must have an understanding of how their society works, why it works, what can be changed and how. Transmission writing can almost be seen as an attempt to remake the world in one's own image or to one's own specifications. If the child can be involved in decisions about her own society, whether at school or home, then sooner or later opportunities should arise when she needs to write in order to influence events. Third, children must take their own place in society; take responsibility; and recognize difficulties which others face and their own obligation to help. They must genuinely feel concerned about the content of their writing. It is of little value to ask a child to write a protest letter about a new car park taking part of the playground, if even when she fully understands the implications of it she still does not feel strongly about it either for its effect on herself or on others. In other words, children can only write in this transmission model when they are genuinely interested in what they are writing and believe or hope that they can influence others through their writing.

At this stage, to my surprise, I discovered that what I had produced was not a blueprint for alternative writing activities but a manifesto for involving the class much more closely in the management of their own lives; a manifesto which would involve giving them more responsibility, developing their self-confidence and sense of individuality, lessening their reliance on the good opinions of others. Only then would the children begin to feel the need and the confidence to transmit information without expecting a reply. The writing activities would have to rise out of their personal concerns.

Reciprocal writing in the classroom

I suspect this is the model of communication which children writing in school follow most often. The teacher initiates a piece of work, the child carries it out, the teacher responds in one of a variety of ways. After that it may be forgotten or there may be amendments and revisions which lead to a continuation of the dialogue between teacher and taught. At a simple level it may be a worksheet which is filled in and marked. It may be a story or poem to which the teacher responds. It may be letters exchanged between two linked schools. The distinguishing feature is that the initial communication elicits a direct and more or less immediate response. In my class the majority of the writing under this model was the children responding to a stimulus from the teacher. Rarely did children ask if they could write a story or poem and then show it to me. But they did a great deal of writing of one sort or another based on this reciprocal model. In nearly all of it the reason for writing was imposed. In crude terms it could be characterized as the children being told to write because they would need to know how to do it in the future. And if that was not sufficient to motivate them then there was the need to gain approval or avoid censure. That is not to say that the children were not proud or pleased with what they had written. Frequently they were and so was I. But if asked why they had been writing they would have been hard pressed to give an answer. They did not personally feel a need to write.

The model that they and I had been following was very much teacher-dominated. If they were to genuinely feel the need to write I needed to revise my practice to make it more child-centred. This would involve letting the writing which the class did spring more from their own interests and the interests which they were developing as we studied different areas of the curriculum.

Reflective writing in the classroom

Reflective writing in my classroom was virtually non-existent. There was no truly private writing. The children made notes at various times, they wrote journals, but this and all other writing was always open to scrutiny by the teacher and other adults in the school. The children had not experienced reflective writing at school and very few wrote in this way at home. Yet reflective writing is, at least to me, the most important model. It is so easy to become confused in one's thoughts. Writing is invaluable in sorting them out, in playing with ideas that might be unacceptable if made public, in releasing pent-up emotion, in deciding on a shopping list, in keeping a personal journal, in coming to terms with adversity, in escaping temporarily from the demands of the world, in learning how to think. In learning, to quote Wilkinson, 'Who am I? What do I think? What do I feel?'[2]

So far, so bad. I had a whole list of things I thought my class should eventually be able to do and an even longer list of things that I might have been doing to help them but was not, or was doing but should not have been. Where did I go from there? What to do next?

My own role as teacher seemed central to the problem. What was I trying to achieve? How was I trying to achieve it? It seemed to me that I did not adopt one role but a whole series. What were they? Which ones would be useful in trying to guide young writers to their full potential? Which roles had I not adopted in the past?

The role of the teacher

The list of a teacher's roles is endless: friend, facilitator, pedagogue, actor, disciplinarian, bank clerk, administrator, librarian, and so on. If we narrow the scope to those roles which have to do with the teaching of writing, many remain: but we might add specific ones such as story-teller, stationer, oracle, confidante, commentator, critic, audience, typist. Again the list is far from exhaustive.

How many of these roles could help me put the children in situations where they would need to write in the different modes identified, to make them enthusiastic all-round writers, and to give them the skills to write once they had identified their needs?

Examining the roles I was currently adopting towards this end I felt mine were rather limited. So far as teaching the act of writing was concerned, I was not doing too badly. The class was being asked to do many sorts of writing. I was working on their syntax, their spelling and handwriting. I was extending their vocabulary, encouraging them to draft and to rewrite. I was achieving this through poetry, narrative, transactional writing and through cloze procedure, comprehension, prediction exercises, and so on. These latter were chosen carefully by me rather than followed blindly through a published scheme. And as far as it went it was working. The quality of the children's writing was improving, if slowly. But in all this writing work I had only one or two basic roles: pedagogue and audience. However much I took work from the children's own interests, however much I attempted to make it child-centred, in effect I was determining the need and I alone, usually, was judging the outcome. Writing in the class was far too often an end in itself – finish this work, hand it in, forget about it – or was a means to some future goal which was so far over the horizon it was beyond the children's vision. It was rarely a means of achieving something else, which is what communication, like any good tool, should be. It was like asking the children to saw a log *not* because they needed to build a house but because they would need to know at some distant and unspecified time in the future how to saw a log to build a house. How much more meaningful if they had something to do with the planks they had practised on, however imperfect. They might at least then have learnt that they needed to learn to saw better.

How, then, to get the children to take more responsibility for their own learning? And at the same time to tackle the implicit need to recognize that failure is a positive experience not a negative one; that only by trying and sometimes failing do we learn? What roles could I adopt or give more emphasis to?

The teacher as facilitator

Reflective writing was the area where it seemed most difficult to achieve anything. All class writing was in the public domain and, unless destroyed, was likely to be read by any number of people from the governors, to the head, teachers and parents. The children expected their writing to be read. Most saw little need to write purely for themselves or, if they did, could not recognize that need for what it was. Obviously I could not give them a need to write reflectively. All I could hope for was that if they were provided with the opportunity they would either grasp it eagerly or perhaps eventually make something of it. The opportunity I gave them was to write every day, entirely privately, on the strict understanding that nobody would read what they had written unless they decided spontaneously to show it to somebody. This last I felt was important since it would be very difficult for a child to resist approaches from an adult such as 'You don't mind if I have a quick look do you?' This required an act of faith on my part since it meant that I would be unable to monitor how they were responding to the opportunity, except by observations which could easily be misleading and by very circumspect conversations about the experience. The content of the writing would literally be a closed book.

What I did was to suggest to the children that I should give them time each morning to write an entirely private journal in which they could write whatever they liked. The idea was greeted enthusiastically and everybody wanted to start immediately. But even at this stage I found it hard to relinquish the control which becomes second nature to teachers. I suggested that any child who wanted to could also use the journal as a means of privately asking me questions or seeking my opinion, the idea being that I would write my answer in their journal and pass it back to them. At the time I believed that I was trying to benefit the children. Looking back it seems much clearer that I was trying to retain some control over the journals by providing myself with an opportunity to read them with the children's consent. Significantly, none of the children asked me a question or showed me their journal in the year they were written. I made it clear that I would not read them unless the children asked and I promised that no one else would do so. That caused practical problems. Sometimes the children inadvertently left them lying around in the classroom at the end of the day. In tidying up there was a terrible temptation to just flick through them. More difficult was the perfectly reasonable request from the headteacher to see all the children's books. When I explained about the journals and my promise of confidentiality he simply replied that he had not promised. Fortunately the issue was fudged as the request got lost in the welter of other demands on his time. I am sure that with more explanation on my part he would in any case have changed his mind. But if he had not I would have been in a very difficult position. Respect for the children's privacy was obviously a crucial point in my experiment. The incident made me more aware of the difficulties of reconciling the children's needs with those of accountability placed on the teacher. The point was reinforced at the end of the year as parents' evening drew closer. The usual procedure was for all the child's work to be laid out for scrutiny by parents. I was already conscious that this would cause problems with the journals when several of the children asked me themselves what was going to happen to them on parents' evening. To keep my part of the contract I removed them from the folders but what, I wonder, what would have happened if a parent had insisted on seeing a journal?

I do not know to this day what was in any of the journals but the fact that the children were so defensive about them suggests that at least some of them had found in the writing an opportunity to set down thoughts and feelings which they could not share with anyone else. There were other indications that they were fulfilling a genuine need.

When we first started the journals I insisted that everybody wrote in them every day. It became the regular first activity in the morning. Gradually, though, I relaxed the regime and children only wrote when they wanted. None of the children gave up writing the journals altogether, though some spent very little time on them. Most wrote every day and some found opportunities to write more than once a day. Some of the children were incredibly prolific and during the year filled several exercise books. On most days my class also had a period for quiet reading. Without doubt these journals were the most read and reread books in my class.

For some of the time the children were writing their journals Morag Styles was working in my classroom on a Shakespeare project. When she got to know the children she expressed surprise at the willingness of the children to write the diaries, a willingness that was not always evident in other writing they did.

Obviously in all this I could not give the children a need to write for themselves. Nobody could do that. What I suspected was that many children might have such a need but were unable to fulfil it through lack of opportunity. To enable them to fulfil that need and in doing so widen their knowledge of the uses of language – not the content or the process – I had to be not pedagogue but facilitator. I collaborated with the children in what might be seen as a departure from normal school practice. I gave them an opportunity to do something for which there would be no evaluation but their own.

The teacher as instigator

It is hard to get away from the role of teacher as instigator of writing and I saw no reason to do so completely. It is obviously a valuable role in developing writing ability and enjoyment. But it does conflict to some extent with the wish I had expressed earlier to let more of the children's writing develop from their own needs. I could not give the children a personal need to write anything that I suggested. So what could I do to involve them more in teacher-instigated writing? Would widening the audience for their writing help? Would it strengthen their sense of ownership of their writing and give them more commitment to it if they were aware that it was to be read by a wider audience? Alternatively, could I put them in a situation where there would be a use for the writing they produced, where the quality of what they produced would affect their ability to carry out a subsequent task?

My first deliberate attempt along these lines was concerned with autobiographical writing. I did not specifically set out to meet the criteria above. If I had, I would no doubt have designed the project differently. In fact my main concern at the time was to find ways of putting over to the class the importance of self-correction and redrafting in developing their writing skills. I was looking for a stimulus that would encourage the children to look more closely at their writing in the hope that motivation, enthusiasm and quality would all be improved.

The writing sessions that followed took place over about one week and involved writing by me, my class and a colleague's class of first- and second-year juniors. As the stimulus I chose 'School Memories – Good or Bad'. There were various reasons for this choice. First, it seemed immediately accessible to the children and would reduce difficulties about what to write, placing more emphasis on how to write. Second, it was a content area over which I as the teacher could have no control. Although I suggested the stimulus, there my involvement with the content stopped since I had not lived the children's lives.

My own memories of small incidents at school come fairly easily and I sat down at home to write a couple down in a way that I hoped would be appealing to my class and which would stimulate their own writing. It took me several drafts until I was reasonably satisfied. I read the accounts to the class and explained that I would be asking them to write about their own memories. Then, just as I was using my memories to stimulate them, they would be asked to use their written memories to initiate some writing from a first- or second-year with whom they would be paired. They could become the teacher for a while. There was a great deal of enthusiasm for this idea and, without any further guidance, the class sat down and began work on the best or worst things that had happened to them. Even the normally reluctant writers set to with enthusiasm and an unusually high degree of concentration. In fact the quality of these early drafts was pretty much what I would normally have expected though there was a tendency to write more, and more quickly than usual. Many of the experiences recounted were very moving. Few of the children altered this first draft as they were going along. Nevertheless, most of the pieces had a logical structure with a recognizable sequence of events. This was made easier because the autobiographical nature of the writing meant that the children had a clear grasp before putting pen to paper of the overall shape of their narrative.

At this stage all I could conclude was that the prospect of an audience and a purpose behind the writing improved motivation but not necessarily the product. This was reinforced when I asked for a second draft. Enthusiasm, though waning, was still much higher than usual.

As it happened, television that week brought us a showing of Michael Rosen's *The Juice Job* (in the Middle English series). This takes as its theme how various people see the same story in different ways. It emphasizes how descriptions, conversations, scene-setting and characters' thoughts can make writing more alive and exciting. This was a very convenient peg on which to hang a class discussion about ways of improving the autobiographical writing. With that under their belts and with my comments on their first draft (mainly a series of questions, which if answered and incorporated into the text would clarify obscure points for a reader) the class set off on their second drafts.

With their much improved second drafts ready most of the class jibbed at the idea of making any further changes. They groaned loudly at the very suggestion. It seemed time to bring them into contact with the first- and second-years. Each child in my class was paired with a younger pupil with loose instructions to read her story to her partner or to let the partner read it for himself, then to set the younger child off on his own writing, helping where necessary or when requested.

We had thought that this session might take an hour. It actually lasted all afternoon and required virtually no teacher input of any sort. For the most part the children from both classes were totally absorbed and, judging by the hard time which some of my class gave their partners, they were determined that the efforts they had made with their own writing were going to be repaid. The idea of writing for someone other than their teacher seemed to grip the first- and second-years and this was reflected not only in the quality of their work but also in the intensity of their concentration.

The following piece was produced by James, a second-year with severe language difficulties. Although enthusiastic about writing at the time, he normally found it impossible to sequence a story or get his thoughts down on paper. Of course, the comparison is not entirely fair since in this piece he had a considerable amount of help from an able child. Nevertheless it was produced while he was highly motivated and at the end he was very proud of what he had written.

> *One day I went to work with my dad I was five at the time. At my dad's work They use pottery equipment. I asked my dad if I could Make a dinosaur He said of course son. I lick the pottery myself and the gooy suf wos big and gooy I lilk the hed and the fed*

It is easy to see the input which the child in my class put into this writing. It is also easy to spot where she began to tire after what she admitted had been an exhausting afternoon helping James to structure his thoughts more clearly than usual.

I had intended at this point that my class should have a chance to consider the writing which their partners had produced and then suggest ways in which it could be improved. Unfortunately, other pressures intervened and this project ended there, leaving me to draw conclusions about what had been achieved. Having an audience and a purpose for their writing had undoubtedly helped the motivation of all the children. In some cases it had improved the quality. It certainly did not lead to an overnight change in their attitude to self-correction and drafting. But it helped. At the time I debated whether the changes had been wrought mainly because of having an audience or because the writing had a purpose. Reflecting on it now I am certain that it was the need to write which affected the children's attitude to the work. They wanted to be teachers for a day and in order to do so they had to write, and write as well as they could.

Looking at the writing which was produced also reminded me that although earlier I have neatly categorized writing into three separate models of communication, there is often no clear distinction between them. The writing task as set here was clearly reciprocal. The children were writing for an audience from whom they were going to get a very clear and immediate response. And yet the nature of the writing was often very personal. There were some very vivid descriptions of bad moments which had obviously been upsetting. Many of the children enjoyed setting them down. Although writing for an audience, they were obviously also writing for themselves. It reinforced my belief that children need more opportunities for reflective writing. As an example, here is Jane's description of getting into a fight.

> *I was at the pooly. And my sister and michel was with me. And I was siting on the hill. And my friend Lesley was on the swing. And my sister tracy went up to her. And she said. Will you have a fight with Jane. That's me. And she said yes. So we all went behind the hill. I was very sceard because I new she could beet me. I did not want to have a fight with her. She is my best friend. Ad michel said One two three. And the fight started. I was worried. I wonted to say stop because she would hurt me realy badly. I got hold of her jumper and streshed it quit a lot. I got hold of Lesley's hair. And pulled it realy hard. And her face went bright red. And so did her blue eyes. They looked like balls of fire coming towords me. I felt very very friternd. Because she might hurt me realy badly. I new tracy asked because she wanted to see me have a fight. Well she wanted me to wine. I got hold of Lesleys jumper again and swang her around. I fourt wy! did I agree to have a fight. I just said OK i will. I cept swinging her around so she could not hurt me. Thn she shouted. And said stop pulling my jumper. your streching it. But I didernt stop. Then I got hold of her head band took it of her head and threw it to my sister tracy and she snapt it but then she got hold of my arm and dug holes in it and now I have got scars all over my arm*

Since this autobiographical work was completed I have tried other ways of putting the children in a position where they feel a need to write. We contacted another school to write penfriend letters. We used ideas suggested by colleagues involved in this project and which they have described elsewhere in this book. We also received stories written by children at a secondary school, based on *The Iron Man* by Ted Hughes.[3] My class were fascinated by these and read them avidly. When told that the secondary children would like some reactions to them they were delighted to write back with their criticisms. Their writing had a purpose and was being taken seriously.

Although I feel that this type of preorganized project involving new and different audiences is likely to form a large part of what I can hope to achieve in giving more of the children's writing a specific purpose, the most satisfactory and satisfying writing in my classroom has arisen when it has come from a child who has perceived for herself a need to write. That is not something which any teacher can dictate. Instead I have tried to foster it by appreciating the children's needs and making sure that they have opportunities to fulfil them. As other children see what their peers are doing, hopefully they, too, will be encouraged to write.

The flexible teacher

The corollary of what I have just said is that my classroom organization must be flexible enough to allow me to respond to the needs which arise, often at times inconvenient for my preplanned day. Lesson planning must be able to cope with individual children who suddenly express a desire to write. If I could provide this flexibility I hoped an atmosphere would develop in the classroom that writing was something you did when you needed to. As children saw their peers writing because they needed and wanted to then they might become more aware of their own needs and that they would be allowed to fulfil them. That is not to say that everything else was dropped when a child said she wanted to write, but I tried to make it clear that I would find her an opportunity to do so while the iron was still hot.

One February we had a visit at school from two Canadian authors. Monica Hughes, writer of science fiction, talked about the problems she had in starting to write. Jean Little talked to another group about her stories and about how her blindness affected her writing. Whichever group they were in the children were fascinated and the visit made a lasting impression on them. Days later several children expressed a desire to write to the two authors but they were faced with what appeared to them to be insuperable problems. They knew what they wanted to say but they wanted to get it right. They did not want their letters punctuated by spelling mistakes. More importantly, they did not know where to send their letters. I gave them time to write them, helped with presentation and provided addresses. I was not concerned with the content of their letters. Though I was interested to note that even though they were mainly just saying thank you, nearly all the children asked that the author write back to them. This reinforced my view that it is very difficult for children of this age to write purely for transmission. They were neither confident enough nor altruistic enough genuinely to expect no response to their writing.

The teacher as editor, publisher, secretary and agent

However, some children do manage it. Two girls in my class demonstrated this when they came up with a project all their own. Donna and Claire set out to put together a collection of short stories, written by themselves, with the intention of getting them published. In the event they did not get that far but they were driven by a perfectly genuine desire to try. I found their reasons for trying as illuminating as the processes which they went through. Their project amply demonstrated the motivating power which having a real need can give to children's writing. Part-way through their project I interviewed them about it. The comments below are taken from our taped conversation.

GD: I want you to tell me about your project to publish a book. How did you get the idea in the first place?

D: Well because we had all these bits of loose paper that had stories on. We decided to put them together to make a book.

GD: Where did the stories come from? Did you write them at school or at home?

D: Story book. Out of my story book. Pages falling out. So we decided to put them all into a proper story book.

GD: Why did you decide to get them published? What made you think of it?

D: Something creative to do, instead of writing them, forgetting about them, finding them the next year.

C: We had the idea that, um, she [Donna] said that there's not many young writers about so she had the idea to write a book. It was her [Donna's] idea.

GD: How did you feel about it?

C: I don't know I just agreed with her.

GD: What made you think there weren't many young writers about?

D: Well, looked at all these books and there wasn't anyone who was about our age [11] who had written a book.

GD: So when you were reading books you couldn't find anything written by [people like] you.

D: All adults and they don't really know what children like or anything. All they do is pick out from other people get it off other books and that sort of thing. I think children are better because they know all these sorts of things because they're children.

C: They have their imagination.

GD: You know what other children like?

D: Yeah in these days.

GD: What sort of children do you think would like to read the stories you wrote? How old do you think they would be?

D: Nine to eleven, nine to twelve years old.

GD: Even stories which you wrote in the first and second year?

D: Well we didn't put any of them in. We only put some of the sort of, I don't know, adventurous and good.

GD: What do you think the children you are writing for would like about them?

D: Well I don't know really.

C: I don't know.

D: I think we liked adventure stories better 'cos a lot of people like adventure stories. The *Famous Five* or something.

GD: Some of the stories you wrote especially for the book, didn't you?

D: Umm.

GD: Can you tell me about one of them?

D: Umm 'Its a Hard Life'. It's about this girl and it was in a long time ago when they used to have mines and children used to go down them. We talked about how she got pushed around and hurt by the other people that are more experienced. Well the mine got caved in and closed down 'cos it was unsafe.

GD: Who got the idea for that one?
D: Well I wrote it 'cos.
GD: Did you write it all by yourself?
D: Yeah.
GD: What did you do when you'd written it? Did you show it to Claire and say what do you think of this?
D: Yeah, 'cos she wrote one as well but she wanted my one.
GD: What was the one you wrote?
C: It was similar. It was about the mine.

Donna and Claire had very clear ideas about why they were writing for publication. They were fulfilling their own need to write and had perceived a need in their potential readership which they wanted to meet. Once they had decided to do something about it their motivation was incredible. Much of the work was done at home, reminding me of the importance of not seeing the work done in school as a complete entity and of the importance of building on what children do at other times. This project transcended school–home boundaries as Claire and Donna took what they needed from where they could get it. From their home life they took the time which they needed to discuss their ideas, set them down in peace and later to prepare finished copies. From school they took the advice and encouragement that I could give them. I felt that the most important thing I gave them was to take them seriously as writers and by doing so give them faith in their own abilities.

Eventually Claire and Donna had their collection ready. What happened next would have been a disaster to most people, but such was their motivation that they took it in their stride and even managed to find it faintly amusing. At the time when disaster struck they were, at my suggestion, putting together a list of possible publishers.

D: We stopped writing our book for a while and now we're going to start again fresh.
GD: With completely new stories?
D: Well no, we're going to get our stories that we actually done. We not going to write any more new ones and actually get it written out.
C: We were thinking of adding our space stories.
D: Yeah.
GD: What happened to the stories you had got all ready to send to a publisher?
D: Claire typed them and she lost them.
GD: What actually happened to them?
D: Don't ask her please ... I thought ... I was angry with Claire.
C: Well I was absolutely devastated.
D: What did you put them under the bed for?
C: I didn't. I put them in my safe box ...
D: And your mum opened it and put them in the bin.

Apparently Claire kept all their writing under her bed. Her mother had tidied up her room and all their work had been binned. By this time it was nearly the end of the academic year and the girls were going off to secondary school. My involvement with the project came to an end before it was completed but both girls have told me since that they intend to finish it.

What had I contributed? My advice had been mainly to do with the publishing process. The girls rarely asked for comments on their writing and never showed me any of the stories which they wrote outside school. Their attention was focused firmly on the wider audience which publication might bring and, as far as they were concerned, that meant other children. Of course, if and when they get further with the publication process they will discover that adult intervention between young writer and young audience is inevitable.

Claire was a very prolific writer. In addition to these short stories she usually had others on the go which she worked on at home and at school. I became quite used to coming in of a morning to find a manuscript slipped onto my desk for reactions. Occasionally Claire would tell me that she had got up at 6a.m. to write before school or that she had woken at midnight and written under the sheets for two hours. I found myself appointed unofficial unraveller of problems. Usually tricky points in the plot which did not hang together, sometimes an appropriate name for a new character. Claire had ideas pouring out of her and needed no encouragement to write (although she was often reluctant to undertake transactional writing). In fact what she lacked was the confidence to put her writing before an audience. However good I felt her writing to be she was always doubtful about its merits and needed to be reassured. That was why her partnership with Donna, who was a much more confident character, was so successful. But when she was not working with Donna I fulfilled the role of preliminary audience. This necessitated being very honest about her writing. She was much too accomplished a writer to be convinced that everything she wrote was wonderful. At the end of the year I commissioned her to write a story for me. I thought no more about it and imagined that she had forgotten it, too. But sure enough, near the end of term she presented me with a very well-written adventure story about life in a city under the sea. She had chosen the subject because I had once mentioned how much I had enjoyed a novel on a similar theme by Monica Hughes.

Rachel also needed to develop the confidence to write for an audience. She was a very quiet but competent girl who approached all her work seriously. She probably took her personal journal more seriously than anyone else in the class. Talking to her I discovered that she followed Anne Frank's example and regarded her diary as a person to be talked to. All her entries began 'Dear Kitty'. My role was to convince her that she had no need to be shy or ashamed of the writing which obviously gave her a great deal of personal pleasure. This could only be done by gentle persuasion and reassurance over a long period. Yet one more role for me to adopt at appropriate moments.

Notes

1. Andrew Wilkinson, *The Quality of Writing*, Open University Press, 1986.
2. Ibid.
3. Ted Hughes, *The Iron Man*, Faber and Faber, 1968.

4 Listening to children's writing

DAVID SOMERVILLE

Introduction

One of the values of involving children in collaborative writing activities is that it helps to make the processes of writing manifest. When writing is done as a purely private activity then we only see the end result, interesting as that may be. But collaboration means discussion and it is in eavesdropping on these conversations between children or getting involved in them ourselves that we start hearing what is going on in children's minds.

Two children working together at the computer, using a word-processing program to write a story will be discussing and arguing at length over the features of the story that matter to them. They will be talking about spelling and punctuation, clear evidence that they *do* understand about full stops but that they usually are not sufficiently motivated to give them much attention. They will be discussing points of grammar ('done' or 'did'?) and arguing over whether one word would be better than another. Further, they will be talking about the development of the story and about consistency of narrative viewpoint ('Should it be "I" or "she" here?'), the deeper structural considerations that matter if the story is to work. It is these discussions that show us the level of understanding that the children have about the way language works and the important narrative rules and conventions that need to be followed if the end product is to be satisfying both to the authors and to any other readers. Quite young children already have a sophisticated understanding of these matters. These have generally not been explicitly taught by a teacher but have rather been grasped by the children from their own varied experience of language.

Myra Barrs[1] suggests that there is a difference between the writings of children up to about the age of eight – these children 'were generally confident and untroubled about their writing, which often seemed to "come to them" in one piece' – and that of older children, who 'were more inclined to admit to problems of composition, and had begun to make changes in their stories in order to solve some of the narrative problems that they perceived'. She suggests that this runs parallel to a similar change in their attitude to their art work. If she is correct then it would follow that the class whose work I describe below (a mixed-ability class of eight- to nine-year-olds) would be in transition between the two stages and I could expect, given the range of ability and maturity within the class, to find individual children well into the more mature stage with others still predominantly at the less mature stage. There then arise questions about the children's perception of collaboration and of related activities such as redrafting. Could it be that some children are too immature at this age to collaborate in any useful way? Are some not yet able to adopt the critical stance needed for productive redrafting? Do such activities have the desired result of improving the children's image of themselves as writers, or can the opposite occur?

Collaborative tasks have helped me to observe the children working on writing more closely than is usually possible in a busy classroom. They have allowed me to move towards tentative answers to some of these questions. Spontaneous comments point clearly to their enjoyment of collaborative work. This must, then, have a good effect on their attitudes to their writing and the way they see themselves as real writers.

Father Christmas stories: planning together and writing for infants

'It was a bit brilliant, really', Elizabeth said three weeks later. The excitement of the intervening Christmas holidays had not driven from her memory the experience of writing a Father Christmas story with a friend for two of the youngest children in the school and then on the last day of that term going to read it with those children.

About a month before the end of term I suggested to my class that they should write stories for the infants. The idea was taken up with great enthusiasm. We agreed that Christmas would be a suitable topic and that five-year-olds would like stories about Father Christmas. When I suggested that the stories should have as the main characters the children for whom they were to be written my class was at once both more excited and more nervous, anticipating some of the problems this might entail. I told them they could work on their own or with a friend, pointing out that working in pairs might be advisable in view of the considerable amount of work that lay ahead of them. They started organizing themselves. Most elected to work with someone else.

I had already talked with the teacher of the reception class, who was enthusiastic about the project, and she provided me with a list of her class put into friendship pairs, with details of any pets the children might have. I decided against any more biographical detail than this, feeling that my class had enough to deal with as it was.

Once my children had been assigned their infants we were ready to begin. I asked them to plan the story preferably in four chapters (by limiting the number of chapters I hoped the children would find this planning stage less daunting) and to write a brief outline of what would happen in each chapter.

For some this was hard and I started getting complete stories being written. Several pairs needed to talk a lot more in order to sort out and organize their ideas. Planning a story is very difficult for children of this age. The children are developing from the earlier stage more typical of infants where just a few sentences can be a complete story. A story of this length can perhaps be conceived by the child more or less instantaneously; it has the whole story ready in its head. If a child is still working in this way at the age of eight (and some undoubtedly are) it is difficult for him or her to think in terms of a summary when the more satisfying narrative is available to the writer. Indeed it would perhaps seem a rather pointless exercise to the child. Why not just get on and write the story? A child who sees the need to start, as Myra Barrs puts it, to 'solve some of the narrative problems' that arise when writing will perhaps be more able to see the planning stage as something useful. Less mature children do not yet see planning as something that can contribute positively to their writing.

However, we all got started and the children got used to the routine of: writing a section; reading it with partner checking for adherence to storyline, quality, spelling, and so on; reading through with me for further checking; producing a neat copy for the finished product; and related artwork. Most of the time the children found the writing fairly easy to get on with, even though the work spanned a number of writing sessions and so they had to remember their ideas for a long time. Although the actual writing was done individually, the children spontaneously used their partners for advice and assistance when they needed to, thus removing some of the demands on my time. A serious problem that some pairs did encounter was that of ensuring that the different sections fitted together. Not surprisingly, it was the children who had had difficulty planning who sometimes did not give due regard to what their partner was writing. They were being somewhat egocentric in their writing. They found this hard to resolve on their own and needed me to act as arbitrator. It is inevitable that collaborative writing will throw up problems of this nature.

One of the major benefits I found was that I was able to spend relatively long *uninterrupted* periods with each pair, since they were soon at completely different stages of the work. This allowed me to help more effectively than would otherwise have been the case those who were finding it hard to organize themselves. I came to value the opportunity to start discussing, in detail and at length, the plot development. Some of the children found this hard to do – it seems that 'stepping back' from the writing in order to be more objective about it is not easy. It would take several minutes' patient questioning on my part to get them thinking about such matters. For this to work it was important that we were not put off by others waiting to talk to me or by trivial interruptions. Throughout this stage it was always very useful having two children together. When discussing one child's contribution to the story I could ask the other child for its comments on how things were going. In this way many suggestions for improvements arose from the children themselves. They helped each other sort out the problems that had arisen. My role was to keep their ideas flowing by asking questions, rather than to suggest the solutions myself.

Once the stories and front covers were complete it took little encouragement to get the children to embellish them with such extras as autobiographical blurb, prices, invented ISBNs (and supermarket bar codes!), and publishing company logos. Finally we were ready on the last day of term to visit the infant class. It was a delight to see my children in this unfamiliar situation. Several of the boys are already football obsessed and are usually concerned to maintain the associated stereotyped male image. As they led their infants gently by the hand and settled with them into a comfortable corner I felt I was being allowed to see them as they sometimes are at home with baby brothers and sisters. In reading the stories to the infants my class showed how clearly they understood the job of a teacher by asking questions, using the pictures to help the story along and keeping attention from straying! The fact that they were heroes and heroines of the stories was accepted by the infants with a calm pleasure.

Later we talked about the whole experience, what it had been like writing *for* someone else, what it had been like writing *with* someone else, what it had been like reading to the little ones. Peter said:

> Well I felt in some ways it was easier because other people have different ideas, you could put the ideas in different bits so you wouldn't just have your ideas.

Susan wasn't sure about the planning:

> At the start we had to work out what we were going to do. I found it a bit boring because we had to work out what to do. But when I got down into writing it started to go well again.

They had much to say about the actual reading with the infants.

> *Karen:* I felt quite happy about it because I like Melanie and Heather [her infants]. Sometimes Melanie listened and sometimes she laughed and she said 'I like that picture' or 'Oh look, I think you spelt a word wrong' and she started correcting us.
> *Teacher:* Did they like it when they realized they were in the story?
> *Karen:* They started laughing.
> *James:* When they didn't understand something they just didn't take any notice, so you knew when they weren't listening. Martin and I just stopped and asked them what just happened and they didn't have any idea.

I think Peter and Simon learned something about prediction. They are talking here about the way Jonathon used the pictures:

> *Peter:* Jonathon, as soon as he saw the book he said 'This book is about me'. As soon as we got into the book ... Jonathon was very clever, he knew when, um, he was good at guessing.
> *Simon:* When we asked him what was in the pictures.

The children clearly gained much satisfaction from the whole project. I was pleased with the various processes undergone during it and the children were delighted with the end product, a *real* book. Was it a coincidence that back at school after the holidays and 20 minutes into a poetry-writing session, having done the talking and about to start writing someone asked: 'Can we do it with a partner?'? I said yes, and over half the class chose to work that way.

The heroes and heroines of the stories also had their say. What was it like being in a story?

Richard: It made me feel happy.
Zatie: Happy *and* important.

On being shown the books again, the children started retelling bits of the stories.

Keith: At the end we were on a big cliff with Santa and Santa fell off and we had to slide off on this magic slide and we caught him while he was going down.
James: Keith was Santa and I was behind him driving the sledge.
Teacher: Was it exciting?
James: Yes, very!
Teacher: What was the best bit?
James: When Keith fell off the cliff.
Teacher: What happened to Keith at the end?
James: He was all right, all bandaged up.

The final word comes from one of the authors, Ian:

I felt joyful in a way and glad that I was writing for somebody else.

In this project, while I certainly learnt a lot about the children's attitudes to their work and about their ability to plan their writing, I do not feel I gained much insight into the writing process itself. The next writing activity I looked at in detail, however, took me further in this direction.

'Getting into Trouble' – writing together

The children wrote stories about getting into and then out of trouble. This arose from the book I was reading to them, *What Difference Does It Make, Danny?*,[2] in which Danny gets himself into *big* trouble. The previous day the children had explored the theme in drama, working in pairs. This meant that they had already worked out a story on the theme of getting into trouble which could form the basis of a written story if they so wished. It also meant that they had already started collaborating on the story, so I told them they could continue this by working on the writing together if they wished. Some of the class, often the more confident writers, preferred working on their own. I think they felt that their ideas would be diluted if they had to negotiate with others over the story.

As I wanted to use this writing activity to help me gain greater insight into how the children thought about their writing, about the planning they undertook, about what they talked about when the writing was actually under way and about the extent to which the finished piece resembled their plan, I asked for a volunteer pair to be tape-recorded. Jane and Susan were only too happy to oblige.

Within the context of my class Jane and Susan are fairly good writers and readers and well motivated. They began by writing the very first sentence but then stopped and worked through the story *orally*. They talked their way confidently to the end of the story for about five minutes. It was all done amazingly fluently – at times they took over from each other in mid-sentence:

Susan: and then when her Mum said you can have your Smarties she goes ...
Jane: (*gasps*) Where have your Smarties gone? You haven't been eating them?

The language they were using was not the language of conversation, with all its hesitancies, repetitions and half-completed sentences. They were talking already in a language appropriate to story-writing.

Once they had talked their way to the end of the story they immediately started writing it. Susan wrote at first and did most of the retelling, then half-way through Jane took over the writing, although Susan continued to dominate the talking. Twice there were moments of tension, first when Jane felt she was not being allowed to do enough, and second when Susan repeated rather urgently a sentence already worked out that Jane was about to write. But otherwise they got on very efficiently. At times they spoke in perfect chorus as a line already worked out was slowly transcribed. Only once was there any debate about the plot:

Susan: 'So I went out the door'
Jane: 'So I ...' No – 'cos we've got to put what, um, she said 'You haven't eaten them up yet, have you?'

The written version was:

My mum tried it and said 'Yuck it's awful, You haven't eaten them up have you?' said Mum. I stormed out.

I talked to the two authors afterwards. They said they like writing together because they can share ideas, they have someone to discuss with and they feel it improves their work. They said they did not worry too much about spelling. They thought that at times they did discuss how to improve the narrative. This is not really borne out by the tape. The written story almost exactly follows the plot of the oral version. The talking produced a 'perfect' (for them) story. They felt little need to redraft.

What seems significant here is that the importance of the preliminary talking stage is revealed. The story was not first written onto *paper*, it was first written in their *minds*. Paradoxically, it seems as if the talking was the real writing, while the physical act of writing the story down was more akin to a reading of the story. This is shown by the fact that the children spoke the story using the conventions of written narrative rather than oral story-telling. Annabelle Dixon[3] has pointed out the importance to young children of the opportunity to be able to retell the stories they have created (in this case stories that the children have made through creative play with models and toys):

> ... we have found it essential that children re-tell their stories. The verbal re-construction of their stories is not always an easy task. It is in fact a demanding intellectual exercise but there appears to be great motivation to explain the worlds they have just been creating.
>
> ... The listening ear does not necessarily belong to the adult. Children often like to share these stories with other children and having an audience who will offer questions and comments even from an early age has a noticeable effect on clarification of style and content.

It is also of interest that Susan and Jane followed their original idea almost exactly when they wrote the story down, making virtually no attempt to make any substantial changes to the story. It did not occur to them to work on some of the more artificial elements, which would suggest that the children are still at the earlier stage that Myra Barrs identifies. They have not yet reached the point where they worry much about the problems of constructing a narrative. It is still a straightforward task for them. I chose not to intervene at any point in this session since I wanted to observe the children at work on their own. However, Myra Barrs's ideas raise the difficult question of what form useful teacher intervention should take with such children. Should we be encouraging them to develop to the more sophisticated stage of narrative writing by the use of appropriate and searching questions about the plot development, or rather should we let this development take place at its own rate?

'Alone in the Grange': helping each other through drama

I had been very interested in Jane and Susan's collaboration and felt that I had started seeing the nature of their writing much more clearly. I decided to pursue further the idea of creating a story together before any writing is done by means of drama. I used as stimulus the poem 'Alone in the Grange' by Gregory Harrison.[4] The poem, about a lonely old man who lives on his own in a mysterious house and who the children all think is an evil magician, starts thus:

Strange,
Strange,
Is the little old man
Who lives in the Grange.
Old,
Old;
And they say he keeps
A box full of gold.
Bowed,
Bowed,
Is his thin little back
That once was so proud.

I read the poem to the children three times at intervals in a week. The third time I then explored the theme in drama work. After initial mime activities, the children acted out creeping up to the house and then exploring what happened next for themselves. Groups developed different continuations, some violent, some friendly. I then got the children to imagine being at school the next day telling their friends what had happened the night before. In this way each child had the opportunity to tell his or her story. The next day the children were able to start writing straight away. It did not seem necessary to talk about the children's ideas for the stories; they were quite ready to write and approached the task with obvious enthusiasm. I feel that this was because they already had the story in their heads and needed no time to plot out the tale. Certainly the weaker writers approached the task with unwonted keenness and some of them wrote for longer and at greater length than is normal for them.

Their approach to the work confirmed what I had felt from the close analysis of Jane and Susan's 'Getting into Trouble' story. Finding ways to enable the children to tell their stories before they write them certainly seems to be a powerful technique with children of this age. From my own observation, it improves the motivation and concentration of the weaker writers in particular. One of my worries with the Father Christmas stories had been whether all the children would be able to sustain the narrative thread over a long story. But this fear proved groundless. All the children in the class have many stories to tell. It is just getting them onto paper that gives some of them problems. Increasing the amount of talking seems to help them. William Harpin talks of something similar in his book *The Second R*:

> Writing often comes most naturally and freely after the experience on which it feeds has had time to incubate, to become assimilated. A great temptation in the circumstances of school is to call for writing to tread on the heels of experience.[5]

Donald Murray puts it differently:

> I wonder if extensive re-writing is not mostly a failure of pre-writing, or allowing adequate time for rehearsal, a matter of plucking the fruit before it is ripe.[6]

School-time poems: helping each other to redraft

In this session I wanted to look at the way children are able to work together when redrafting a piece of writing. Earlier work with the class had led me to consider how best to intervene usefully in the writing activity given the age and stage of development of the children. Morag Styles and I decided to set up an activity where the children themselves would be helped to collaborate on redrafting. We hoped that this would give insight into what the children are capable of in terms of becoming more objective about their own work, and to show the extent to which children are prepared to accept another person's reaction to their writing. The ways in which children are prepared to intervene in another child's writing should give us suggestions as to how to intervene sensitively and sympathetically as teachers.

During this writing activity I was able to observe, as Morag Styles led the session. She talked with the children about school-time and read poems on the subject. They were asked then to write a poem themselves about their own school experiences. As we were looking for very individual and personal responses to the subject the children did this first stage of writing on their own. Collaboration took place after the first draft. As children finished they were paired off and sent to work on each other's drafts. First they were to read their partner's poem and underline anything they particularly liked (explaining why they felt this) then put a dotted line under things that could be improved (again explaining why they felt this). Then they were to write under the poem what they thought of it, having perhaps negotiated changes or improvements. They were encouraged to worry about spelling last of all. Then the poem's owner was to write a comment in reply to her or his partner's report. Finally they were to write out the redrafted poem. We were careful to stress the need for positive comments, looking for what they liked in each other's writing rather than negative criticism.

The children are well used to the idea that a piece of writing can be done in rough first and then worked on. However, I have found it hard with this age range (eight- to nine-year-olds) to get beyond working just on the surface features of the writing. There seems to be a reluctance to undertake deeper structural change once something has been written. I was interested to see how this more complicated redrafting process, something quite new to them, would work out in practice.

We were making considerable demands of eight-year-old children. We were asking them not only to identify what they felt about a piece of writing but also to attempt to explain *why* they felt this way. We were expecting each to respect the feelings of the other writer, to show their appreciation of the writing as well as perform that difficult balancing act of adopting a helpful critical stance towards the writing. As teachers we sometimes find this hard. Would it all be too much for eight-year-olds? Perhaps the novelty of the activity helped, but I was reassured by the maturity which they showed. Even the less able children appeared to enjoy the task and made a good attempt at it. I feel sure this is largely because of the genuine pleasure children get from reading or hearing each other's writing.

In this session I spent time observing neutrally and at times participating in the discussions that ensued. George (who lacks confidence as a writer) worked with William (a capable writer and speller). The two versions of George's poem are as follows:

ROUNDERS	ROUNDERS
The bouler bouls,	*The bouler bouls,*
I hit the ball,	*I whacked the ball,*
It's hi in the air,	*It's high in the air,*
Jonny caches me out.	*Jonny cought me out.*
now it's Mickeyes turn,	*now it's Mickeyes hit,*
The bouler bouls Micky hits	*The bouler bouls Micky hits*
It goe's over the outher side	*It zooms over the outher*
of the pitch	*side of the pitch*
Micky races round the pousts	*Micky races round the posts*
the feilder throughs the ball	*the fielder lobs the ball*
Mickey on the last come	*Micky is on the last cone*
the feilder stames him out.	*the feilder stamps him out.*
at the end of	*At the end of the game*
the game the	*The scores were*
scouse were 36–1.	*36–1!*

They changed words for effect. 'Hit' was changed to 'whacked'. 'Goe's' became 'thunders' then 'zooms'. 'Turn' became 'hit'. George expressed concern about the fact that William seemed to use better words, but in fact William's suggestions seemed to trigger off George's own vocabulary – he reached deeper into himself. 'Whacked' was William's suggestion, but 'zooms' was George's. 'Throws' became 'chucks' then 'lobs'. William made spelling corrections, but this was done quickly and with little comment. Discussion centred on deeper features of the writing. A grammatical change was made ('caches' to 'cought') and William rewrote George's last verse for greater effect in layout. At one point a technical discussion of rounders was held. Interestingly, the poem started with more consistent use of tense than it finished with. Another stage of drafting would be needed to clear up details such as this.

William's written comment was as follows:

I like the way George says Micky races round the posts. I put whacked instead of hit because it sounds more exciting. And the same with some other words. Altogether very good.

George's written reply:

I think the report is very good altogether. Thanks to William.

Certainly this technique of redrafting another child's work was of benefit to the children. It provided them with a tight structure in which to work. This helped them to keep their thoughts and comments relevant. While much of the redrafting stayed on a superficial level there were some indications of deeper thought, for instance when William reorganized one of George's verses. Redrafting is clearly very difficult for children of this age. Since this was the first time the children had engaged in any type of structured redrafting, their approach to the activity gives some clues as to their natural untutored inclinations in this area. Not surprisingly, they were concerned about spelling, but they showed genuine interest in the story that each poem told. Their suggested changes may not be thought of as improvements by an adult, but if the changes have come from considered probing of the text this is of little concern. Their judgement will improve over time.

When Morag summoned them all back to the carpet at the end of the morning I heard Duncan say: 'I must say that's the best sentence I've ever ...'. I do not know whether the last word was going to be 'written' or 'read' (it got drowned in the general hubbub) but it hardly matters. The opportunity to spend time looking hard at a small piece of writing had produced a significant reaction in him.

Later I asked the children how they felt when they were working together on a piece of writing. They found it easy to identify the features in each other's writing that they enjoyed, but several expressed reservations about being asked to make suggestions for improving a friend's writing. They said that they felt they were hurting the other person's feelings.

Teacher: Do you think that working with someone else makes your own writing better?
Child: Yes, if I look at someone's who's cleverer than I am, I can get ideas.
Child: Well if they've got neater handwriting it can help.
Child: I think when you look at other people's writing and they're good it makes me feel mine isn't as good as theirs. But it encourages me to try harder.
Child: When you look at someone's who's better than you it makes you feel jealous.

These comments raise a difficult issue. The only justification for working in this way is if it helps to develop the children's own self-confidence as writers and their understanding of writing. The children themselves have seen some of the pitfalls that could arise if the whole process is not handled with sensitivity. To develop work in this way will require that we regularly talk about what is going on, why we are doing it and how we all feel about it and who works with whom.

I asked if I should continue getting children working together on their writing next year with my new class. They were adamant that I should. It makes it easier to write and makes the writing better, they claim.

I was interested in their explanations about the difficulties of suggesting improvements. Here Donald Murray, a professional writer, talks about how he feels when a piece of writing he is doing is redrafted by someone else:

> Steph pointed out ... that I incorrectly used 'for' in the second paragraph. She suggested 'because'. My reaction was normal; I rejected her suggestion, as I would any editor's suggestion. I over-reacted and re-wrote the whole paragraph. When I receive criticism, I normally put the draft aside and start a new one. It is probably the way I re-establish control over my territory. Childish. But the paragraph was better. 'For' became 'who'.[7]

Donald Murray accuses himself of being childish. Perhaps child-like, a non-pejorative word, would be more accurate. The children themselves are aware of how easy it is to hurt someone else's feelings. Writing is a very personal experience and as adults most of us know how nervous we feel when we show something we have written to someone else for comment. During the writing session described above I had written my own poem about my school day. I can still remember how much I wanted the children to like it when I read it out to them.

At the end of his introspection Donald Murray knows that the paragraph is better. He has not necessarily followed his editor's advice, but that advice has led to a new version that he still feels in charge of. Donald Graves comments on his co-author's self-analysis:

> Rebellion is not the exclusive property of the professional writer. I find it a healthy sign when children rebel in order to maintain control of their information or language. The child may be 'wrong' but the greater issue in the long run will be the child's sense of control of the writing process. We are experts at stealing children's writing voices.[8]

It is perhaps when we do not show how much we *value* a child's writing that our well-intentioned attempts to 'improve' the writing are at their most destructive. It is then that the children will start to sense an attempt to wrest control of the writing away from them. The children by their comments showed me how aware of this problem they are. Our job as teachers is to maintain this sensitivity to the individual in order that we may help that individual gain ever more control over his or her own writing.

Conclusion

The activities described above took place over one academic year with one class of second-year juniors. I did not embark on the project with any preconceived theory of writing that I wished to test. I was merely hoping that I would gain further insight into the nature of the process of the writing, how children view writing and how they see themselves as writers.

The complex relationship between talking, writing and reading was illuminated in the work we did. With children of this age it seems as if the true writing of the story is done before pencil is put to paper, while the transcription of the story is more akin to a reading of the story.

I do not believe that what I have described in any way proves that collaboration necessarily produces 'better' writing. However, I think it is clear that the activities have enabled the children to reflect on their own writing and to talk about the writing both among themselves and with me. This discussion has helped them to develop their own images of themselves as real writers. Collaboration has given me a chance to see the writing more clearly from the children's point of view. I have no doubt that at times it helped the weaker writers to write with greater concentration and motivation and at greater length. Above all, though, they enjoyed it.

Notes

1. Myra Barrs, 'Knowing by Becoming' in Margaret Meek and Jane Miller (eds), *Changing English*, Heinemann, 1984.
2. Helen Young, *What Difference Does It Make, Danny?* Fontana Young Lions, 1983.
3. Annabelle Dixon, 'Storyboxes – supporting the case for narrative in the primary school', *Cambridge Journal of Education*, vol. 17, no. 3, Michaelmas 1987.
4. Gregory Harrison, 'Alone in the Grange' in *The Night of the Wild Horses*, Oxford University Press.
5. William Harpin, *The Second R*, Allen and Unwin, 1976.
6. Donald Murray and Donald Graves, 'Revision in the Writer's Workshop and in the Classroom' in Helen Cowie (ed.), *The Development of Children's Imaginative Writing*, Croom Helm, 1984.
7. Ibid.
8. Ibid.

5 Profiling in English: the potential for real teacher–pupil collaboration in assessment

NICK BROWN

It would be good to think that this particular chapter could become dated very quickly. The ideas behind profiling are not new and much of what follows would no doubt be accepted without raised eyebrows by many English teachers. Her Majesty's Inspectorate was in 1979 prepared to concede that pupils '*could* show an ability to make a shrewd evaluation of their work'[1] and Chater sensibly comments on this sentence: 'By ignoring what pupils think of their own ... writing and talk' – why not listening and reading too, though? – 'the teacher denies his pupils valuable learning experiences and himself a rich source of information about their achievements.'[2] It is true that this comes at the start of a chapter entitled 'Pupil Participation in Assessment' which only glances (in a section called 'Setting up a dialogue between teacher and pupil' – my theme for this chapter) at the value to be obtained from formalizing the whole process of self-assessment; nevertheless, the book is sufficiently mainstream in its approach to be regarded as fairly representing standard enlightened good practice at the time of its publication in 1984.

So why, given the apparent acceptance of the general idea, should it need emphasizing now? There are several answers to this and, briefly, there are two that interest me at the moment.

First, there seems to me to be little doubt that, in the near future, considerable pressure is bound to be placed on English teachers to ignore considerations of the role of pupil collaboration in assessment. To view it as *fundamentally* important is unlikely, for example, to be consistent with a national curriculum monitored by national testing at seven, 11, 14 and 16, let alone within the model of English we can begin to guess might be recommended as being part of that national curriculum. Second, although the idea of profiling and self-assessment may be widely accepted, the actual practice may not, of course, be sufficiently soundly established to be able to withstand the thinking which might prevail.

The whole problem with relying on external, objective assessment, as Thornton comments, is, quite simply, the complexity of language – 'the complexity of its structure and functional nature, of what it is as a human attribute and the part it plays in human life'.[3] Of course, most practising English teachers recognize that any form of assessment that tries even to define the competences that students might be acquiring, let alone rank their abilities in these in some kind of order, is at best simplifying this complexity and at worst totally misrepresenting and distorting the abilities of their students. And it does not take very much of a glance at the responses to the *English from 5 to 16*[4] document in English or the difficulties caused by GCSE criteria to English departments across the country to begin to appreciate the problems that formalizing objective testing nationally poses, whether it is a question of setting up the bench-marks that students 'should' be achieving or in defining their capacities for achieving them.

One might, of course, say that if teachers and other professionals find difficulties in such assessment, why shift such a burden onto the pupils themselves, who are surely going to be even less competent than the 'experts'? But this, of course, overlooks the crucial point that probably the only viable form of assessment is that in which the pupil does learn or discover something of value, something other than the usual, self-determining, simple or subtly presented fact that he or she may be thought of by others as a relative success or failure. It is pupils' perceptions of themselves, what they *feel* they have learnt and mastered, what they *think* they need to know – however sharp or however inaccurate such observations may seem to be objectively – that are ultimately infinitely more useful and important, to them or others, in 'raising standards' than anything 'objective' that could be devised.

What follows is, therefore, an attempt to reformulate at least one of the real alternatives to any form of assessment that fails to see the student as an important collaborator in his or her own learning and progress. It is largely an account of the assessment system obtaining in one particular English Department at the present time and anyone interested in how our scheme has developed can trace it through Burgess and Adams's *Outcomes of Education*[5] and Blanchard's *Out in the Open*.[6] But times have changed and, especially for those unfamiliar with these books, let me outline briefly what has remained of the system described there and also explain what developments have since taken place.

This assessment system, then, is almost entirely based throughout the five years on coursework, self-assessment on the part of the pupil and teacher statement in response. This has been so in the Lower School for some time and GCSE has provided the perfect opportunity to extend the whole scheme consistently through the five years. Formative assessment involving of necessity collaboration between teacher and pupil remains an area of high priority, though progress has also been made in fusing formative with the summative assessment designed for the information of those outside the classroom, be they parents, future employers, other teachers including those in further education, school governors or whoever, and traditionally represented by the grade on the exam certificate. As Blanchard writes: 'It is important to realise ... that formative assessments may have an enduring value. Equally, summative assessments may quickly outlive their usefulness and, crucially, their validity.'[7] The arrival of records of achievement and the advent of GCSE should enable us to minimize the gap between the two, first, by maintaining a periodic summary of, and judgement on, performance within the context of a course that is dedicated to an individual's positive achievement; and second, by adopting a course reliant on coursework whereby it is the quality of the best achievement that is preserved for assessment. Putting it simply, with pupils collecting their best work and continually reflecting on it, it is possible for outsiders simply to eavesdrop on the whole process – a process in continual evolution rather than one of categorization – and make their own judgements.

It should be possible to avoid 'the destructive implication that it is only possible for some to succeed at the expense of others'.[8] Sadly, the government's lip-service to the ideas of records of achievement:

> The Government aims to set in place by 1990 national arrangements for the introduction of records of achievement for school leavers. Such records, which are at present being piloted in a number of areas ... will have an important role in recording performance and profiling a pupil's achievements across and beyond the national curriculum.[9]

seems totally undermined by an apparent primary aim in assessment not merely to rank pupils definitively within a form or school but between schools and ultimately within a whole national age-group:

> Pupils and parents should know what individual pupils are being taught in each year ... They also need to know how the individual pupil has performed against the attainment targets, and by comparison with the range of marks achieved by pupils in his or her class – for example, 10% got grade 1, 20% grade 2, 30% grade 3.
>
> Teachers should know how individual pupils are progressing so that they can decide on appropriate next steps for their learning; and how pupils in their class overall are doing as compared with the attainment targets, with other similar classes in the school, and with other schools, particularly in the same LEA and with the national average.[10]

The centre of our scheme of assessment remains the pupil's folder. In the Lower School this is a ring binder where all the best pieces of work over the three years, together with the pupil's comments made during that period, are collected. In the Upper School it is a folder containing the GCSE pieces for submission, accumulated as the course progresses, with the comments of both pupil and teacher on achievement in each unit of work comprising the formative aspect of the record of achievement.

Pupils in the Lower School write statements on and reviews of their work using guidelines that concentrate on three areas. To simplify somewhat, these entail reflecting on what they have done, what they have learned and what they feel they need to do to make progress.

The coursework element used to be a major factor in deciding the groups that each pupil would be placed in but because of the extension of mixed-ability teaching within the Department, folders are no longer used for direct comparison of pupil with pupil for the purposes of setting. Pupils now simply collect their best pieces, whatever those might be, and their increased responsibility for reflecting on what those might be, what does represent them at their best, is at least arguably an advantage to the system. Teachers now no longer have to categorize their pupils into four areas of competence and group them accordingly and it seems entirely within the spirit of what was set up as a 'non-graded, criterion-referenced, descriptive, non-competitive, pupil-involving assessment'[11] scheme that this use of the scheme (to compare and grade and set pupils) – a use quickly appreciated by pupils themselves and pushed very much to the forefront of their thinking – should vanish.

To show something of how pupils respond to this, there follows a number of statements and extracts of statements from a class of first-year pupils at the end of their first term who have had no previous experience of reflecting formally on their own achievement.

One of the most interesting of these, particularly in terms of actual collaboration and potential collaboration, is Paul's. Paul finds enormous difficulty with all aspects of reading and writing and has little confidence orally. He has, with others, support from the Head of Special Needs in two of his five English lessons per week and he achieved this statement by dictating his response to the guidelines to her and then copying out her written transcriptions (any errors are errors of transcription on his part).

in English this year I have read books written a poem and about Christus filled in the gaps in stories listened people reading in class from Tyke tyler and Mrs. frisbee. I wrote a poem abous snow that was publidhed in the frs1. year poemy magazine and I wrote about my first street. I also did work on using my dictonry. The thing I enjoyed most was writing about my street. it was good to think about where I live. I thought it was easy becase I had lots of ideas. I least enjoyed reading the two books because Im no good at reading. It was okay to listen to the stories when other people read them out. My handwriting has got better it is neater. I have lent to use a dictonry. Now I know my alphabet. My reading is improving. Now I can read lots of new words. I look forward to doing more writing next term I would like to write about tractors.

There seems to me to be an enormous sense of achievement about what he writes – the pride in the published poem and the real satisfaction in having reflected on his surroundings, for example. There is a quiet simple pride and sense of confidence in his honest and entirely accurate statements about his progress: his handwriting *is* neater; he *has* learned how to use a dictionary and does now know his alphabet; his reading *is* improving and he can read lots of new words; above all, he does look forward to writing next term (and will, of course, be given the chance to write about tractors!). Interesting, too, is his lack of confidence over reading among his peers (something he does not have to do but clearly feels uncomfortable about) and his therefore muted lip-service to having enjoyed the shared experience of the texts – a pointer and challenge to the teacher. Clearly, it seems to me anyway, he has benefited enormously from being integrated into a mixed-ability classroom with support from outside and it was a fine moment when, in another context and in totally unconscious but gloriously complete refutation of everything that national testing stands for, he was asked to grade his attainment in English on a four-point scale of 'very good', 'good', 'acceptable' or 'cause for concern' he chose, with remarkable perception and accuracy: 'very good'.

But what about others in the group? What can we learn from their responses, both individually and collectively? Consider the reflections of two pupils, first Jennie:

We started at the beginning of term doing some work on using our eyes and describing things. Then we started thinking about books and what we like to read. We also worked on making up our own riddles and they were shown in a booklet which was sold at the Words and Music evening. We did a topic on writing thriller stories and I thought that was good. Then we were presented our dictionarys and we were taught how to use them ... I have most enjoyed the reading as a group in English because when a certain point came up in the book we talked about it and people had their own say in things. I least enjoyed 'filling in the gaps' work because it was boring ... I look forward to doing more group work in the future because people learn to work together and discuss things together ... I could use my dictionary. Listening to people is also good because you can learn things from what people say.

and now Simon:

... We have a library reading lesson, class reading and of course reading at home. We did some work on filling in gaps from passages after that, we used the computer while doing a similar project. I enjoy using the computer because you get to do some work on words and the way you put them together without putting pen to paper. I also like writing stories because you can let your imagination run riot. I hate working from English text books because you have to write the right answer and not what you'd like to put.

In English this term I have learnt about presenting my work more neatly and more about punctuation. I also learnt about preparing your work like writing down some notes so when you come to write it it is easier. My handwriting has improved slightly. I look forward to English usually but not when we are working from books. I can develop my English by dramatically improving my handwriting which I am trying at the moment.

There are certain things that stand out clearly for a teacher here. First, there are always the issues of what each pupil *chooses* to write about in a statement, what he or she considers to be important or even remembers – and omissions *can* be as interesting and fruitful as the comments themselves. This can be on a class level or on an individual level. (Look at Simon's perfunctory remarks about his own reading, for example, but also the fascinating remarks on note-taking, a skill the class had spent a little time on but only he had mentioned presumably because he, perhaps unlike others, had found it useful or important.) Remember that, although pupils have the guidelines, they are left free to write about their experiences in any way they choose. So marked differences of response between individuals (who have, after all, experienced the 'same' term's work, in the broadest sense) are always significant for the potential development of those individuals and marked similarities of response are always clear indicators to the teacher of group feelings that he or she can scarcely ignore. For example, in this case the emphasis that the pupils themselves place on their own collaboration is fascinating. Jennie's comments on collaboration were echoed throughout the class in different ways. Here's Cassie:

> *The thing I have most enjoyed in English this term was probably the reading and the work that followed on from it, as the books were both good and I liked the way we read it, having different parts each and taking it in turn to read. Doing it like this made me enjoy the books even more because in our old school the books were all read by the teacher and I found it boring but this way everyone has a chance to read and its fun to listen to.*

and here's Mark:

> *I've most enjoyed working on the computer with everybody. I like working in a group getting different ideas and thoughts.*

One of the most interesting aspects of this is the unprompted enthusiasm for group work. Is it nothing more than the dutiful response to previously articulated teacherly comment? Very unlikely! Even if this were the case, it would seem to have been internalized quite naturally through genuine response, for if there is one thing that emerges from pupils' writing their own statements it is that only what they are enthusiastic about and have actually responded to will be enthusiastically reviewed. Perhaps one important collaboration that is indicated as necessary by these comments, though, is the one between secondary school and feeder primary school since part of these first years' enthusiasm appears to be generated by some novelty of the experience. Can this be true?

In a sense, this may also be the lesson to be learned from the multiple thumbs-down for textbooks expressed so vociferously by most members of the class. Simon's dislike of English textbooks was echoed by Ian:

> *I did not like using the english exercise book I found it uninteresting.*

and Scott:

> *I didn't like the work out of a book with some set questions that we have to do sometimes. I found it boring because I done it at my old school and didn't like it then.*

Another consideration in looking at these statements, it seems to me, though, is the *way* pupils write about their experiences in English. There are always sections of cliché and received undigested repetition from peers, parents, siblings and teachers – dead, meaningless sentiments, sometimes even as empty as a grade – and, without knowing the pupils, it is perhaps possible to spot some of these in the above examples. I think they are inevitable. But so, fortunately, are the genuine and revelatory comments. Take this, for example, from a shy little first-year girl, Natalie, who had considerable difficulty in adapting from her primary school:

> *I read out the poem to the hole of the 1st years and I enjoyed it very much.*

or Simon's actually very precise realization:

> *I enjoy using the computer because you get to do some work on words and the way you put them together without putting pen to paper.*

or Jennie's threefold repetition of her discovery that talking and listening are important to her. Is she, incidentally, telling herself, or trying a bit of propaganda – very common and useful in statements? Is she rehearsing what she has heard to see if it fits, or because she thinks it is what the teacher wants to hear? Or is she making a genuine discovery for herself at this point? Such questions abound in every statement and it is partly the fact that the teacher *needs* to make such interpretations that give them a considerable part of their value, it seems to me.

Finally, from this first-year group, some extracts from Scott's statement:

> *We read as different people and spoke when the person you are speakes in the book ... I had never done this before and didn't like it much ... but I surpose that was because I don't like reading much ... The first book we read was Tyke Tyler. I had read the beginning of it before, but I didn't like it much so I put it down. It wasn't much better this time either ... The second book we read was Mrs Frisby and the Rats of Nimh. This wasn't very good at the beginning but I realy enjoyed it near the end ... I enjoyed the work on the computor ... because I like working computors and it was a change from reading and writing. I didn't like the work out of a book with some set questions that we have to do sometimes. I found it boring because I done it at my old school and didn't like it then. I think I have improved on my reading but nothing else. ... I am looking forward to using the computor again and I am dreading writing storys. I could help my English by speaking out aloud alot*

more as I hardly ever put my hand up and answer questions. I also think I should read alot more which I am starting to do.

Could anyone devise any kind of test that could tell us a fraction of what Scott himself is prepared to, either consciously or unconsciously?

But what about the implications of this for GCSE? For us, this whole Lower School approach now naturally extends itself into the Upper School where, with the adoption of records of achievement and the arrival of GCSE, the welcome emphasis on coursework and criterion-based marking, it seemed for the first time feasible to make the whole five-year scheme coherent and begin to avoid the schizophrenic lurch into exam-centred education that previously used to afflict students.

In order to marry the demands of GCSE with those of records of achievement we set up a system whereby pupils not only built up a folder of coursework for their GCSE assessment in clearly defined stages but periodically reflected on their achievements in the course and set themselves targets for the future as well. The reflection necessary for both processes was intended to be mutually supporting. Naturally, parents, who receive the statements and for whom the folders are available for inspection on parents' evenings, are thus in a position to be closely involved and far more fully informed.

There is a good deal of detail to reflect on in these statements even if the style is sometimes more formal than might be genuinely helpful. Pupils are, of course, intensely aware that these Upper School statements are potentially very *public* utterances and it is difficult to see how the cold influence of this realization can easily be avoided. As an example, take this statement by Siân, a GCSE pupil:

A large amount of time this term has been given to studying our Literature text book 'On the Black Hill' by Bruce Chatwin ... I enjoy reading, and in any available time I have had, I read The Magic Cottage by James Herbert, and I am in the middle of the controversial book 'Spycatcher' by Peter Wright.

Most of the discussions taken place were about chapters in the 'Black Hill', which I contributed to as much as I was able ... I am more confident in smaller groups maybe because you are not intimidated by anyone. Another topic discussed was Childhood. I participated in a good discussion about children's fears, and how they affect them. Following this, I wrote a piece about how the fear of dark can affect a child's imagination. I was pleasesd with this imaginative story, as I find being able to write freely and imaginatively much easier and more fun than for example book reviews or other 'controlled pieces'.

The 'Old Age' topic was also imaginative so I enjoyed writing it. The topic made me aware of how old people can become to feal rejected and very lonely, if their family does not take an active interest in them. Since I wrote this piece I have been involved in taking old people shopping. The topic became a reality, saddening in some cases, as we talked to the old people, and they expressed their feelings about being sent into care.

> While we were reading 'On the Black Hill' tasks were allotted to us including making a family tree, and a timeline for the book. These tasks were quite difficult, but fun, as I had to locate exact dates, and investigate who was related to whom for the tree. Reading the book 'On the Black Hill' made me aware of how it relates to people nowadays. It shows how peoples feeling towards others are communicated in different ways, and a view of community life.
>
> The language in the book, and that of other books I have read has influenced my writing (I think!) I learn new vocabulary and phrases from the books and use them in my stories/reviews. New vocabulary also influences my ability to communicate my views and ideas clearly. I have improved in this respect and am able to hold discussions with others, stating my point of view and listening to theirs much better.
>
> I find that it is important to choose the correct style of writing or speech for different audiences. For formal adresses my style of communication differs greatly from that for children. I have done a lot of work with children recently, and I am able to talk to them in simple language so they are able to understand.
>
> To improve my English in the future I will continue to read more books of differing styles, to acquire varied vocab. My spelling has improved but I can still look up words so I am sure that every piece of work I hand in is correct. For my Literature exam I need to re-read the texts and revise my notes so I can obtain a good grade. My English course has given me a good background for the future. I am able to write good imaginative pieces which has shown me I have an imagination which can be used for amusing children. I can write a formal letter (or informal) which will show my qualities off to my best, perhaps for a future employer.
>
> Although I do not think I will study English A level, the ability to write essays and understand literature will be useful for later life

In the meantime, teachers were preparing for their side of the statement and assessing what they believed to be the actual level of skills achieved by pupils in GCSE terms by assessing submitted pieces of work using our own design of assessment sheet (see Figure 5.1) which attempted to make manageable the complexities of officially imposed GCSE criteria. Similar methods of assessment obtained in the Department for oral work and literature. However, it soon became clear that attempting to merge GCSE assessment demands with those of records of achievement in the way we had was to bring its own problems. Criterion referencing is an enormous improvement but a good deal depends, of course, on the criteria being used. In English, for example, at GCSE, writing was supposed to satisfy any of the above criteria at one of the levels indicated. Our problem as teachers, and a very crucial one, was to respond to pupils' *own* perceptions of their own progress and needs within a GCSE course while also feeding back to them a helpful kind of 'official-based' judgement.

Figure 5.1 Assessment criteria

1. *Understanding and conveying information*
   v.straightforward/straightforward/more complex/quite complex/complex

2. *Understanding and conveying ideas and opinions*
   v.basic/basic/coherent/clear and accurate/ordered, clear and accurate

3. *Selecting and commenting on material*
   simple comment/literal comment/detailed comment/detailed comment evaluated/ specific purpose evaluation/detailed specific purpose evaluation

4. *Describing experience, reflecting on it and expressing what is felt and what is imagined*
   basic/concrete/detailed/effective/reflective/detailed and analysing feelings

5. *Recognising meanings and attitudes*
   v.explicit/explicit/more obvious/implicit/subtle

6. *Awareness of variety of uses of language*
   some/sense of audience/understanding appropriate use

7. *Sentence and paragraph structure*
   simple/clear/varied/correct/appropriate/accurate/well constructed/full range.

Two fundamental problems quickly emerged. First, a new schizophrenia was engendered whereby, while students were assessing their own work within a framework of what they had done, what they had learnt and in what ways they could make progress, teachers were using an entirely different framework, unintelligible to their students and often to an extent themselves, too. Or, to put it more kindly and accurately, when assumptions as to the significance of the terms above were questioned, it became clear that English teachers had widely differing interpretations of certain key areas. Second, and significantly, the criteria failed in very important respects not only to match what the pupils were doing but to reflect the actual 'levels' they were supposed to be doing it at. For example, it proves quite impossible to 'measure' a student's ability to convey information on a level of complexity; it is quite obvious that in most real instances the most effective way to convey information is as straightforwardly as possible and that any attempts to introduce the complexity so valued by GCSE criteria would probably only confuse the recipient unnecessarily. More crucially, it was also quickly apparent that much of the, for example, imaginative writing produced by students was impossible to assess adequately using the categories and criteria extracted – possibly inadequately – from the syllabus and represented in Figure 5.1.

It was clear that, if we wanted to obtain a system whereby the requirements of GCSE coursework and the principles behind self-assessment were not entirely mutually exclusive, considerable redesigning would be necessary. What we have arrived at now enables pupils to write about each of the major pieces of work they intend to submit for GCSE by describing what they set out to do and then reflecting on their successes in completing the work. To help them decide on how successful they were, they are invited to consider the criteria teachers themselves will be using in assessing their work. It is probably unnecessary to say that these will be far from the only criteria that pupils will use about themselves but it does help in assessing their own work to consider what framework will be applied by others and might therefore usefully be applied by themselves. To be clear *for themselves* about the actual skills they are in the process of developing is surely an important principle of the whole business and one sadly neglected by more conventional assessment.

It is interesting to note some of the difficulties, therefore, involved in making the terminology of such skills accessible to pupils. To take one example, a concept such as 'a sense of audience' may quite rightly be a key notion within GCSE practice but how well do pupils grasp the extent to which, in a small group discussion, they have shown, for example, 'sensitivity to the audience and situation in the use of the appropriate speech style and in the manner of presentation'? One may say that it is the responsibility of *teachers* to assess this and all the fine distinctions involved in GCSE assessment but it is also the job of the teacher to enable the pupil to understand what he or she is trying to achieve in any task: if a pupil does not understand what he or she is trying to do, how is he or she to be successful in achieving it? And is it not unreasonable of a teacher, then, to assess it in such terms? Pupils in this case, therefore, could be invited to consider to what extent such a discussion was 'right for listeners' in such a context.

No doubt, certain things are lost in such simplifications. Questions of audibility, intelligibility, style tone, intonation and pace may all be subsumed under a label such as 'performance skills', a label open to misinterpretation without discussion. Important changes take place, too, in adapting GCSE criteria to a human framework. It is hard to prevent subjective elements from striding unashamedly in, ignoring the pseudo-scientific objective stance of the exam boards. It is surely right for both pupil and teacher to consider to what extent a piece of writing might be, say, 'interesting' or 'original' rather than get bogged down in the minutiae of the extent to which such pieces are 'describing and reflecting upon experience and detailing and analysing effectively what is felt and imagined'.

Some reading this may feel, as I do, that there are uneasy compromises involved in any system that tries to reconcile such diverse goals as genuine teacher–pupil collaboration with the demands, say, of an exam course and its certification and with the need to communicate in a real and valuable way with those outside the process. This is undoubtedly so, though a more important consideration may simply be about the way in which pupils respond to such a scheme in practice. To what extent does what they write show a valuable level of reflection? What opportunities for genuinely collaborative learning can we find in what they write for us? In what senses can we see the process encouraging pupils to take themselves seriously as writers, talkers, human beings? Whatever the answers to these, we need, it seems to me, both from a human and educational perspective, to question through alternative practical models such as the one I have suggested above, the insidious and, for many, tempting proposal that 'established national standards ... [are] a proven and essential way towards raising standards of achievement'; we need to question any assessment system pitched against such 'national standards' that claims for itself that 'at the *heart* [*sic*] of the assessment process there will be nationally prescribed tests'; we need to question whether any of this could genuinely 'enable teachers and parents to ensure that he or she [the pupil] is making adequate *progress*'[21]; and instead we may need to learn to listen more closely and quite explicitly to the children themselves.

Notes

1. DES, *Aspects of Secondary Education in England*, HMSO, 1979.
2. Pauline Chater, *Marking and Assessment in English*, Methuen, 1984.
3. Geoffrey Thornton, *Language, Ignorance and Education*, Edward Arnold, 1986.
4. DES, *English from 5 to 16*, Curriculum Matters 1, HMSO, 1984.
5. Anthony Adams and Antony Burgess (eds), *Outcomes of Education*, Macmillan, 1980.
6. John Blanchard, *Out in the Open*, Cambridge University Press, 1986.
7. Ibid.
8. Ibid.
9. DES, *The National Curriculum*, HMSO, 1987.
10. Ibid.
11. Blanchard, *Out in the Open*.
12. DES, *The National Curriculum*.

PART TWO
Cross-phase writing exchanges

6 Four examples of cross-phase collaboration

Edited by MORAG STYLES[1]

I 'Seven Up'

'Seven Up' was one of the first collaborations between members of our writing group while we were investigating different ways of approaching autobiographical writing with children. From the start the interactions between primary and secondary teachers were dynamic. They were learning from each other, eager to find out how writing was tackled, how pupils 'tick' at different stages of schooling. To explore this further, all sorts of exchanges between pupils and teachers were being set up. Perhaps the most exciting collaboration at this stage was that between Mary Hilton and Nick Brown. The combination of the quiet, reflective Nick, a very experienced Head of English in a secondary school and the passionate, lively Mary, a mother of three in her first year of primary teaching, was electric. Descriptions of their pupils' activities dominated early meetings and we were all gripped by the inventiveness of this exchange. They came up with a scheme which would enable their respective eight- and 14-year-olds to communicate with each other. The younger children would write to the older, telling them what they thought life would be like when they were 14. Meanwhile, the secondary pupils explored memories of being about seven through different types of writing. Here's Nick Brown on the origins of the project:

> The idea behind the work my fourth-year secondary pupils produced really sprang from a conjunction of two factors: the first was that I was paired with Mary's eight-year-olds; the second was the fact that my pupils were involved in a Film Studies course, were about to look at the notion of documentary, primarily through the 'Seven Up' programmes produced for television which charted the lives of various individuals from the age of seven through seven-year stages to the age of 28. Since the theme we were exploring was autobiography and since the pupils concerned were themselves very close to the first and second stages of the film's age gap, the opportunity for some kind of mutual work seemed ideal.
>
> From my end, I had already become interested in the implications of this particular documentary for my own pupils. What the film does successfully is open up real windows into what it is like to be a seven-year old and act as a very

sharp reminder to my 14-year-olds of an age which, for them, already seems like a foreign country. I wanted to see if they too could produce 'documentaries' in the broadest sense of their own or others' lives at the age of seven or 14 using as 'documents' interviews, reminiscences or imaginative constructions or reconstructions. The fact that they were to have a specific audience of younger children added purpose to the enterprise.

The film itself provoked considerable discussion and thought – more so by a long way than any other material we had so far explored and at a deeper, highly involved level. We looked at issues of class (another aspect of the film that is dealt with very powerfully) – something of a red herring in terms of subsequent work, but fascinating in the questions it raised about the relative influence that background seemed to have on character and attitude, both of which are *seen* to develop over 21 years in a way that could not be shown in any other medium or by any other method, with such clarity and ease at any rate.

They were then given a wide range of tasks and options to explore either jointly or individually. These included interviewing seven-year-olds (they composed questions that echoed quite closely the concerns of the original film on fighting, discipline, the opposite sex, race, money, class, plans for the future). Many found the interviewing surprisingly difficult in comparison with the TV smoothies! They interviewed each other and their friends on the same questions to explore different attitudes of different ages. Some wrote series of autobiographical sketches, some wrote poems, some re-created short scenes of their younger lives in play form (mostly based on remembered arguments). One group derived great pleasure from the songs and skipping rhymes they had sung as youngsters in the playground. One girl devoted a lot of time to interviewing parents of younger children to find out how they (adults) thought young minds ticked. Here are some examples:

MY SCHOOL LIFE AT SEVEN
My name is John and I am seven years old. I live in suburban London and I live about half a mile away from my middle school. My mum doesn't let me walk to school on my own so my friend's mum and my mum take it in turns to take me.

Once I've got to school, me and my best friend, Colin go to our classroom. After our teacher has called the register we usually have a discussion about what is happening in the news. Our teacher always asks us to listen to the news and read the newspapers because she says we should know what was happening in the world. I never listen to the news – apart from the football results because it's boring.

At school we have a gang. My best friend Colin is the leader. There are five people in our gang and we never let anyone else in it.

At lunch times we play kiss chase with the girls but we never really kiss the girls because we don't like them much. School dinners are really disgusting but worst of all is mashed potato. Last week our gang had a mashed potato fight with another gang, so now we are not allowed to have school dinners. The highlight of my year at school is always the school play because for a whole three weeks at the end of the

Autumn term we don't do any schoolwork and just spend all our time working on the play. This year I have got an important part and I've got loads of lines to learn so I'd better go and do it now.

WHO'S THE BEST AT HIDE AND SEEK AND WARS? [extract]
A small boy sits behind a fallen tree trunk in a large wood, not moving, not making a sound. He could hear the others calling him but he was the best at this game.

Chris: (as Chris shrugs and calls again) Come on Sam we all give up.
Sam: (sighs) O.K. I'm over here.
Chris: You knew we had all been caught. It's no good playing with you.
Sam: No, I didn't.
John: (Turns to see the others walking away . . .) Now what's happened?
Sam: Who wants to play with them anyway? (pause) Let's play wars

SEVEN AGAIN
Seven year olds are extremely intelligent. The quotation 'Give me a child until he is seven and I'll give you the man' is very true. A seven year old's daily life would begin by getting himself dressed. This is a timely task yet to be properly mastered is something which is pressed upon seven year olds by their parents.

Friends are of great importance to seven year olds and sometimes it would seem as if your whole life revolved around being asked to play in a game. If not asked it would be drastic.

Little responsibility is given at this age but usual things like feeding rabbits, cats or other pets. Rights is another important issue in a 7 year old's life. Whether you are right or wrong, arguments can spring up all over the place when seven year olds discover someone is wrong for what ever reason a great crowd of them against you and no matter how hard you try and get in with them, they still push you away.

Imagination also plays a big part, thinking up good games. A favourite game is witches and wizards or doctors and nurses. Seven years olds love to dress up and put on face paints so they can act 'big'. Seven year olds do not really care about the opposite sex nor are they racist in any way towards any nationality.

That once was me
young and afraid, my life spins round
My clothes hang limp.
No friends, no family.
I need care and love, but no-one wants me
That once was me.

Older, but not wiser
School, no way! Just laze the day away.
One friend one life
My life is a dream
The world is a dream
That once was me.

Old and trapped
Feeble and frail
Limp and soggy
What a life what a world
That once was me.

By this stage of the project, the notion of audience had become central. We had always known that writing for others, a real audience, was important. James Britton and others had made us aware of this in the early 1970s.[2] But we were sharply reminded that when real learning is to take place, we generally have to reinvent the wheel for ourselves. We *knew* that audience was important, but did we really carry that knowledge into our daily endeavours with children?

Mary Hilton is one of the most sensitive teachers I have ever seen work with children. She takes children and their learning very seriously and treats them with respect. But even Mary, in this instance, failed to realize till it was too late that it was only reasonable for her class to know *for whom* they were writing:

Although the general theme of the group was autobiography, the children in my class had already written several pieces about themselves so we decided to experiment with collaboration. My children would write about what they expected life would be like when they reached fourteen and Nick's pupils would then be able to respond with their comments and their own pieces about their lives when they were seven.

To get them talking and thinking first I asked my class whether they thought life would improve for them as they grew to be 14. Several of them had older brothers and sisters. At first they were quite sure that it would. In fact they represented life at 14 as a sort of adult Nirvana – a life of luxury, autonomy, free from care and responsibility. You could have money, clothes, teenage excitements and power – people wouldn't 'boss you around'. However, one of the more thoughtful children mentioned school reports. At this they all seemed to veer over to a notion of retributive providence whose central theme was school which would become alien and punitive with a frightening extension into home by means of school reports. In all this and in their writing they were rather detached from obvious sources of fact, such as older brothers and sisters. They preferred to invent their own versions of the future. Indeed, some of the more inventive first-years became quite carried away with the idea of being everything to everyone and wrote of buying a car and taking their (presumably aged) parents around the town. Going down town was a recurring theme.

I hope my life will be interesting when I am fourteen. I hope not to get any detentions or lines or to late reports home for my mum or dad I am not going to smoke or get into to much trouble ... I want to pass my exams and have a good job like nursery school teacher securtery and many other things ... I dont want to be really tall or really small I want to be normal hight like all my classmates ... I don't think it will be better being 14 than 9 years old I would stay up later I would worry about if I didn't pass my exams and get a good job.

When I am fourteen you can drink lots of lemonade and go out to clubs in the night. You have to work harder. You will write more . . . If you daydream you get a report card.

I have another 4 or 5 years to go till I am fourteen. Probley I might have a boyfriend to go out with.

All in all, they were extremely hazy about being 14. Even the oldest children could not grasp the feel and limits of being 14 with any precision. As it turned out this variety of incomprehension turned out to be extremely comical to actual 14 year olds.

I feel very strongly that the detachment of my children from the idea that they were being asked to explore was not a feature of the potential quality of their understanding. It was much more to do with the way the writing task was presented – that is somewhat baldly by me – but more important was the idea of audience. In fact, at first I couldn't see why they were so curious to know who this unseen group of 14 year olds actually were. 'What school is it?' they kept asking. When I said I had forgotten they pretended they knew. 'It's Chesterton isn't it?' they said. 'No', I said. 'Well, it must be Manor.' (It wasn't!) They were quite obsessed by this and foolishly I brushed it aside. I now realize how crucial it was to their response to the writing task and their engagement with it.

As Mary notes, why should children put their hearts into writing for people they do not know: people who might be critical? Why should they take risks in sharing their feelings, hopes and fears? Why should the powerful adult hold on to the secret of the real audience while the 'little ones' get on with their writing about themselves? Mary was quick to realize her mistake and felt that her pupils' work had not, on this occasion, matched their normal standards. The writing had all the hallmarks of self-preservation rather then genuine personal engagement. However, the exchange continued and their writing was sent to Nick's school. Nick takes up the story:

The next stage, we hoped, was for these two classes to meet to discuss one-to-one each other's writing. Because of the organizational problems, this was judged to be too difficult and as a substitute – definitely inferior as it turned out – it was decided that my group would make a video of their own work and include some of Mary's pupils' materials as a kind of audio-visual postcard to send to her class.

The video proved far more difficult to make than I had anticipated. A week of work produced a surprisingly high level of self-consciousness and technical hitches that certainly highlighted for me the problems of working with one camera and 26 teenagers with unexpectedly massive problems of either intra or extraversion . . . A hurried re-take was necessary the next week and the result, somewhat stilted and stodgy by now, was apparently received with total blankness by the younger pupils.

As Nick stated, Mary's class were not entirely happy with the video of their work. The natural boisterousness, on the one hand, and embarrassment, on the other, of adolescents made their portrayal of younger children's writing appear to the latter trivialized and 'sent up'. This was certainly not the intention of the older pupils, most of whom genuinely appreciated the younger group's work.

We learned a lot from this experience, which is often the case when things do not go as planned in teaching. First of all, it underlined things about writing we all knew, but needed to keep in the forefront of our minds. How exposed we feel as writers, even as young as eight. It highlighted the importance of not keeping children in the dark when it is not absolutely necessary. It showed us the significance of audience – how the younger pupils *needed* to know for whom they were writing.

We were beginning to learn how pupils and teachers at different phases of education operated. We were observing children closely, reflecting on our experiences and benefiting from our mistakes. We were convinced beyond doubt of the value of real writing for a real readership. And one of our number had used the collaboration as a starting point for an innovative piece of media studies. The last word belongs to Nick Brown:

As a postscript, it is worth saying that this last experience served to inspire this particular class to proper video-making. Immediately afterwards, with considerable financial help from our local Arts Association, they went on to plan and execute a highly successful and professional-looking video about a week's work experience. This video is now used regularly in our school to stimulate other pupils to undertake similar projects.

II   Mapping our world

CATHY POMPE

When Jo Southon and I met each other during the writing project we found that, although we taught different age groups, we shared a similar outlook to children and teaching. My eight- to nine-year-old pupils were writing books for the younger children in the school and Jo had a class of 13-year-olds in need of a boost. They had written a collective novel in the previous year, and were now in the last pocket of pre-GCSE time. The age gap was big enough to avoid contemptuous familiarity, small enough to ensure something could be shared. We were linking a rural secondary world to an urban primary one.

My class received a graciously penned letter from Jo asking for their help, offering the services of her class for tailor-made stories and inviting them to write back with enough details about themselves to provide the means to send each member of the class on exactly the right kind of adventure: in the company of the right friends, bedevilled by their very own personalized enemies and hedged about by all the actual circumstances of their own lives.

We discussed this unique offer, the children accepted, a little bemused, and set about making booklets to introduce themselves and maps showing significant personal landmarks. We collected up categories of what would be useful information, and I produced a duplicated guide sheet collating suggestions, from 'Favourite Clothes' to 'Worst TV', from 'Things That Get Me Down', to 'Favourite Time in History', 'What I'm Rotten At' and 'Friends, Enemies and Frienemies' ...

Some details I made compulsory, the rest I left to the children to select or design as they felt comfortable. If the unique flavour of each child was to come across they had to be left some privacy and scope to express themselves. Also I did not enforce a stringent 'your best handwriting, please' policy. This was not an exercise carried out to satisfy me, but the sending of real messages that would yield their own results in the outside world. Looking back at the little booklets, many of them inelegantly scribbled, I feel this casualness might have inadvertently backfired on my pupils and conveyed an impression that they were younger than they would like to be considered. The quaint spellings and childish script endeared the eight-year-olds to their secondary 'siblings', but also belied the sophistication and complexities of children who were at an age where written powers of expression lag far behind thought processes at the best of times. In their thoughtful attempts to target their stories for these unknown creatures, some of Jo's pupils aimed a little 'young' and wrote dear stories with deliberately simple plots for children who, like themselves, hardly blink when watching *Jaws* and follow *EastEnders* with absorption. Significantly, though, the secondary pupils were struck with the quality of the eight-year-olds' drawings, one area where the not yet so inhibited primary pupil often manages to convey subtlety, and feels less lame than with the written word.

Take the example of the impression given by one leading light in my class to the attentive adolescent from Jo's class who pored over his work. Here is Mastermind Robin, an eight-year-old in my class frequently to be found in the lunch hour finishing off work he has failed to believe he can tackle, plagued with difficult pencil grip and what he believes to be the world's vilest handwriting, chained to his desk like a convict, muttering imprecations, writhing with furious boredom and self-contempt, conveying that he would rather be sent to the galleys, or be allowed to make a quick end of it all. His are the pictures that are illicitly removed from displays on the wall and found torn up in the bin, and who always needs at least two pieces of paper for a job, one to crumple up after the first minutes of work. His booklet begins:

Me
 Well Im a norty person if I could change anything it would be my hight 1m 25cms and 9 years old!
 Me I am midget man

Here is Lucie who was moved to 'adopt' him, who pondered so very hard on ways to tackle Midget Man's personalized story: how to celebrate smallness, but not make too big an issue of it, and yet also provide an element of wish-fulfilment which is the unique power of fiction. I think she succeeds admirably in 'The Hot Summer's Day':

> ... *Robin felt sorry for the wizard and said 'Why don't you use your magic spells to get her out.'*
> *'Yes but which one? I've so many I don't know which one to use' said the wizard. Robin looked around the room for ages until he said 'Ah! What about this one, to make yourself small.'*
> *'What help is that?' said the wizard.*
> *'Well I could take some* [we see Robin is not that small, since he needs spell help to become really small ...] *and creep into the dungeon and through the bars of the locked door and nobody would notice me* [small is very useful]. *Then I would give your daughter some and she would be small as well and we could escape and not get caught.' said Robin.*
> *'That's a brilliant idea, why didn't I think of that. Well done!' said the wizard. ...*
> *... The wizard was very pleased to see his daughter and said 'What can I do to thank you.' said the wizard.*
> *'Well I've always wanted to be taller because I'm short for my age.' said Robin.*
> [The painfulness of the subject is acknowledged in a discreet way.]
> *'Yes of course, but I can't make you taller all of a sudden because everybody would notice, but I'll cast a spell so that you will be the right height for your age when you have finished growing and nobody can pick on you anymore.' said the wizard.*
> [Side-stepping the cruel gap between fiction and reality, it's the perfect kind of low-tech magic that offers both wish-fulfilment and real hope.]
> *'Can you do me another favour? Can you send me back to the sea-side where I belong.' said Robin.* [The story moves swiftly on, no violins are playing ...]

Here is Robin's typically honest and cheerful thank you letter:

> *I liked the story and the book on you but it seems like you thout I was a baby I'm starting to hate Mrs Pompe She biased on girls.*

And later:

> *We have disided to write stories about you as well and I would like to know what you like because if you like olden day stuf we have a problem ...*

Was Lucie able to untangle from the immature script and missed-out words, the only evidence available to her, the small telling clues that reveal the self-assured thinker: the intended irony of listing among his 'hobies' 'haveing 200 or more jobs to do', the succinct reference to the wide range that exists between TV 'best' and 'worts' programmes by adding that 'Im geting to old for he man', the spunk implied by daring to top the list of his enemies with the name of his teacher, with illustration of dagger plunged into heart of villain and assortment of space weaponry circling about her person, the vigour of the concise literary style: 'food chart – yuk: mash poteto – mmm: crisps ... '? *I* can hear Robin's articulate and expressive voice as I read this, but how could Lucie?

When I met her we discussed how she interpreted Robin's writings:

L: He likes to point out what he can't do, like the drawing, he said 'this doesn't look like me' ... 'I can't spell very well' ... He's putting it forward to me ... He's telling me that he's trying ...
CP: What does that say about the way he is – how does it come across to you?
L: That he can't help it ...
CP: What do you attribute that to?

Lucie felt he was probably someone who was 'struggling on all levels' with his work.

Yet she was also sure of what Robin's comment that 'it seems like you thout I was a baby' meant: 'I think I was talking down to him'. It was clear Lucie had thought and worried a lot about these questions before. It was difficult to get it right:

L: I can't quite remember what he's like at that age. When you're older you think different.
CP: Do you think that if you talked as you normally talk they would be lost?
L: That was what ... I suppose that if I talked normally I was afraid they wouldn't understand.

Lucie hated the idea of 'talking down', she wanted to relate as an equal, 'at the same level', but 'the way he writes I thought he couldn't, you know ... '. Talking about the story:

CP: Do you think because of the writing you pitched it quite simple?
L: At a lower level, yes.

Lucie 'didn't want to make it really simple like "the cat sat on the mat"', but tried to make the plot 'without complications or anything, because he might get confused'.

> He wouldn't be able to understand the story, and I wanted him to enjoy the story, [and not] chuck it on the floor ... It's ever so hard if you don't know what that age group is like. I don't talk to that age group, do I ...

The slight anxiety at not being able to get it 'quite right' touchingly hints at the familiar vulnerability of the 'older' towards the brazen carefree 'younger generation'. This is probably what made Jo suggest that her pupils had enjoyed the 'communicating without meeting': the mediation of the written word protected them from being exposed, and found wanting, as they imagined they would be. Jo's class were at that middle stage in a school career where you are nobody special, and as a class they did not perceive themselves as good pupils: self-confidence did not ride particularly high.

To return to a chronological account of our collaboration, and the early stages when my class were responding to Jo's first letter, my class had had a week or so to fill in their booklets, and make a large Map of the World as related to them. As with Jo's class the project was an easy option for those who did not put a lot of themselves into it, and some of my pupils' booklets were thin in content. Likewise, when the stories came tumbling in from the secondary school, some of my pupils felt sold short to receive a low-effort production, when other classmates had had their every wish and circumstance lavishly embroidered into a fat book. Alas, it was not the case that this low-effort retribution fell upon the minimalists in my own class. However, the disappointment was never mentioned aloud, such was the climate of gratitude for the generous efforts made on our behalf.

Jo received our booklets, read them, took notes, and distributed them to the bidders in her class ('I am glad that you like Queen as I do as well. I think we have a lot in common, but I don't like American football much' wrote Big David to little Jack). The booklets and maps were read around the class with delight.

Here is a flavour from the world maps of the eight-year-olds:

Miracles: *Once I found a pece of paper saying that I was going to be good at writing and since then I have???*
Favourite time in history: *when I was born*
Not jobs: *I would not like to be a nurse. And I would not like to work in a hospital. No I would not!*

Jo's class held involved discussions about how to deal with sensitive issues: did you mention or ignore the information that a child's father had died? Do you magic away a child's unhappy fatness? Responses varied in maturity, but Jo was impressed by the maternal and big-brotherly feelings aroused.

Jo's class found they needed to know more about their adopted eight-year-old, and sent out feelers: affectionate letters of introduction were written, with thoughtful questionnaires devised to minimize the amount of laborious writing needed to answer the queries.

These letters won over the hearts of the eight-year-olds at a stroke: astonishment, deep absorption, a buzz of compared notes... Nothing else could be done in the class for a very long while, as individuals weighed up the personalities that had entered their lives, at once mysterious and strangely intimate. Robin, shocked rigid, was at the centre of a pool of admiration, for Lucie had not only written a letter, but had made her own booklet about herself for him, with exquisite and painstaking illustrations, which caused a flurry and drew gasps of wonder from even the art 'gods' in the class. The traumatizing mixture of being chosen by a girl at the same time as being the recipient of attentions from such a prestigious being was a comical sight, but, intrigued and philosophical, Robin rallied to and faced the Lucie challenge.

Jo's class now became a part of the family: we wondered how we could show them the play we had just produced, or write it up as a book for them. We already visualized the summer picnic we would have together on the giant playing fields the secondary pupils had described to us ...

When Jo's class had processed our responses they were under some pressure to produce their stories: Christmas was drawing near, and two days into the new term I was due to leave my class to go on a long course, which was the first of the breaks in continuity which marred the project. The elder children wrote most of their stories during the Christmas holidays, a feat in itself.

'I kept re-writing it ... ': Anne-Marie worried about whether she was 'putting things straight' enough, or 'whether they wouldn't like it'. 'First of all I'd see how I would read it, then I changed it quite a lot.' Anne-Marie and Robin's Lucie had shared a desk at English lessons and were intimately familiar with each other's 'penpal' – when I spoke to them it was obvious they had talked a lot over the task they faced, as they had with other friends. They had enjoyed the project very much and found it a real challenge:

> I find it like in a way more educating than reading a book and writing about it as we would normally.

'Communicating with another age group' was 'pretty different', you had to 'think of the words', 'their interests', and so on ...

A difficult task, yet easier too. Reading the stories, all of them well structured, it is clear that the constraint of dropping to a 'lower level' also affords a sense of mastery which is liberating, and releases all sorts of ingenuity. This was definitely noticeable when my own pupils wrote their stories for younger children, well structured, with consciously used style, where otherwise they might have drowned in a sea of over-ambitious ideas.

The bulk of the stories reached my class before I left for my course. A disappointing silence for Jo's class must have ensued. When I returned and we received a second batch of stories, we reimmersed ourselves, read our stories out and read sections of the serialized novel Jo's class had written the previous year.

Not all of the stories had been agonized over, but the mixture of fantasy and accurate personal detail in all the stories had a powerful effect. The children glowed. 'Inspector Tom in the Jungle of Doom' brought together Tom's bird-watching and his obsession with detective stories. For Sarah who collects ducks and wants to run a market stall when she grows up, an atmospheric opening scene:

> *The plastic ducks that she was selling were covered in frost, and the stickers were damp, and the paper on the backs of them were wet. The market place looked empty and it was mainly because it was too cold for people to come out ...*

Something emerged strongly from all these stories: every central character, the child for whom the story was written, had been immensely valued and boosted. Strong and autonomous, wise yet ordinary, these child-heroes carry responsibilities, act decisively and perform adventurous deeds. It was the great succession of impressive young female heroes in particular which first drew my attention to the distinctive flavour of these stories: there is nothing supernatural about these children characters, but they are self-realized. Here is an extract from Anne-Marie's story:

> *Katie lay asleep on her wooden bed in her den, which is on the edge of a wood behind her house. It had taken her and her dad two months to build it. Her mom and dad didn't usually let her sleep alone, but now her birthday had just gone, they let her just the once. It was about 11 p.m. when Katie heard a scream for help. She jumped up in a start. The scream came again. Katie quickly got dressed and went outside to find where it came from and why ...*

And here is one from Samantha's:

> *Eleanor sat in his car and they were talking when Nigel [Mansell] said 'I don't feel like driving today, I feel very ill and tired.' Eleanor said 'Well, I'll drive for you if you show me how'.*

Melina wrote to Clare to thank her:

> *... it was brilliant ... Your handwriting was easy to read, not like some others I might mention.*

Struggling to decipher some of the stories, the children realized that poor handwriting was a major deterrent to wanting to read a story, however brilliant the style. Some of the older pupils' jewels were only properly discovered when I read them out.

With a few days of term left we wanted to convey our gratitude: the children painstakingly made little Easter baskets filled with school-made sweets and wrote big thank-you letters. The closely timed operation that followed marked the high point of the project: the gifts reached Jo's class on the last day of term. They had probably almost forgotten us by then, and were deeply touched, for little ever happens in secondary schools that bears any resemblance to the world of the primary school Easter egg basket. It brought out the child in the 14-year-old, and created a holiday atmosphere in the class which bonded them as a group. Jo's pupils spontaneously collected up money to buy us an Easter present, and designed picture letters and Easter puzzles during the rest of the lesson. In the lunch hour, five pupils whose names had come up in a draw piled into the back of Jo's car and drove into town with bags of sweets and letters to deliver to us.

An awesome awkward moment, as the five tall teenagers (all of them shy people) looked down at the swarm of tongue-tied little children, teachers cheerily trying to keep the conversation going. In another rash of thank-you letters, the eight-year-olds adopted the picture-letter-writing devices the adolescents had initiated.

At this point the connection faded. Jo's school got very busy. By the time we received an answer, it was late in the year and we had become too involved in another large project. The outing to Jo's school we had long imagined had been replaced by two days' work in a television studio. Each of us juggling too many balls, not knowing each other very well, and at times misunderstanding each other's silences, we had failed to link up at the right times. The threads were lost.

In writing this account, looking through the correspondence and rereading the fine-detailed stories with more care than I ever did in the classroom, I feel that in the normal run of events teachers can have no real conception of how much thought a pupil might put into a piece of work or a relationship like the ones Jo and I initiated. Because these relationships were individual and private, we perhaps did not understand or honour them sufficiently. Because children do not have much power to decide what they do at school, they follow where we lead them. When, as teachers, we did not bring our collaboration to a celebrated conclusion, we probably did not realize as I do now that our unfinished exchange had left many unsatisfied longings in some deeply involved children.

I remember Katie in my class saying that her 'pen sister' Anne-Marie had written to her at home, and sent her a present. When I met Anne-Marie at Jo's school, much later, and questioned her quite searchingly, I understood that she had written because she was angry that things had come to a standstill.

The disappointment was in fact a symptom of the gains made. The collaboration was an opportunity to see beyond appearances. Insecure or less popular pupils were recognized as caring people and brilliant authors by children who had never met them, and little people used to kicking at their own limitations were accepted wholeheartedly for what they were. For many, too, it was an initiation to the joys of letter-writing. I conclude with a few choice exchanges. Marc in Jo's class wrote to Tom G. in mine:

Why don't you like girls? ... You may find this unusual but I dress up smartly when I see a film at the cinema. There's one thing you and me have in common and that is we don't like tidying our bedrooms.

Tom G. wrote in reply:

Girls are not bad but I think they are a bit boring ... I would like to point out I do not dress cool.

Melina, whom we encountered earlier, made a generous offer to Clare:

My kitten hasn't had kittens yet but would you like one there going to be half siamees because we know the father.

Finally, here is Tom C.'s punctilious little note to Alan setting an important matter straight:

To Alan
The illustration on page 3 is wrong I do have some striped pygamas but the stripes are the other way ... otherwise it is a brilliant story.
From Tom.

III Heroes and heroines
GABRIELLE CLIFF HODGES

In 1986 the theme for Children's Book Week was 'Heroes and Heroines'. I wanted the third-year class I was teaching at the time to do some work on that theme and so I suggested the idea of a collaboration with a primary class of nine- to ten-year-olds. The younger pupils jotted down a few autobiographical details, then my class wrote an individual story for each of them, making him or her a hero or heroine.

The details the primary schoolchildren sent us were very useful and never seemed to act as constraints on the writing. Most, if not all, of my class ended up writing the type of story they wanted to, on a subject which appealed to them as well as to their 'central characters'.

Duncan, whose chief hobbies are fishing and football, wrote a story called 'The Scale Breaker' about a boy catching a 150-pound, 50-year-old pike in the local gravel pits, a popular fishing haunt with which he and his hero, Christopher, were both very familiar. Later on Duncan wrote this in his journal:

> *When we were first told of this project I didn't think it was going to be any good. I didn't think it was going to be any good because I'm not very good at making up stories. But when you were [telling] us about the children and their hobbies and one with fishing, the title* Scale Breaker *popped into my head and the 150 pound pike. So I eagerly put up my hand when you mentioned Christopher.*

Once the writing had started the pupils often stopped to read 'the story so far' to each other, and to do some redrafting which seemed to carry greater significance in the light of who would finally be reading these stories. Katie said:

> *You have to be a lot more careful when writing for somebody else. If you've made a lot of mistakes it will spoil the story for them ... I was glad I redrafted it ... when you go over it you realise a lot of things aren't good ideas after all.*

For several others the sense of their central character being 'real' made this writing unusual despite the fact that they hadn't met their heroes or heroines and that their stories were fictional. Lucy wrote in her journal:

> *It's different from writing other stories because you are writing about a real person, who has family, feelings, and so on.*

The two heroes in Adrian's story 'Gauntlet (Out of Order)' got stuck inside a complicated computer game and at one stage he seemed unable to work out how the story could possibly continue. After some discussion he solved the problem but he obviously sensed a difference in his writing because he was working with 'real' characters:

It is not just any old story with the characters invented, letting you do what you want. But you MUST work with a real person's character. This is very good because it helps you to work to guidelines and also you have no 'easy way out' of a situation as you have not invented the character so you cannot mention 'quirks' in his past which enable you to escape writing lengthy stories.

Although making their finished stories into booklets did take some people quite a long time I met with surprisingly little opposition – most wanted the opportunity to write their stories out more neatly and also to do some illustrations.

My reason for wanting them to be made into booklets was primarily that I wanted to encourage and maintain the class's already growing sense of themselves as *real writers* for *real readers*, a sense which could be added to by putting covers on their booklets, dedicating them to someone and writing a brief bit about the author on the back cover. Also, because the two schools are three miles or so apart we had made no plans for the children to meet each other or for my class to read the stories aloud to their respective heroes and heroines.

Finally the stories were ready to be sent off. One thing remained to be sorted out before they went: who owned the stories? Who would the booklets belong to? Were they the property of the writers or of the readers, the central characters, the people for whom they were written and to whom they were dedicated? It was a problem enjoyable to discuss but difficult to solve. What the children were discovering is described here by Aidan Chambers:

> 'The birth of the reader is at the cost of the death of the author', and my whole experience of writing and of reading convinces me that this is true. The books are finished events; the person who wrote them is no more. He has a biography, as the writing of his books has a history. But he has no extra-terrestrial presence, and the books, as texts, stand on their own, having a life independent of their author, but dependent for their continued existence on the readers who make them their own.[3]

My pupils eagerly awaited a response to their stories and each of them eventually received a letter. I also passed on to them information from the teacher about how the booklets had been read and shared and what the children's response to finding themselves as central characters in a story had been.

The letters are unusual in that they are effectively book reviews written in the first person.

The bit I liked best was when we were at the haunted house when we were awake all night terrified on what was going to happen to us.

Dear Catherine,
    Thank you very much for the story you wrote to me. The bit about Clare's party was quite true, Clare does have a disco party but it ends at 9.00 because 10.30 is too late for us. I liked the way you described things like the ghost and things like that. I liked the bit where I stuck my tongue out at Lisa and she pulled a face back at

me. The illustration on the front is good and I like the way you've scribbled black and grey felt tip pen over the picture to make it look dark and as if it's in the middle of the night. The only thing I'm afraid of in the book is I hope it never happens to me.
  Yours sincerely,
    Zoe

Audrey's story proved a success, too:

Thank you very much for writing me a story. I thought it was very good ... It wasn't too scary although I'm glad I got home in the end ...

Robert wrote:

Dear Alan,
  I was intrigued by your marvellous story about me, Ashley, Michael, Tina, Tango and all the rest of my pets. At the front you wrote 'I hope you like my story'. Well I really did enjoy it, especially where I say 'SHUT UP'. I really enjoyed it ...

Allan obviously liked Katie's football story:

Dear Katie,
  I thought that the story was very interesting and very well written and I liked the cover and it was a pity that Liverpool went down to the Fourth Division. But the best part was when Liverpool scored a goal and I thought that the pictures were very good too.
  From Allan.

Although I am sure there would have been much to be gained from the children being able to meet and talk to each other they were, nevertheless, participating in the most common experience of any writer and reader of fiction when the distance between two people is bridged by the written word. It challenged my pupils (who minded very much what impression would be received by the third-year juniors, both of their stories and of themselves) to be particularly careful with their writing. For my part I enjoyed observing the blurring of lines between the author, the hero or heroine and the reader, between fiction and reality, and between desire and fulfilment. Duncan's 'The Scale Breaker' perhaps illustrates this best. His story of the great pike catch is as much his own wish fulfilled as it is his younger reader's, and their common enthusiasm is shared in the story itself. This is how it begins:

THE SCALE BREAKER
by Duncan
for Christopher
On Friday the 26th of September, Christopher was dreaming of catching a pike. Through the years of fishing he had tried to catch a pike, but no such reward came. He dreamt, feeling the fight of the pike pulling to get away. But after a battling half

> hour, the pike gave in and so he pulled the pike out of the water, with his landing net and then pulled the hook out of its mouth with a disgorger, and then hit the fish with a bit of wood to put it out of its misery. He then dreamt of taking the fish home, showing his mother and father and getting his name in the newspaper for the largest fish ever caught in the gravel pits. But then his dream was washed away because he thought he had no hope of catching a pike.

The dream is 'washed away' but Duncan, invested with all the powers of the storyteller, can make that dream come true for his fictional Christopher. First of all, Christopher spots a large pike well known by the locals to be 50 years old, then he spends a day in thorough preparation for the great fishing expedition, another night dreaming about it (this time a nightmare in the style of *Jaws*) until the day comes when finally he succeeds in catching it. His name does indeed make all the newspapers with a photograph of him next to the fish.

The real Christopher's thank-you letter reminds us of the strange twilight world where reader and writer, truth and fiction meet, a world perhaps not so very different from the dream within the story where 'The Scale Breaker' began:

> *Dear Duncan,*
> *I liked the story mostly the bit when I shot the pike and blood went spurting everywhere. I wish that there was a fifty year old pike and it did weigh 150lbs and I caught it ...*

As D. W. Harding suggests,

> The more sophisticated reader knows that he is in social communication of a special sort with the author, and he bears in mind that the represented participants (in the story) are only part of a convention by which the author discusses, and proposes an evaluation of, possible human experience.[4]

IV Animation across the divide
CATHY POMPE

A few years ago, an international group of producers of television programmes for schools, working in the upper primary age range, evolved a format for putting their school audiences in touch with children from other countries. Each producer was to commission some film footage from every other country's producer, incorporate the material around a theme that would best arouse children's interest in other countries, and also feature an exchange of parcels and letters taking place between individual schools from different nations.

I had worked on making animated films with schoolchildren, and was drawn into this project because animation is potentially a powerful medium of communication between children who do not speak the same language. The British producer involved had experimented with schools in Britain corresponding with each other through the writing of four-part serialized stories, each group or class writing one section of the story, and sending it off to be continued at the other school, like a literary game of consequences by post. There was a possibility of doing something similar with animation, which my class might help pilot.

When I joined the European group of producers for a conference taking place in England, my class had prepared by request the first part of two possible four-episode stories. One format was to use a universally known story, which would act as a common reference. The other story was a home-grown space adventure.

These 'animated openings' were designed as a suggestion that might meet the interests and suit the unusual approach of the producers of the Swedish school series *Hanteras varsamt* ('Handle with Care'): these enthusiastic producers had evolved a sensitive and open-ended approach to programme-making, allowing ideas and events which arose from the situations they helped to initiate in schools and elsewhere to shape the actual content of the programmes. Thus in the series which illustrated a multi-media exchange between schoolchildren from different backgrounds within Sweden, the programmes recorded and re-created the real quirky events which arose in the course of the exchanges, focused on the feelings and circumstances of individual children, homed in on their concerns, allowed them to speak to the cameras, and helped them to develop their ideas and enhance their work in such a way as to make it broadcastworthy. This particular project was therefore a mixture of promoting exchanges between schools, and a method of working with young people by giving them access to television broadcasting: a step towards real children's television.

It was now my task to live up to a similar project on an international scale. The Swedish producers had liked our space story 'Pied Piper'. We were teamed up with a school in the Southern city of Kalmar, where the unusual initiative of the municipal museum curator had resulted in city children producing 200 films during an animation season she had organized with the help of Swedish television.

By the time the Swedish school had processed our letters and film, I was already teaching my next class, unlike the Swedish teachers, who were spending three years with the same children. The project, fraught with difficulties on my side, but most enriching, is now in its third year, and a small group of devotees has kept it alive long after the television producers finished with us.

My original class had enjoyed making up the 'Pied Piper' story together, a great deal of thought and negotiation had taken place, and the story had a strong grip over us. It told of a child going to bed at the top of her house, and finding a parcel on her bed. It contains a doll, and a Mars bar which she eats with delight. As she sleeps contentedly, the doll changes into a little alien who transforms the bedroom into a space capsule. Finally, the roof of the house parts open, and the top of the house blasts off into outer space, heading for an unknown destination.

We had decided to send our hero alone into space, despite the wrangles about having to decide on whether it should be a boy or a girl, for we thought that if there were two children they might have tended to be self-sufficient in their adventures, rescuing each other in turn, and not offer so much scope for the writers of the next instalment.

The next stage involved introducing ourselves to the Swedish school, who luckily were already learning English. We sent a portrait gallery of ourselves and of our teachers, an account of school life in a large collaged map of the school, peppered with *Beano*-type detail of what happened in the various corners of the institution, letters and drawings. The children started to reflect on what would be relevant or interesting to people who did not know England, wrote about it, and brought in tiny trinkets to send off: stamps, badges, tiny smelly rubbers and football stickers.

The Swedish school welcomed our parcel, they tossed out their drab English-language textbooks, and different classes scrabbled for the privilege of working with us. I was later to feel that our side of the collaboration fell short of the involvement they were longing for from us. Throughout the project, whatever their expectations might have been, Klaes, the main teacher who worked on the 'Pied Piper' story with us, and his colleagues and pupils, beamed out warmth and unconditional acceptance to us. It spoke to us of a completely different kind of schooling system, one where teachers and children related in much more informal and comfortable ways, and one where a project like this would be given much background support and a real place in the curriculum.

By the time we heard from Kalmar, I was taking over a new class of eight-year-olds, who were yet again starting from scratch with animation. The Kalmar children were heading for their twelfth and thirteenth birthdays. Nevertheless, this class's contact with the Kalmar children had a profound impact. In the year also marked by the 1985–6 famine in Ethiopia, the 'Pied Piper' story turned us into citizens of the world.

Kalmar's second instalment of the 'Pied Piper' featured children from different parts of the globe being whisked off into space in their idiosyncratic ways, after accidentally consuming a magical Mars bar. We had to send the Swedish children a supply of English Mars bars and wrappers as the Swedish version is retailed as 'Japp'. This also became a fetish: there was nothing more delicious in the world for my 32 pupils than one-sixteenth of a Japp bar! The cliffhanger for the end of 'Pied Piper' Part Two featured the medley of earthling children left circling round a giant planet Mars.

Kalmar had sent us the storyboarded plans of the film before it was made, so that we could plan the next phase. Letters arrived addressed to individuals from my previous class, with photos, maps and tourist guides to Kalmar. A Christmas parcel arrived, full of exotic Swedish Christmas decorations, with large paintings and explanations of strange and wonderful Christmas traditions, streamers of little Swedish flags and card models of the Kalmar school to cut out and construct ourselves.

The children studied the letters and documentation with attention: they were written in imperfect English, which reassured those of us daunted with the task of corresponding with teenagers.

In time we gathered together a large parcel: it contained little presents from each child, including a one-year supply of the *Beano*, copies of the books we were reading in class, an anthology of Mike Rosen poems, little sweets and a child's own breathtaking chainmail costume from our Normans and Saxons Christmas play, knitted in string for her by her mother: a spontaneous gesture of generosity echoing something we had seen take place in one of the Swedish 'Handle with Care' programmes we had seen on our video. Then the father of one of my pupils, travelling to Stockholm on business, struggled to Sweden with the enormous parcel. He returned with a stock of Japp bars commissioned by his daughter, an assortment of coins and bus tickets, and several rolls of pictures he had taken of Swedish town and countryside for us ...

We now prepared to tell the rest of the school about this project. We were in the middle of a big Space topic. We devised an assembly featuring beings from a distant planet, looking with alien eyes at the strange institutions and habits of earthlings, focusing on a city in the European continent: Kalmar. The models, paintings and photographs we had received from Klaes's pupils were mounted and labelled with comments and notes of explanation made by the bemused aliens. The class, festooned with streamers of little Swedish flags, bristled with large (cardboard) monitors screening scenes of Earth and Mars, and Swedish robots that spewed printouts of Swedish words ...

Before the BBC came to film the footage of our school commissioned by the Swedish producers for their programme about the 'Pied Piper', and on their own initiative, a group of girls bought a length of cloth, and spent a week-end decorating a large banner to wave in front of the cameras. The filming was more than a moment of personal glory, it was the most direct link we had had the chance to make. The giant 'Hello Kalmar' sign painted on the banner the girls held up to the cameras was beaming out their own message. A small background detail, but significant: they were learning to use the media for their own purposes.

In Sweden, too, work had grown. Klaes's pupils had shared the task of continuing the 'Pied Piper' story with others. It had been an opportunity to visit the tiniest children in the school. They had held a screening of our film for the infant class, and carefully listened to their suggestions about how the story should evolve. Then when the programme 'Handle with Care' was made for Swedish Television for schools, it featured the first two parts of 'Pied Piper', refilmed professionally on 16mm film. Viewers were asked to write in to the school with their suggestions about how to continue the story.

Back in England, 'Pied Piper' Part Three was brewing. We had looked at the original Pied Piper story, in Browning's version, and written about it. We speculated on whether our space Pied Piper would be trustworthy or malicious, and whether we would be able to know this when we met him or her. Had the Earth children been summoned to this chocolate planet Mars for a mission, or were they being lured into the deceptive pleasures of a false paradise where rivers of toffee flow under marmalade skies?

During the year our class had followed an international trail that had led from the conquest of England by the Normans to the growth of the American nation, and to ecological concerns, a world we had entered through Laura Ingalls Wilder's book *Little House in the Big Woods*.[5] During our space topic I had read the children an Isaac Asimov[6] story about the colonizing of a planet in space, inhabited by intelligent beings the colonizers refused to recognize as such. Then when Olof Palme, the Swedish Prime Minister, was assassinated, the children felt deeply involved and wrote letters of condolence to Kalmar. The class had an eye on international affairs, and scoured the papers for Swedish news.

Now a Senegalese drummer came to work with our class over six weeks, and he became our very own Pied Piper, the graceful and dignified stranger we learned to love and trust. In a year where Africa had made grim headlines, he offered us a different and powerful glimpse of Africa, which deeply affected the children.

Out of all these strands 'Pied Piper' Part Three evolved: the Earthling children would land on the chocolate planet, follow a little green alien through underground tunnels to the headquarters of the careworn Pied Piper, a large green-striped alien, who was surveying scenes of trouble and warfare in different parts of the Universe through the many screens and monitors in the room.

The children were to help the Pied Piper with the conflict between the Mars people and the Sram folk, which was raging in pitched battles in the underground part of the planet, fought with a lethal arsenal of sweets: jelly diamond spears, toffee traps and gobstopper cannon balls ...

In Kalmar, Klaes was working away: the organization of the school was such that he was able to work with a small group of nine children for a whole morning every week. We had sent storyboards of Part Three, and pictures and models of Srams, Marses and the Pied Piper. A new Kalmar team took over the filming of Part Four, which was duly completed and posted to us: Srams and Marses, reconciled, feasted with the Pipelings and Earth children.

The children who finished the film in Sweden were a group who had had some difficulties in school. They also sent us a string of little video films about themselves, which they had scripted and filmed entirely on their own during their sessions with Klaes. A considerable achievement, especially as the programmes were made for us in English. We wrote letters back to Klaes, whose pupils were now about to fly off to secondary school. An era was ending, but links are still alive.

The last big highlight of the project occurred when I was teaching yet another new batch of eight-year-olds, who had not been involved in the project. Out of the blue, a smiling 14-year-old turned up at our school one lunchtime: it was Nina, from Kalmar, on a trip to England with her father, who had travelled to us specially by train, bearing a video copy of the completed 'Handle with Care' programme, as it was broadcast in Sweden. I still entertain the dream of taking a few of my old pupils to Kalmar one day, to visit the places and people we seem to know so well already.

Tom Stanier, the British television producer in this European link-up, organized his own European project around the theme of Winter festivals, with three British schools piloting exchanges with schools in Sweden, Finland and the Netherlands. Since that time 1200 schools have linked up, 600 of them British.

Most of them are success stories, though some schools badly let their counterparts down. The secret is to strike while the iron is hot, Tom Stanier says. The latest he had heard was from a class in a primary school in Gloucestershire who were setting off to visit their Dutch counterparts. The Winter festival series is being broadcast again, and next a programme about Hungary will extend the project into Eastern Europe, with plans to create links with schools in Russia. The wider vista glimpsed here intimates that there is something greater at stake here than teachers merely looking for a project to occupy their classes. It hints of children preparing for their responsibilities as future citizens of a fragile planet.

Notes

1. Based on work undertaken by Nick Brown and Mary Hilton.
2. James Britton, *Language and Learning*, Penguin, 1970.
3. Aidan Chambers, *Booktalk: Occasional Writing on Literature and Children*, Bodley Head, 1985.
4. D. W. Harding, 'What happens when we read?' in M. Meek (ed.), *The Cool Web*, Bodley Head, 1977.
5. Laura Ingalls Wilder, *Little House in the Big Woods*, Methuen, 1956.
6. Isaac Asimov, *The Heavenly Host*, Puffin, 1978.

7 Collaboration at transition

'By pupils, for pupils': An alternative information booklet for incoming first years.

FRANCES D. FINDLAY

- Are there enough opportunities for children to write for an audience other than a red-pen toting teacher?
- Are the children aware of the purpose of the writing?
- Are they aware of the differences in language necessary for different audiences?
- Is work ever published?
- Does the redrafting go beyond 'manicuring the corpse'?

Knott[1]

Writing for a recognised audience encourages children to see themselves as writers.

Horner[2]

Introduction

I currently teach in an 11–18 rural comprehensive school with 1350 pupils who transfer from five primary feeder schools. In early June, for the past three years, English teachers have visited all the fourth-year pupils in their primary schools. During a one-hour session, we have asked the junior pupils to write letters to our first-years in which they ask the questions which they would like answering. This gives the primary pupils the opportunity to identify what is of genuine interest to them and not the points which teachers think they ought to know. Then our first-year pupils write the replies and the letters are returned to the primary pupils within ten days. The experience of talking about the transfer with both primary and secondary pupils over a period of time led me to try a more ambitious project. Maybe if junior school pupils could know more about the school as seen through the pupils' eyes, some of the anxieties about transfer could be reduced. I was also keen to try a collaborative project with a first-year class since they were being taught in a mixed-ability group for the first time. Prior to the recent period of industrial action good relationships were beginning to emerge with the feeder schools and I was anxious to build on these promising beginnings.

During the autumn term, we had shared a poet for a short-term residency with one of the feeder primary schools, so we had got to know one another. It is important to establish the context in which it was possible to consider asking first-year pupils to write an information booklet for the incoming juniors: the primary schools were likely to be supportive and welcome this initiative.

Preparing the booklet

Stage 1: Whole-class discussion

I spent some time introducing the topic to the first-year pupils and stressed its purpose, the nature of the audience and the tight time-scale we had to keep to. Our aim was to produce a booklet containing relevant information presented in a reassuring way. I reminded them of the contents of the official school booklet which they had all received 12 months previously. I read them examples of letters written by fourth-year juniors and first-year secondary pupils under the scheme referred to earlier. We started to discuss what incoming pupils feared and what they would want to know.

Stage 2: Brainstorming

During the next lesson we moved on to discuss what made a good working group and decided that (for the purposes of this project) a group would need at least one person who could draw, one person who could write neatly and at least one person with good ideas. Amidst noisy negotiations, groups of four or five were finally formed. Each group then brainstormed all the ideas they had concerning any topics which could be contained in a booklet. Then, they discussed suggestions for group organization. How were decisions going to be made? Was each person in the group going to have a particular responsibility or could they actually discuss, compose and write together? In pairs? Would they be flexible and work according to the demands of the different tasks? The 'brainstorming' lists produced many suggestions which, because of the constraints of time, I pared down; I made judgements about the distribution of interests and pupils' abilities and shared out the more demanding tasks fairly. We decided to tackle topics as various as PE facilities and what to do if you felt ill; punishment and the bikesheds; school dinners and homework; exams, reports and lockers.

Stage 3: Preparing questions, taping interviews

The pupils recognized the need for hard information concerning the arrangements for next year's first-years. Each group devised questions to ask the appropriate teachers, wrote letters of explanation, conducted an interview and made contacts with the pastoral system.

Stage 4: Principles

Three principles were underlined: first, don't forget your audience – they are exactly one year younger than you are. Select carefully, but don't talk down to them. Write as if writing to a friend. Second, ask yourself as you're writing: does this tell me everything I wanted to know last September? Third, ask yourself as you're writing: if it was my *first* day at this school, would I understand this?

Stage 5: The cover and title

During the time the pupils were working in groups we returned to a full-class grouping on two occasions. On the first of these occasions, we talked about the cover and the title for this unofficial school guide. Each pupil then designed a cover which included the title. These were displayed so that everyone could see the range of ideas. The Head of Year chose 'Come On Over to Our Place', which, although a little corny, nevertheless seemed to hit the right note of equality. It avoided the idea that transfer to secondary school is going *up*.

Stage 6: Rough drafts

The project took roughly a month, including the preparation time as already outlined. We were working in 'real time' with a real deadline. The booklet had to be printed, collated, stapled and delivered to the primary schools before the incoming pupils visited the school. English teachers had also asked all primary schools to write a letter to a first-year pupil. Transfer was being given a high profile.

I was forced by the pressures of time to take on the role of editor. Given a longer period of time and/or older pupils, this job would have been better carried out by a small editorial group, for the class, chosen by the pupils themselves. As it was, groups prepared their work and reported to me in lesson-time on their progress and problems. I helped them, as a group, to rethink and redraft. For one session, the groups reported back to the whole class, reading their work aloud and showing it to them. During another session, each pupil wrote a short report including what he or she felt had been achieved so far and what future targets were in view. I also discussed tape-recording and interviewing techniques with the members of each group separately.

Stage 7: Good finished copy

The final stages of the booklet-making were rushed as a result of working to a tight deadline. Some important aspects of life in the school were either unrepresented or missed out. Nevertheless, a booklet with 34 A4 pages, printed on paper of a wide variety of colours, was produced in time using offset-litho. The pages were printed using pupils' own handwriting; some 25 topics were covered and a welcoming letter from the whole class was printed on the first page. Almost all the pages included drawings, diagrams, boxes and cartoons so as to break up the blocks of print. Among the topics which figured largely and represented the pupil angle on school survival was 'Equipment and Survival Kit for the First Day', written and illustrated by a low achiever; a page called 'Where Do I Go If I Feel Ill?' contained some very sensible, reassuring information. The pages dealing with school uniform were clear and well illustrated – so were 'Where to Hang About at Dinnertime', 'Notes to School' and 'Important Places' (toilets, office, medical room), 'School Buses', 'How Not to Get Lost'. A simplified map showed toilets, where to eat packed lunches, the rear entrance to the school used by pupils, office and dining hall as well as the classroom bases. The booklet had a similar flavour to the letters I had read: when pupils choose the topics, the real experience of school life emerged.

The booklet was collated by the whole class working in the library. We produced 300 copies, one for each of the fourth-years and one for each of the members of the class.

Stage 8: The visit

The following day the class was split into four groups: three small groups were taken by teachers to deliver the booklets to the village schools while a Vice Principal drove 15 pupils in the school mini-bus to distribute the booklet to the two primary schools in the town. In each school, the first-years spent about 20 minutes talking to the junior school pupils in informal groups. A pupil from each group wrote a thank-you letter to the teachers who had given up their time to transport the pupils. The Head of Year wrote a kind letter to the whole class ('I hope next year's pupils are as nice to know as you') and put up a display of pages from the booklet in the main corridor of the school and a notice congratulating the whole class on their achievement. I took photographs of all the stages of the making of the booklet, as well as the visit to the primary schools and the new pupils on the visit Day. These were displayed in the classroom, where the first-years had done the work, alongside the pages of the booklet itself. They were left on display for the new first-years to see the process of making the booklet and to see photographs of themselves during the visit when they arrived in September.

Perspectives

I tried to find out the views of a number of different people involved in this project: I hoped, thereby, to cover a range of people, some directly involved in the projects, others who saw it 'from the outside'. I was lucky enough to be able to use one of the English Inspectors for Cambridgeshire to do some interviewing in this context. She could take on the role of an objective outsider who was interested in the project itself but not involved in its detail.

The writers' point of view

First of all, she talked to six pupils representing the ability range in the first-year class and with varying levels of commitment to the project. She tape-recorded a discussion with the pupils a week after they had delivered the booklets. The pupils showed a marked degree of sophistication about the nature of the activity they had been involved in. They were able to make constructive suggestions about how the project could have been improved. They were very aware of how groups had functioned and why some had faced problems: 'We argued about who should do what 'cos everyone wanted to do the nicer things.' 'We argued about who should be the leader.' Advice was plentiful for working in groups in the future:

> Don't just go with your friends ... People you can get on with but not too friendly. You've always got a joker in the group.

The pupils were perceptive about their own intentions and fluent in finding a language to describe them. They knew what they had found unhelpful in the official booklet and why they had chosen to alter certain items rather than miss them out: they were very lucid about why the official, teacher-drawn map of the extensive school buildings was both misleading and offered so much information that it was unclear. Two pupils voiced an uncertainty about the degree of control which the groups could exercise over their new way of working: 'I think that the work should be given out to people' was the first rather long-suffering offering here, followed up sharply by another pupil adding: 'because some people did more work than others'. The six pupils were equally perceptive about the practical problems of interviewing adults. They were easily able to list points of advice they could put into operation in future: how to compile questions; necessity for multiple copies of questions for all involved; making notes of responses as well as tape-recording; the problems of asking questions, listening fully to the replies so that the interview is a two-way process. Would there be a change in their attitude and behaviour towards the next first year? Yes, they agreed that there would be a change; after all, 'We've only just got over it. Only just got through it, so we're likely to be more sympathetic.' One pupil owned up to being 'tempted' to exploit the situation of being a year older and more experienced. As first-years, they'd felt like 'servants', 'bottom of the pile' and 'guinea pigs', as they'd been asked to try out new ideas: 'it's the first time this booklet's been tried'. There was considerable discussion about the ways in which attending a small village primary school produced more problems during the adjustment period than for those who transferred from the larger town schools. The pupils spoke clearly about the arrangements for distributing the booklet. They stressed that the junior school pupils had been interested in the booklet but were disappointed that they had not been asked many questions. They recognized that it might have been helpful to work as an individual with a small group of school pupils in order to encourage a more open discussion.

Finally, these pupils were most surprised that other teachers involved in the project had responded very positively to the booklet and the form's achievement in producing it. The English Inspector was impressed by the children's candour and perception about the processes they had been involved in and how supportive they were of each other's contributions. This perception derives largely from the collaborative nature of the work they had undertaken: they had a very clear goal, which was to communicate information in a reassuring positive way to a very particular, identified audience and within a demanding time schedule. They were proud of seeing their work in print and of their capacity to produce something which could be of value to other pupils whom they had met, face to face. It was not writing for the teacher. It was not writing that was 'marked' in the conventional, school sense. There had been a purpose to the drafting procedures as the need to communicate clearly and accurately was obvious to all concerned. It was pupil-to-pupil contact. They had learnt much about the pleasures and the pitfalls of group work; their ability to articulate the problems as well as the advantages is likely to make them more successful in other group work in many curriculum areas in the future.

An English teacher's point of view

I had learnt that a mixed-ability group can produce a group product which reflects a wide range of children's contributions. There are 23 different writers in the booklet; it was not dominated by the more able pupils. The less able did contribute successfully, particularly as they were writing from their own experience, with the help of discussion and support from other pupils in their group. One girl who was an isolate in almost all school activities throughout the year joined a group for the first time without too much negotiation on my part. She produced a page on 'What to Bring on the First Day' which was highlighted by one of the teachers as being well received by primary pupils.

On reflection, I should have made sure that an editorial group of pupils took responsibility for the whole production from the start. Similarly, it would have been beneficial to deliver the booklets and leave them in the primary school for half a day before the visit.

A primary headteacher's point of view

The English Inspector spoke to one of the headteachers of a large town feeder school and a Language Co-ordinator on the same day that she interviewed the pupils. The headteacher emphasized the novelty of the visit by the first-years when they delivered the booklets. The photographs taken of the occasion indicate the degree of activity which there was in the classroom when, after a slightly tense couple of minutes, 15 first-years started to mingle with more than 60 junior school pupils. The primary school staff stressed that the booklet and the visit by familiar faces on their territory helped to prepare the pupils for their day visit to the secondary school. In the past many had been apprehensive about the visit, but they were 'bubbling' and looking forward to the day. The headteacher was also very pleased with the pupils' responses to the letters. These had been read in near silence, then swopped and sections read aloud to each other. She was impressed by the way in which the secondary pupils had made such an effort to answer the primary school pupils' letters in a personalized way.

The Language Co-ordinator's point of view

The Language Co-ordinator in the other large primary school spoke highly of particular items in the booklet which the pupils had immediately found more useful than those in the official booklet: for example, the map and drawings of the school uniform. Similarly, they had liked the subtitle of the booklet 'A Guide to —— School By Pupils, For Pupils', which stressed the relationship between the pupil writers and pupil audience as recipients. They also had liked the very practical perspective of pages such as 'What to Bring on Your First Day'. On the day visit three school days after the delivery, all pupils from this school had started off with their pupil-written booklet; only some had brought the official booklet with them!

The Head of First Year's point of view

When I interviewed the Head of First Year, she told me she'd welcomed the perspective which the current first-years had given her. She had been surprised and encouraged by the enthusiasm and commitment of the pupils in their application to the task. They had taken it very seriously. She had accompanied one group of pupils in the delivery of booklets to a small rural primary school. She had previously visited in a more 'official' capacity and this second visit was much more relaxed and welcoming. She had been proud of the poised and confident behaviour of the delivery team. She indicated correctly that there was room for improvement in the booklet: there were gaps in the information. She felt there was insufficient informed commentary on the new learning opportunities which the secondary school offered. This brought us to a discussion about censorship. Should children be allowed to write exactly what they think and in the way they want to express it when the writing could be read by the whole community of parents, teachers and pupils? Is the abandonment of adult censorship the price of giving children more control over their own learning? Where is our accountability as professionals?

The Vice Principal's point of view

This was an issue which I raised again with the Vice Principal who had accompanied 15 of the first-years on the delivery run. He spoke warmly of its 'freshness' and the clarity of its sense of audience. As a teacher who has reservations about mixed-ability grouping, he emphasized that it was impossible to know that the booklet was produced by children from a full ability range. He liked the idea that so many different voices and forms of presentation were represented. We agreed that, as a learning activity, it was very different from most first-year classroom experiences as a result of its scope, scale, use of a real audience and the encouragement of active and group learning. Like the Head of Year, he wondered whether there was almost too much information and that some of it was rather arbitrary. It is a booklet in which the school's facilities are not as fairly represented as they would be if teachers had compiled it. On the other hand, the booklet represents what this mixed-ability group of 12-year-olds could compile at this point in their school learning. Just as there is a risk in not censoring children's writing, so the emphasis has to be on the *process* which the pupils went through in order to achieve a reasonably acceptable product. In assessing what the children have gained in terms of learning, the emphasis must be on 'how' they have learned and less on 'what' is learned. This is crucial principle of collaborative learning.

Collaboration as liaison? Whither curriculum continuity?

The good reception which this project received from the writers as well as the recipients, the pastoral, administrative and primary school staffs, gave me the courage to pursue more ambitious projects with my colleagues during the current academic year. We are now involved in a reading and 'paired story-writing' project with all five primary schools which spans the whole academic year. In addition, for the first time, secondary pupils are reading, writing and making books for pupils in the infant department of one of our feeder schools as part of their GCSE coursework.

The making of the alternative school guide led to valuable collaboration at the transition for pupils in both phases, teachers in both phases and those with a designated responsibility for transition. The secondary school pupils worked collaboratively in their groups; they collaborated with primary pupils during their visit to the primary schools; the three secondary teachers who were directly involved in the project certainly shared more common ground in this context than on previous occasions.

Creasey, Findlay and Walsh[3] define 'continuity' as being concerned with content and methodology whereas 'liaison' is largely concerned with processes and procedures which can facilitate that continuity. Liaison happens 'in real time', largely in the summer term, and is mostly concerned with the exchanging of information on individual pupils. This process itself can be problematic, but it is considerably more trouble-free than exchanging information about the curriculum offered by the different institutions involved. The exchange of information about individual pupils can be negotiated and accepted for what it is: a snapshot, partial view of a child's retrospective achievement. To convey a manageable view of the pupils' experience and expectations before and after transfer is a huge task. There may still be large gaps between a teacher's intentions and the experiences which the child receives; there may be large differences both between and within institutions in the curriculum which they offer. Teachers can swop policy statements, list content, concept areas, skills and methods of assessment. The child's experience still remains more than the sum of these diffuse parts; and these lists do not indicate where particular experiences fit into the individual's development.

This information-swopping, whether it concerns individual pupils or curriculum statements, has recognizable limitations. Moreover, a small-scale survey I carried out with colleagues in Peterborough primary and secondary schools in 1981 indicated that there was a great deal of activity concerning liaison: this included considerable swopping of information and pupil visits. Half the primary schools had also sent on samples of written work and lists of books read recently. There was also some exchange of policy documents, but no reaction to the information. It was not used in the planning and policy-making in schools for either phase. This situation is borne out by the Primary Survey of 1978[4] which concluded that the importance of continuity was 'largely overlooked'. Joan Dean says 'We have paid lip-service to the idea of continuity for many years'.[5] Plowden in 1967 offered as an item on the agenda for continuity 'to discuss and comment on the curriculum of the secondary school'.[6] Bullock was not arguing 'for the transmitted knowledge of a particular pupil's capabilities and needs but for the mutual understanding of what has been and will be involved in his experience of language'.[7] Marland cynically refers to attempts at closer liaison as 'romantic vaguenesses' and as 'one of the hardest things to achieve ... consum[ing] considerable time to little effect'.[8] In *Better Schools*, the DES addresses the issue in a prescriptive tone: 'The 5–16 curriculum needs to be constructed and delivered as a continuous and coherent whole, in which the primary phase prepares for the secondary phase and the latter builds on the former.'[9]

Elsewhere,[10] I have argued the need for teachers to experience the curriculum in transaction in each other's schools. Teachers need to respect the practices of other schools but also to react to this knowledge. This does not diminish the importance of transfer information, whether about individual pupils or policies; rather, it places this information in the larger contexts of the curriculum transaction. Teachers need the chance to develop shared reference points as specialist language teachers so as to promote and foster initiatives for curriculum continuity. The information needs contexts: these develop more fruitfully in collaboration on a joint activity. The collaboration is between equals and should, at best, be developed over a period of time and not be limited to 'one-off' occasions. Discussion of policy documents or individual pupils has its place but the process of education rather than its products can best be understood when there is a shared context for the activity and the teachers collaborate as equals. Writing for a real audience within a pyramid of schools is an example of this. The primary pupils had a genuine need for information and the first-years needed to know that their audience would receive their information and use it. The primary schoolchildren needed to feel that it was written 'by pupils, for pupils'. The teachers concerned needed to feel that the activity was mutually beneficial. Feedback from the recipients is an essential part of the process.

The follow-up activities in which we have been involved this year were made possible by the alternative guide to the school. It opened the door. A reading and writing for infants project carried out by fourth-year secondary pupils has led to discussion about reading and group work with a primary headteacher and infant teachers. The GCSE pupils are writing stories which the infants are commissioning from them, centred on their own interests and involving them as appropriate. The older pupils will write with the real audience of individual children in view, children they have met and spoken to; they will return to the infant school to read the stories to the children. Copies of the stories will be in GCSE folders as well as adding to the resources of the infant classrooms. The fourth-year pupils are keeping journals alongside the production of the story so that they are reflecting on the experiences they are both having and creating for others.

The 'paired story-writing' activity puts the primary and secondary schools in a more demanding relationship. During one session of a half-day, school-based Grant-Related In-service Training (GRIST) meeting, supported financially by the LEA, we made a list of some 12 ideas for 'paired-writing'. For example:

1. 30 opening sentences are provided by one school; paired school writers write the middles of the stories; the original school finished off the stories; they are then read in both schools.
2. Sound story. One school makes up a sound tape which the paired school writers use as a basis for narrative stories.

The project will require much goodwill, tenacity and administration if it is to survive successfully, but it has already started in a positive way with considerable support from the primary headteachers and teachers as well as the secondary English staff.

Real writing and real writers in the secondary school

When pupils write for a real audience, they see themselves as real writers, facing up to the responsibilities which this entails: to be able to persuade, influence, inform, give pleasure. Writing is a purposeful activity. Both the pastoral Head of Year and the Vice Principal, neither of them English teachers, commented on the commitment of the pupils in creating the alternative guide. Pupils' work was not trapped in exercise books with only a teacher as its reader/assessor. Pupils can be motivated to recognize that drafting and redrafting and presentation have a genuine purpose. Sustained work over a period of time is more likely to be possible. These activities can generate a collection of shared experiences for the teachers from the different phases to review: methodologies and expectations are likely to be discussed more readily and with greater understanding of the curriculum in transaction.

The authority invested in being in control of what you write makes the writer more independent, a genuine partner in the reader–writer relationship. Writing is powerful in these circumstances. The implications of the release this control brings to the writer and the ways in which the writer takes more control require different materials and different contexts in which to work. Pupils need different lengths of time to tackle tasks and different strategies for dealing with the written work. To allow first-years to write for a real audience and to work collaboratively on one occasion in the last month of their first year in secondary school is not enough! The implications for setting up writing opportunities across the curriculum and across the five years of secondary education are enormous and could be grasped by a teacher with responsibility for INSET. As the invaluable publications of the National Writing Project have continually stressed, the teacher becomes a fellow collaborator and a facilitator rather than being a controller, initiator and assessor since the final criterion for success is shifted from the teacher's mark book and is in the audience's response. Pupils can become more independent of their teachers. Writing has a different purpose since the writer is not now writing to tell the teacher what the teacher already knows.

Notes

1. Richard Knott, *The English Department in a Changing World*, Open University Press, 1985.
2. Sue Horner, *Writing and Liaison*, National Writing Project, 1986.
3. Martin Creasey, Frances Findlay, Brian Walsh, *Language across the Transition*, Longman/Schools Council, 1983.
4. DES, *Primary Education in England*, HMSO, 1978.
5. Joan Dean, 'Continuity' in C. Richards, *Primary Education: Issues for the 80's*, A. & C. Black, 1980.
6. DES, *Children in their Primary Schools*, HMSO, 1967.
7. DES, *A Language for Life*, HMSO, 1975, para. 14.12.
8. Michael Marland, *Language across the Curriculum*, Heinemann, 1977.
9. DES, *Better Schools*, HMSO, 1983, para. 65.
10. Frances Findlay, 'Continuity and Liaison in Language', *Education 3–13*, vol. 2, no. 1, 1983.

PART THREE
Strategies promoting collaboration

8 Writing without a pencil

GARETH DAVIES

The trouble with computers is that they often offer more than you want. They have such a wide range of capabilities that it is often difficult to decide how best to use them. The temptation is to plump for the flashiest, most sophisticated application rather than first assessing needs and then finding the package that will best meet them. That was how I felt when I first found myself in a school with a computer, a wide variety of programs at my disposal and a limited amount of time to use them, as the equipment had to be shared with other classes. All the programs sounded good and I could have justified using many of them. But I did not want the software to dictate how I used the computer. I thought that I should decide on my teaching aims and then find programs that would help me to achieve them.

I decided that I wanted to concentrate on programs which allowed the children to use the computer as a tool rather than those which made it into an electronic guru, set questions and gave out the right answers when asked. I developed a particular aversion to programs such as those which tested tables knowledge or spelling not only because they gave the entirely false impression that computers are infallible masters rather than very fallible servants but because with the limited time at my disposal they did not make best use of resources. Of the programs available which avoided such pitfalls the word processor seemed one which was immediately accessible and I began to use it extensively. In the process I became very interested in the interaction between children working together at the computer and how it compared with other types of collaborative writing which I had initiated. In this chapter I have tried to outline the conclusions I reached, though not in the order they occurred. Unfortunately life just isn't that simple!

Collaboration in theory

One of the aims which I set myself was to give my third- and fourth-year juniors enjoyable writing experiences. One of my strategies was to allow pairs or groups of children to write stories together. Nothing new in schools, of course; but in terms of published fiction, collaboration between writers is rare. On a purely organizational level it was easy to ask the children to write together. They had the advantage over most adult writers of being in the same place for a considerable part of each day. There was also their own wish to work together springing from the close friendship patterns which develop in schools.

But being in the right place at the right time was not necessarily a justification for allowing the children to work together. Motivation was. One of the benefits I expected from collaborative writing was increased enthusiasm for the task and an extra confidence in tackling it, on the basis that a problem shared is a problem halved. The difficulties I expected were the usual ones faced by inexperienced writers – what to say, how to say it, the physical effort of concentrating on and transcribing an extended piece. I also had some hopes that the product of a joint effort might in some way be an improvement on the usual standard of either individual. At that time I was far from clear as to what sort of improvement I had in mind but with some results of collaborations to look at I was able to form the conclusions which are set out later in this chapter.

It was not just the product of the collaborations which interested me. I was equally, if not more, anxious to observe the processes which the children went through in writing. Frank Smith[1] has identified three stages – pre-writing, writing and re-writing. The problem with monitoring the pre-writing stage is that it is invariably unspoken and, therefore, unobservable, although it is sometimes possible to trace the gestation of a piece of writing by looking at the eventual product. If, on the fairly simple level, I took pre-writing to be the process during which an idea emerges, is given shape and undergoes numerous transformations and refinements as the writer becomes more involved with it, would having joint authors make that process more explicit? Would it be possible for me to see how ideas were developing and how involvement was growing, by monitoring the conversations which the children would have to have in order to reach an agreed starting point for their story? Similarly, as the writing progressed to transcription and rewriting, would the dialogue between the writers reflect the constant questioning and answering, trial and error, acceptance and rejection which goes on in the mind of the individual author as his or her work progresses? My own experience told me that every individual writer has an image in the mind of the kind of audience for whom he or she is writing. As the writing develops there is a continuous, if subconscious, reference back to the needs of that invisible audience and as a result a continuous reworking not only of what has already been written but of what will be written in the next sentence or paragraph. Does the work live up to the perceived expectations of that invisible audience? How visible would that process become when the writing was collaborative and there was a real audience sitting at the individual writer's shoulder ready to comment instantly on each word or sentence as it was produced? Or would the collaboration limit the process? It was possible that having an on-the-spot audience in the shape of a collaborator would reduce the need to consider the requirements of a diverse and imaginary readership because the work would be tailored to the needs of that individual. In other words, each collaborator might try and write for the other and not for a wider audience.

Collaboration in practice

As I had expected, the children were, mostly, very enthusiastic about writing together, though there were exceptions. Certain children were very anxious to write individually at all times. In some cases this was because they disliked their work being made public. These were the children who built a shield of arms or books round their work and were reluctant to submit it to scrutiny. Others preferred to work by themselves because they were confident of their own ability.

For those who did choose to work together the increased motivation and commitment were immediately apparent. Concentration spans lengthened and as noise levels increased so too did an atmosphere of purposefulness rather different to that which often surrounded the less enthusiastic writers. Collaborators spent a very long time talking, much longer than they would have spent preparing to write a story of their own. There was a great deal of hubbub, but tuning into individual conversations it was obvious that even those children who normally tended to avoid writing were talking almost exclusively about the work and there was lively debate about the stories and, particularly, about possible plots. Often the debate was joined by adjacent groups as a stray phrase caught their attention and brought a fresh idea to mind which they either passed on for what it was worth or purloined for their own use. It did indeed seem that the usually silent pre-writing process was coming alive in the classroom. It seemed also that conversation was speeding up the process. Whereas normally the pre-writing stage might last days or weeks as ideas were picked up from here or there and juggled around, the children were brainstorming in a way that produced plenty of instant ideas and just as many changes of direction before an overall shape for the work was decided upon. I interviewed some of the children later to see what differences they noticed.

Kirsty and Sally were particularly articulate.

GD: Why is it different writing stories together?
S: More ideas.
K: Because you can share ideas and you've got someone to compete with instead of just saying it's my idea and I like it.

They also talked about the strategy they adopted when there was a conflict of ideas.

S: When you write down an idea and show it to someone they might say 'Ughhh that's rotten and awful' but me and Sally got on well. Sort of shared the ideas.
GD: Did you ever have different ideas for the next bit of the story?
S and K: Yeah, definitely.
GD: How did you decide whose idea was going to go or did you compromise?
K: We actually asked somebody else.
GD: Who did you ask?
K: Melanie.
GD: You asked her to choose which idea?
K: Yeah.

GD:	Was she working with you as well?
S and K:	No.
S:	We just consulted her to see which was the best idea.
K:	And she was fair.
GD:	Did you tell her which idea was whose?
K:	No, that might have ...
S:	If you told her which one it might have influenced her.

So here were two children working through a lengthy period of pre-writing. More than that, they were bearing in mind the needs of an audience and on occasion using a representative of that audience as a means to decide how their writing should proceed.

When it came to actually writing the stories which had emerged from the discussions there were a variety of approaches. At one extreme, one partner did all the physical transcription while the other sat almost entirely silent, looking on. At the other, partners took it in turns to share the transcription task and were simultaneously holding a conversation about the writing. In between there was a whole range of levels of involvement but the balance seemed weighted towards groups where one partner dominated the transcription process. It was impossible to judge accurately whether the dominant partners were faithfully reproducing the fruits of the earlier discussion or whether they were using the transcription process to make the writing their own. Certainly the latter was the case with some pairs who had not developed such sophisticated adjudication procedures as Sally and Kirsty.

There was a steady stream of complaints that X was hogging all the work or ignoring what Y said. These tended to come from pairs who were not closely matched in ability. The more able child would dominate the writing; the less able would either take a back seat or be constantly overruled when he or she put forward a suggestion. Generally there was little discussion during the writing stage about particular aspects of the work. Little was altered once it was committed to paper and major re-writing was not attempted. This was true even of the more sophisticated writers who were usually very particular about getting things right. In the latter case I suspected that this lack of revision was due to the pre-writing discussion which had clarified their thoughts more than usual.

Once the stories were finished there was a marked reluctance among most pairs to write out a neat copy, to correct spellings or to revise the work in any way. In marked contrast to the enthusiasm of the initial conversations many children now seemed to have lost all interest in the stories. Suggestions that they might write it out again so that each partner could have a copy were resisted. Protestations by each that the other could keep the existing copy and that they did not want it seemed to be a defence mechanism against the threat of more transcribing. The waning of enthusiasm was so noticeable that I wondered what factors might have prompted it. Had the stories simply gone on too long? Was handwriting a problem? If the pairs were unbalanced did one partner feel that he or she had no stake in the work, while the other felt hampered by having to collaborate? I had no immediate answers to these questions, though the work I did later using the word processor shed some light on them.

The quality of the product

Some parts of the process the children had gone through in their paired writing had proved very satisfactory, others less so. But what about the product of their collaborations? Were they 'better' in any perceptible way than their individual writing? To try and determine this I carried out a close comparison of several pieces of collaborative writing and individual work by the same children. The writing of Scott and Darren was fairly typical of what I found. These two boys were among the less able writers but the relative level of improvement was fairly standard across the ability range where the writers were well matched. At the time of writing both boys had just become fourth-year juniors. They were evenly matched in ability and in normally lacking motivation to write. I was surprised when they chose to work together as they were not particularly close friends in class.

When set the task of writing together they became very excited and seemed eager to get on with it. I had left them a free choice of subject for their story and this caused them initial difficulty. They asked for help and, after I had mentioned possible genres – adventure, space, ghosts – immediately chose a ghost story. I did not see them again until they had written two pages at which point they were bursting with pride and eager that I should read the story so far. I did so over lunchtime. That afternoon they added another two pages and, not content with their ending, started planning a second chapter. By the next day they had completely lost interest and the second chapter was never written. Nevertheless they had already amazed me by concentrating on a writing task for nearly a whole day. Compare that with Darren's space story, written a little while earlier, also in chapters. The first draft of the first chapter ran to one page and took over a week of desultory work to complete. Even that was after a false start which ran to only four lines and with which Darren initially declared himself entirely happy. The motivating power of the collaboration was in little doubt, but what about the quality of the writing? I found it useful to consider it in terms of organization and structure, appropriateness and awareness of the reader, lexis, syntax and presentation.

Organization

On a superficial reading I immediately thought how much better written was Darren and Scott's joint story than anything either of them had written by himself. Darren by himself opened his space story with:

> *My Name is Robbet I gooing to Leaving Earth. Because I don't Like my frind or my mum or my dad*

Together Darren and Scott started:

One day John and his frineds were playing tig. They said Lets go over the woods.

Although this seemed to read better, on closer examination of the pieces it was apparent that in terms of their organization the two pieces were in some ways very similar. Both continued in a strictly chronological sequence giving each story a very simple structure. At no stage in the stories were previous events referred back to or future events predicted.

Reader

What was improved in the joint writing was the sense that there was an audience which had to be satisfied. The opening of Darren and Scott's joint work is, for instance, much more convincing than Darren's solo effort, in which 'Robbet's' reasons for leaving home simply did not ring true. The improvement was, I suspected, largely a result of having two writers, one of whom was also acting as audience. When one writer made a suggestion the other would accept it as a good idea or, if he did not understand it, would question the idea and suggest alternatives until it would stand the readership test. This sensitivity to the needs of potential readers was demonstrated by the way in which Darren and Scott linked the different episodes in their story. Darren by himself had envisaged a series of events but felt no obligation to explain why or how his characters moved from one to another.

I runed away and I came to an earport the rookit was aBout to go of I went it stole it then a man canted down 10 9 8 7 6 5 4 3 2 1 Lift of the rook was in the ear I went in a room

Darren and Scott together leave fewer unanswered questions

John was lony he was walking and he stopet and looket and he saw an old house Then he walked over to it and he knot on the door. The door crek and it open

There were no missing episodes in this narrative. There was even an attempt to assign a motive for John's going to the house – he was 'lony' – on which the rest of the story hung. We even had the detail that he knocked on the door. The impression given is that the writers were enjoying following the slow progress of their adventure. They were savouring it, not trying to get to the end as quickly as possible, which is the impression left by Darren's breathless narrative.

Where Darren and Scott were less successful was in mastering the genre in which they had decided to write. They set out to write a ghost story but, in fact, what they came up with was something nearer to the *Babes in the Wood*. Although there were odd ghostly touches such as creaking doors, what the characters find inside the house could as well have been witch, wizard, dragon or monster since the ghost when it appeared was not required to display any of the features normally associated with its kind – walking through walls, voices from the past and so on. In fact it simply indulged in the kind of chase which could equally have been managed by a malevolent human. As reluctant readers, Darren and Scott had apparently not soaked up enough of the essence of ghost stories to be able to produce a convincing one of their own. They had not internalized the language and conventions of the genre. This feeling was echoed in Darren's individual space story. Substitute the words 'home' for 'Earth', 'plane' for 'rocket' and it could have been a story about almost anything. Only the '10 9 8 7 6 5 4 3 2 1 Lift of' was directly related to the genre.

Lexis

The vocabulary of Darren's piece was extremely limited. His verbs were mainly restricted to all-purpose ones – 'go', 'went', 'got'. His nouns were invariably unspecific – 'room', 'place' – and nowhere in the whole of the first chapter was there an adjective or an adverb. 'Then' was the only temporal linking word which he employed.

In the collaborative writing there was a difference. Although the verbs were still mainly very general there were variations – 'creaked', 'answered', 'slammed', 'glow', 'disappeared': small signs that extra effort had been put into finding appropriate words. There were still many wildly unspecific nouns – 'a white *thing*', '*something* stopped him', 'he saw *something* next to it', 'he fell in *some water*'. But there was evidence of more care in 'lantern' and 'candle' not just 'light'. The improvement was more noticeable in the adjectives.

> *He walk it to the liveing room it was dark and glueme and clod*
>
> *He saw a Big Black door with a red hadall*
>
> *The burning candall*

And although there were no adverbs, there was one adverbial phrase

> *he hit the ground with a thump*

and one metaphor

> *He ran like a Bulat from a gun just go off*

Both Darren and Scott were delighted with this piece of description which they told me about as soon as they had written it and which I took as further evidence of the considerable thought and effort which both were putting into the work.

Syntax

Although Darren's writing had very little punctuation (and what there was mainly erroneous) it was essentially written in short sentences.

We found some food

There were only two subordinate clauses in the first chapter and they were both in the same sentence although Darren punctuated them to stand alone.

I gooing to Leaving Earth. Because I don't Like my frind or my mum or my dad. Because they go of with people.

Darren and Scott did no better together, managing only

No wan anedud him so he went in

Presentation

The spelling in both pieces of work reflected the boys' individual standards. Their attempts at words they did not know reflected their own speech patterns which tended to give them difficulties in correctly interpreting initial sounds and vowels. There were less errors in the joint writing but I was not aware of any particular extra effort on the writers' part to ensure that their writing was completely accessible to an audience. I put the improvements down to the fact that between them they had a larger stock of correct spellings and that they were checking each other as they went along. They wanted to get the writing right but had not taken a conscious decision to concentrate on the spelling.

Although both pieces of writing compared here were intended only as first drafts and I had stressed that presentation was not the most important factor at that stage, it was noticeable that Darren's handwriting was markedly neater and more careful in the collaborative writing than in his individual work.

Perceived problems

I felt that the collaborative writing had gone a long way, but not all the way towards meeting my initial optimistic expectations. As far as the pre-writing went it had been wonderfully motivating for most children and the quality of the discussions had been excellent. After that it was a gradual slide through writing and re-writing and the difficulties at those stages had reduced rather than enhanced the enjoyment for some children. This was particularly apparent when I came to consider the question of ownership of the writing. In many groups neither child felt that he or she really owned it. In others, one child felt that it was exclusively hers. In such cases the partners felt left out and were even more disgruntled that where their ideas had been incorporated they had been appropriated by the more dominant writer. It seemed clear that when collaborative writing was being carried out using paper and pencil, ownership of the writing depended largely on who held the pen during the transcription process.

In terms of content, the joint work showed improvements in areas where the initial discussion was obviously of value – consistency of plot, overall structure, characterization, and so on – but improvements were less apparent in those areas which might be regarded as the 'tools' of writing – spelling, syntax, and so on. Here the writing tended to reflect more the normal standard of whichever child was holding the pencil.

Removing the pencil

The less satisfactory aspects of collaborative writing often stemmed from the fact that the child holding the pencil had more power: he or she controlled the writing. The word processor offered a way out of this difficulty. It also offered extra motivation for the writers. Partly this was because computers were still comparatively unusual in school and there was considerable competition to use them. Whatever the reason, the children writing on the word processor retained their high level of interest throughout the writing process, not just in the initial stages. Enthusiasm was such that it backfired on me at first. Once children knew that they were going to use the computer they were so eager to begin that the pre-writing discussion, which had been such a positive feature of previous work, went by the board as they rushed to type something, anything. In the long term I would have expected this over-enthusiasm to have toned itself down as the computer became less of a novelty but in the meantime I had to insist that the children carried out their story-planning away from the computer.

Keeping the use of the word processor simple at first and ignoring most of its more powerful editing capabilities was also helpful in reinforcing the idea that at this stage I wanted first drafts and not polished writing. Nevertheless, most of the groups worked out for themselves the simpler editing functions, notably how to delete what they had written. This had unfortunate consequences sometimes.

> GD: Are there any problems about writing at the computer?
> Sally: Remember that time ...
> Kirsty: She pressed the button and it deleted the whole thing.

The interactions between the children once they were sitting at the keyboard were varied and illuminating. First, who controlled the keyboard? It was certainly not the same children who had dominated paper-and-pencil collaborations. This time pre-eminence was based not on writing ability but on familiarity with computers. Children who had them at home tended to take over the keyboard when paired with those who did not, almost irrespective of writing ability. But such one-sided relationships were rarer than in collaborations using pencil and paper. Most pairs developed strategies for sharing the work out. Sally and Kirsty came up with a symbiotic relationship which, although inefficient, suited them.

> *S*: Its good 'cos she does half the board and I do half. We split the board in two. We split the keys up and she does ...
> *K*: We do a word at a time.
> *S*: And if you actually say the word.
> *K*: She'll be ready to do one word and when she's finished it I do the space and then I do another word.

Sally's reference here to 'saying the word' was significant. It was quite usual for the children at the computer to vocalize what they were writing even when they were doing the typing. It was almost as if they were telling the computer the story. As well as providing a means of transcription it seemed to be an initial, uncritical audience. At this stage, indeed, I noticed a big difference from the earlier collaborations. Irrespective of who was controlling the keyboard it simply did not happen that one child took over control of the content of the story and the composition process. Quite often the task of composition was as equally shared as the mechanical task of keying in the words. Each child in turn would have responsibility for composing a sentence, a few lines or a paragraph. Not that relationships stayed so clear cut, even when that was the mutually agreed arrangement. It was common for one partner to take over and finish a sentence begun by the other, to suggest alternatives and additions, and even to draw attention to inconsistencies with what had already been written. Although I had stressed that it was not important at this stage, there was a lot of discussion about spellings.

In practice, as Frank Smith suggests, there were no clear distinctions between the pre-writing, writing and re-writing stages. The word processor further blurred the distinctions because it was so easy for the children to delete and replace without ending up with a messy and unreadable script. Watching the children at the computer, the blurring became obvious. Although they had an overall idea of where their stories were going, both writers were constantly involved in renegotiating the text as the writing progressed. This could only happen to the extent that it did because the writing was in the public domain. It was written large on the screen that both writers could see easily and it was in the handwriting of neither. It was impossible for either writer to claim sole ownership and the element of impersonality in the presentation helped to foster the feeling of joint ownership of the content. This seemed essential if both partners were to find collaborative writing fully satisfying. Here are Kirsty and Sally again:

> *GD*: Imagine that you were writing a story together and that you were having to write it down. What would be the problems? [They had had this experience.]
> *S*: You'd have to have really two pieces of work.
> *GD*: Why?

K: Well it would be a bit cramped on one piece of paper and you're all trying to write down your ideas.
S: Yeah. You'll be shoving each other out of the way.
K: Two pencils, two rubbers.
GD: So having it on screen means that you can both see it without any problem?
S: You sit right in front of it.
K: And you don't need to push it away to see and give it to the other person to see.

The continuous discussions between the collaborators meant that what they eventually produced required little, if any, revision. Major elements such as plot and setting were sorted out as the work progressed and re-writing was done immediately. An extra pair of eyes looking at the work usually spotted parts which were unsatisfactory before they were finished. The more pairs of eyes there were looking at the work the more carefully it was crafted. In groups larger than two there was quite often at least one child who seemed to be paying very little attention. But suddenly they would speak up and draw attention to some inconsistency, or point out that some element already written in ruled out the options being discussed for the next section. Eavesdropping on conversations it was quite usual to hear sentences beginning 'We can't say that because up here it says ... '.

Occasionally the groups or pairs would write themselves into a corner from which it was impossible logically to reach their planned ending. When this happened with individual writers I found that they usually adopted one of two main strategies. The less able carried on without worrying about logic or consistency and introduced some totally improbable device which allowed them to reach their ending. The more thoughtful writers simply changed their endings. There was a universal reluctance to re-write the story from the point at which it started going wrong and the strength of the reluctance increased with the quantity of writing which had been done since that point was passed. This was equally true of collaborative story-writing, whether using a pencil or the word processor. Whatever the means of transcription, there was no enthusiasm for the unravelling, re-writing option. With collaborations using pencil and paper the choice between changing the ending and logical inconsistency depended on the attitude of the child controlling the writing. On the word processor, however, the invariable choice was to change the ending. Somehow the discussion between partners made improbable devices unsatisfactory even for the less able. But the problem was in any case minimized because the two pairs of eyes tended to notice things going wrong much earlier:

GD: What things about the story you wrote together were better than if you had written by yourselves?
S: Umm. They fit together easier than when you work by yourself. You make two good ideas but there's no link in the middle whereas if you work together then someone else may have them.
K: If you have two good ideas but nothing to go in the middle. If you have two good ideas but there's something missing.

Output from the word processor

I considered the output from the children through the computer in terms of its content and presentation. Presentation was by far the easier to assess. The word processor had a huge advantage over the children's handwriting in both legibility and layout. It was also much less physically tiring. In particular, children who had untidy or poorly formed handwriting were able to produce work which was visually pleasing to themselves and others. That their story was printed made it seem more like the writing in published books and did a great deal to enhance its status. This was reflected in the eagerness of other children to read what had been produced. Use of the printer also meant that multiple copies could be produced in seconds with very little additional effort for the writers. Not only could each child have his or her own copy but each copy was a top copy. This reinforced the sense of joint authorship and joint ownership of the writing. Further copies could also be produced for inclusion in a class book or for display. Once multiple copies were available the potential audience increased, the status of the work was enhanced and the children's pride and satisfaction in their work were reinforced.

> *GD*: So whose story was it at the end, when you had finished it? Was it yours, Kirsty? Or was it yours, Sally?
> *K*: Both.
> *S*: Both.
> *GD*: Were you as proud, it being both of yours, as you would have been if you had written it yourself?
> *K*: Yeah, 'cos we both done it together and we thought it was different. Not many people write together.

An analysis of the content of some of the work produced on the word processor led me to conclusions similar to those I had reached after analysing the content of collaborations using pencil and paper. Improvements over individual work tended to reflect the differing abilities of the participants in the writing task, in that they pooled their strengths to produce something slightly above their average, particularly in areas such as reader awareness. In other areas the improvements were slight. Vocabulary did not improve dramatically, and although Kirsty and Sally could produce descriptions like:

There was a fountain that sprayed golden water and parlm trees that swayed in the breeze. The trees had money growing from them. And huge marquees that are full of food and drink. There are sand, sun and sea plus big swimming pools and sunbeds. There were small rivers with Italin gondolas with full champagne bottles in them.

this was no more than I would have normally expected from them. Their spelling had improved somewhat but they remained shaky in other areas: in the way, for instance, they varied their tenses and split sentences in two.

Generally the analyses of content were inconclusive. I found it impossible to say that using the word processor had improved this aspect of the writing. It had certainly not wrought any dramatic improvements. On the other hand, it had maintained the improvements which had sprung from the act of collaboration. It was encouraging enough to leave open the possibility that greater improvements would spring from greater familiarity with the use of the word processor.

Conclusion

My experiences of collaborative writing convinced me that it was a very powerful weapon in my teaching armoury. It improved motivation for the writing task and satisfaction with the written product. It also helped tighten up some aspects of the story content. But its potential benefits were much enhanced by linking it to the use of a word processor. The children's enthusiasm was extended further and maintained right through the process of pre-writing, writing and re-writing. As they went through this process they were learning more about the strategies adopted by mature writers. That is not to say that they were turned into excellent writers overnight. They were not. The word processor by itself often made little impact on the quality of the writing. Nor did the high profile given to the writing process feed back immediately into an individual's own writing. The children did not instantly improve as individual writers because they had the opportunity to collaborate either with a pencil or the word processor (though it would be interesting to know if they would ultimately do so given frequent and regular opportunities). What the combination of collaboration and the word processor did provide for the children was a satisfying writing experience and an end product of which they could feel justifiably proud. If I could build on this then the task of improving other aspects of their writing would be a much simpler and more enjoyable one. In the meantime I had found a way of harnessing the power of the computer to a task which fitted perfectly with some of the teaching aims I had set myself.

Note

1. Frank Smith, *Writing and the Writer*, Heinemann, 1982.

9 'Which Way Now?' A whole-class collaboration to write a novel

JO SOUTHON

My aim was to produce a single, coherent novel by means of collaboration between thirty-one 12–13-year-old authors. I felt they were at an age when they could begin to explore the construction of a novel and there seemed no better way to do this than by writing one. Each child's written work would have to measure up, not only to the partner he or she was working with, but also to the group as a whole. I felt the novel would provide a strong motive, not only for the improvement of narrative writing skills, but also for achieving greater technical accuracy. I had worked on a 'class novel' with a second-year group before and found it an ideal time for group collaboration. They feel they belong in the school but are not yet too cynical to show enthusiasm for school work.

It was essential that they should feel in control of their novel, but I had to define a structure for them to work in without imposing my ideas. In groups of four they had to select a plot which took one main character away from home on a journey: a journey of sufficient length and complexity to allow for 15 chapters to be written as separate but connecting stages of the whole novel. Each group presented their ideas to the class, and then they voted to choose a single plot. This democratic procedure was vital to the whole project. Any major decision had to be made by the group as a whole for them to feel it was their novel. Every decision was put to the ballot: a procedure the class accepted and respected readily.

I had to learn to suppress my tendency to be judgemental in favour of becoming an adviser or technical assistant, as it were. I wanted the children to look to each other for approval rather than to me, so that they could develop their critical faculties and self-confidence. This meant taking the time required for the democratic process to work although I knew many of the voting sessions would be laborious. It meant there would be no absolute timetable for the project: it would take the time the group chose to spend on it. It meant much talk to produce a relatively small amount of writing: but the results were certainly worth it.

The second-year English groups in my school are divided into ability bands.

'WHICH WAY NOW?' 107

The group I chose to work with was the top-ability band and this made me slightly anxious. My previous class 'novel' 'Scotland Bound' had been by a middle-ability group which had enjoyed writing collaboratively. As they were in the middle band the children did not perceive themselves as 'good writers' but were greatly enthused by the project which gave their writing value and purpose. The quality of the writing was greatly improved by the drafting by and criticism it received from the pairs in collaboration. These were children who were inclined to show more concern about getting the page filled than the quality of their writing, so they were pleased to share the responsibility of creating ideas and expressing them with one another. With the new group I knew it would be different. There were some individuals who were very self-assured writers already. How would they take to having to collaborate with others whose ideas may not be as good as their own? Wouldn't a plot agreed by committee be inevitably banal?

Setting up the project: the plot

The plot of the novel was, clearly, of great importance. It had to allow for 30 authors to construct 15 separate chapters which had integrity when read as a complete novel. A completely open brief was impossible so the following instructions were given for homework:

1. Outline a plot involving the journey of one main character. This journey is to span the novel so each chapter can be set in a different location.
2. The plot will need to be attractive to the class as a whole and allow each pair of writers the freedom to be creative within their own chapter.

In the following lessons they were to discuss these plots in groups of four, choosing one plot to present to the class as a whole.

Group collaboration: choosing a plot

I had allowed the children to develop their own plot outlines at home. I knew they would find it difficult to fulfil the second part of the task: there was a danger they would conceive of plots with too narrow a scope or minority appeal. They were not as used to collaboration in writing as they were in improvised drama. I hoped they would deal with these problems in the group discussions. The friendship groups they had formed turned out to be single-sex, except for one mixed group I had thrust together out of the stragglers.

They began by taking it in turns to outline their individual plots. Some of the discussion became quite heated when someone would defend their story against attack or derision from others. However, some groups decided to build up their plot by democratic means rather than choose the plot of an individual. This involved reaching agreement on each detail at a time, laboriously building up a plot piece by piece. One such group spent ten minutes earnestly reciting every female forename they could think of before voting: a process I found rather depressing. The following transcript will give you an idea of this type of discussion:

108 COLLABORATION AND WRITING

Natasha: Where's this journey going to start from?
Jenny: Not America, *please*!
Natasha: All right, everyone does America ...
Belinda: Say we start the story from Devon ...
Natasha: Why don't we do it from the highlands of Scotland ...
Jenny: Wales!
Rachel: No.
Belinda: Say it's from Devon and then it was to Scotland ...
Rachel: Derbyshire.
Jenny: (*in Birmingham accent*) Birmingham!
Natasha: (*echoing*) Birmingham!
Rachel: (*singsong*) Derby-shire.
Jenny: Say we started from Wales ...
Natasha: Not Wales!
Belinda: I didn't say Wales!
Natasha: Wales is a boring place.
Jenny: No it isn't!
Belinda: What about Somerset?
Natasha: What about ... *Dundee*!
Jenny: No!

However, they warmed to the task and were later able to make some quite sensible decisions in less than a minute of collaborative talk. Here are the four girls from the previous extract, working on their plot idea, deciding on the age of their main character:

Jenny: How old?
Rachel: Eighteen.
Belinda: Eleven.
Natasha: Not as young as eleven, and not as old as eighteen.
Jenny: We don't want eighteen because you can do what you like when you are eighteen. Well, virtually.
Natasha: Fourteen.
Rachel: Yeah.
Belinda: But you'd still be a schoolgirl ...
Jenny: So?
Natasha: But you could run away.
Belinda: But they can run away.
Jenny: It would give more sort of 'oomph' to the story.
Natasha: They might not be running away but it gives ...
Belinda: Why are they running away?
Natasha: Not eighteen, it's too old.
Jenny: Eighteen is boring.
Rachel: Ten.
Belinda: Sixteen.
Jenny: Sixteen's too old.
Natasha: You can get married and do everything that you do when you get married.
Rachel: All right, we'll have fourteen then.

Group plots presented to class

The next task was for each group to present its plot to the class as a whole, to 'sell' its ideas. I was pleased to see that after a short while they stopped looking to me for approval, but presented their ideas to the whole group, arguing their case, defending their position.

What soon became obvious was that the type of plot fell into two categories according to the gender of the group. The boys favoured science fiction or fantasy while the girls wanted emotional drama. The two poles are evident in the following extracts.

Alex: Within the next 50 years the sun will turn into a supernova and in this time a boy or girl has been chosen to find a planet where human life is possible. He or she has been chosen for skill with computers and knowledge of science. Geography of the world has changed and the Med's now twice as large as it was. England's now joined to France and North and South America have split. He or she goes out in a light spacecraft equipped with computers and all the latest in technology. He or she goes through all kinds of things – these are just suggestions – black holes, asteroid showers, loss of communication, space cyclones and land on planets with strange people, volcanoes and things like that. Maybe he or she can get back and the world can be saved. He or she is blonde haired (nearly gold), eyes are pale blue; he or she's patient and waits for the right moment to act; he or she's not very strong but has skill knowledge and ...

Richard: ingenuity ...

Alex: which helps him or her get out of trouble.

Richard: They do actually find the planet where the people can move to and they somehow move ...

Alex: they don't have to move, but they might.

Teacher: So possibly the end of the novel might be them finding the planet?

Alex: Yes.

Shervin: Even if they do find it, it'll take much more time to build a spaceship to take the whole population of the earth.

Alex: No, they're building the spaceship in advance.

Richard: ... while this girl ...

Alex: or boy ...

Richard: ... is out in space looking for it.

Jenny: How am I going to write about something like asteroid belts ...

Girl: Yeah ...

Jenny: I haven't got a clue about them ... (*murmur of female agreement*)

Boy: Just make it up.

Cathy: This is set about a hundred years ago in California, when they had black slaves. There's a rich house and a servant called Henrietta and she was caught stealing something so she was sacked, so they got someone to replace her called Jacko who is black as well. The girl who lived in the house, the rich white girl, is called Francesca Claydon ...

Class: (*titters*)

Cathy: (*indignant*) Shut up! And she got really friendly with this Jacko and um ...

Girl: Ooh er ...

Cathy: It's not a romance, or anything. Her father found out and he got really cross... It's not funny, it's really sad! And he sacked Jacko and Francesca told her parents that she would keep seeing him and they got really cross because they didn't approve of him because he was black. So she ran away with him. They go to lots of villages and things. Sometimes they have to go into hiding because her father sent out some men on horseback who chase them across California. One time the men on horseback come in and they ask the people who are hiding them if they have come and there's a really tense atmosphere because they think they're going to get caught, but they don't. There's another bit where they try to get across a bridge and it's really rickety and it nearly falls down and it keeps swaying but they manage to get across it. And um, you can decide how it ends. It might be sad because Jacko might be killed or something or it might be happy because she convinces her father not to be so racist.

Stuart: I think most of the boys wouldn't want to be writing these sort of love stories.

Girl: But it's not a love story...

Stuart: It's a love story, running away with a boy...

Cathy: It's not going to be a romance, it's more like ... friends ... and showing how racist people can be.

John: Could there be, in a story like that, as if they're hunting for something, treasure or something ...

Girl: Oh no!

Teacher: Well, why do you feel you need to do that?

John: Well, at the moment I don't think it's appealing to the boys, really.

Natasha: (*chanting*) Sexist ... sexist ...

Boy: Then it would give them something to go away for ...

At this point I felt I might have spoiled the whole thing by allowing them to develop strong attachments to their gender-based ideas. I might have anticipated such an outcome if I had paid more attention to the answers on a questionnaire I had given them at the beginning of the year. They were asked to name books they had enjoyed reading. The titles speak for themselves:

BOYS
Way of the Tiger
William – The Bold
Master of the Grove

GIRLS
Six Ponies
Long Time between Kisses
Flight from Heartbreak

It was with some trepidation that I set up the secret ballot for the plot. The winning plot came out with a clear majority. Here is a transcript of its presentation:

Helen: There's this girl called Jennifer Kimble who's seventeen and has come from Scotland and she gets a letter from her lawyer to say that her Granny's died over in Australia and she's been given a certain amount of money to go over there and collect her will. In this letter there's this family jewel but nobody really knows what it is and her cousin is in the house at the time, and she's twenty, or it could be a he, and he's twenty, and he

'WHICH WAY NOW?' 111

overhears and he follows her and on all the trains and everything he tries to murder her to try and get the jewel. She's also got some money in the envelope as well but she doesn't know how much, She's got to go and collect some more from her Granny, or Grandpa, or whatever. They're trying to murder her to get all the money from her.

Sean: She gets there and it's only just a brooch or like a personal thing.
Teacher: Oh, so you mean it's nothing of any value.
Sean: No. It's all about the journey over to Australia and how this bloke is trying to kill her.
Teacher: In other words the story is made up of the journey to Australia and involves the heroine being chased by the cousin who is after what she is carrying with her. Yeah?
Sean: No.
Teacher: Oh, she gets it when she gets to Australia?
Sean: She left this brooch 'cause it's a personal thing to her granddaughter to keep to give to her grandchildren.
Teacher: But ... but where is the brooch?
Helen: She's got it ...
Sean: In Australia ...
Teacher: Oh, you don't agree about this. I thought there was some confusion. The brooch is ...
Helen: She's got it with her and she's going to collect some more money, from Australia.
Sean: What?
Helen: There'd be nothing to steal, otherwise.
Teacher: A little confusion here, actually. It needs sorting out.
Mark: Why does it have to be a girl who ...
Girl: Oh, Mark!
Boy: The cousin's a boy.
Boy: We can decide that later.
Boy: Why does it have to be a boy?

I felt it was rather a weak and undeveloped plot and wondered whether there was any significance in the fact that it was the only one developed by a mixed-gender group!

As the plot was so thin, we had to hold a further session of whole-class voting, which, as it happened, changed matters considerably. When I did 'Scotland Bound' we had determined the plot in a spontaneous way, with individuals making proposals which were summarized on the board and then voted on. In many ways, this technique was more successful as people had not had the opportunity to become possessive about their ideas and the whole session had an electricity generated by the magic of constructing plot, character and motive in a double lesson. On this occasion I felt it important to act as the facilitator of their ideas; to accept, without prejudice, whatever proposals were made, hoping they would spot the impracticalities for themselves. They accepted the virtues of the ballot system and there was little demur after the result was declared.

So Jennifer Kimble became Charlotte Kimble; the grandmother became an author of adventure stories from Scotland; her will set Charlotte off on a treasure-hunt around Britain and the complication of the dastardly cousin was eliminated.

At around this time the school had a visit from Joan Lingard, who spoke about how she had made the mistake as a 13-year-old author of setting her novel in Australia. She told them how she uses the people and places she is familiar with to create her novels: the very stuff she had thought 'boring' as an adolescent. Fortunately, some of the class picked up on this advice, so we had a clutch of chapters set in East Anglia or places people had been to on holiday.

First draft: collaboration in pairs

After all these preliminaries, the class were very keen to start writing, so there were grumbles when I insisted that they wrote a plot outline before they began the text itself. The decision about which order the chapters took had to be made later by me as I worked out a logical route from the list of place names. The children had to start writing with Charlotte in location: they had no notion of where she had been in the previous chapter. They also needed to write the clue to be slotted into the previous chapter and discovered by Charlotte, providing the links for her journey. I emphasized how each chapter had to be a self-contained adventure. Charlotte could meet all kinds of people and face any doubts and dangers, but she must be free to move on to the next location at the end.

Each pair chose their own method of collaboration. The majority worked out a detailed plan and individually wrote sections which jigsawed together to make the whole. Six pairs wrote each word collaboratively, doing their homework together at each other's houses or in the library during lunch hours. Whichever method was used, there was a good deal of mutual criticism and revision. It took a while for the pairs to settle into a working pattern they could follow with confidence. In the following transcript, you can see Sean and Alex's hesitancy in the first session:

Alex: We can't do the journey yet 'cause we don't know where she comes from.
Sean: Yeah, I know.
Alex: So if we start um ...
Sean: From where she gets ... no ...
Alex: When she gets to the castle.
   (*pause*)
Alex: 'She saw the castle.'
Sean: We've got to describe the castle, really. Right. What it is, when you go in, there's a little book ...
Alex: Don't worry about that ...
Sean: There's a little stall thing and then there's stairs, big wooden stairs going up to the castle.
Alex: Right, um ... 'She saw the ... then she ... '
Sean: It stood ...
Alex: Hill ...

Sean: It's quite good ... Hold on, don't write anything.
Alex: I'm just putting 'hill'. I just thought I'd put it in.
Sean: All right. Really we should describe this hill.
Alex: No ...
Sean: Yeah.
Alex: Not really. A hill's a hill.
Sean: No, not the hill, I mean the castle.
Alex: Yeah (*laughter*).
Alex: How many turrets, or whatever?
Sean: Four. Right, write in the back. Shall we describe the castle and then put it into a sentence? Yeah, might as well.
Alex: No, just carry on, because we're doing it in rough in the front.

Sean is the one with the information while Alex appears more preoccupied with finding the written form. Sean was reluctant to commit his writing to 'the front of the book'. He was typical of many in the group.

Alex is quite dismissive of Sean's contributions: 'They don't really want to know about that ...'; Sean seems to lack confidence with the written form, preferring to contribute ideas rather than sentences. One of the fundamental problems they were having was that they had not formulated their plot but were trying to construct one, sentence by sentence. Later, they became more enthusiastic when they abandoned the writing in favour of agreeing on the plot. Enthusiasm sounded in their voices and they gave an equal contribution, rewarding and encouraging each other as they seesawed the idea from one to the other.

Sean: They shout! They shout down there to see if there's anyone down there ...
Alex: And they brick it back over ...
Sean: So they brick it back over ...
Alex: They put a board over, they put a board over to ...
Sean: Yeah!
Alex: and then she wakes up and finds it all covered up ...
Sean: and its all dark and everything, she can't see a thing ...
Alex: ... so she has to go down the tunnel ...
Sean: No. Say the tunnel wasn't there yet and she's leaning against it and the tunnel starts to crack ...
Alex: Yeah ...
Sean: It sort of cracks, and she can feel the crack down her back and um, and then the tunnel ...
Alex: and the tunnel ...
Sean: the tunnel all of a sudden it gives way and she's straight through.
Alex: Yeah, and finds the cave
Sean: and finds the tunnel ...
Alex: Yeah.

The majority of groups worked by agreeing to write individual sections which would fit together. Richard and Ian worked in this way. The tape from which the following extract is taken was made after both boys had written part of the agreed chapter for homework. They were supposed to be criticizing each other's work and agreeing on a final version. They took it in turns to read out their part of the chapter. The comments were not what I would call critical:

Ian: That's all I've got.
Richard: Excellent.
Ian: Brilliant.

but they improved:

Richard: Now the only trouble with mine is, I keep putting 'She, she, she,'
Ian: Yeah, but ...
Richard: I should put 'Charlotte, Charlotte, Charlotte'.
Ian: Well, I suppose we both – You've got to keep a balance of it 'cos you can't keep going 'Shesheshe' all the time, but on the other hand you can't go 'Charlotte this'...
Richard: ... 'Charlotte that'...
Ian: ... 'Charlotte everything'.
Richard: Yeah.
Ian: Now, yours and mine are totally different. I think they're totally different ways of writing, so we've gotta be careful. Now, what was she like? Courageous.
Richard: Yeah.

After a while, I took the class's books in. I was able to devote more than average time to commenting on the development of their chapters as there were 15 scripts instead of 30. Furthermore, as we had only just begun the process of writing, I knew my comments had a real purpose: they would be revising what they had written in the light of specific comment. So often, we write on work which the child has finished. There is little point in seeing what one *should* have done when it is too late to change it.

It was clear that many of the chapters suffered from similar weaknesses. The majority started well, but the standard of writing deteriorated as the chapter progressed. I decided to address the problem to the group as a whole, to see if they could spot the weaknesses themselves.

Improving the first draft: class collaboration and teacher intervention

I typed a page from Richard and Ian's chapter using the original spelling. Before handing back any of their books with my comments, I gave each pair a copy and asked them to do the following: read it through carefully; identify the best section of writing; correct spelling and punctuation errors; tick good expressions and vocabulary; identify any weak sections of writing; and make any suggestions and comments which would help improve the work. I realized that I was submitting Richard and Ian to quite an ordeal by allowing the children to dissect their work in class so I made a point of telling them that I could have chosen any chapter to treat in this way. In fact, I had picked Richard and Ian's because they showed

'Which Way Now?' 115

potential in the first part of the chapter and I felt they could take the criticism. Their first draft read as follows:

> *The atmosphere in York Station at the rush hour was electric, people were scurrying here and there boarding and departing Inter-City 125's. A tired looking girl slowly stumbled off the inter city train from———. It was Charlotte. Heavly weighted down by rucsacs and bags. She ambled through the station gazing endlously a the ornimental bridges and carvings in such a modern station. As she was nearing the entrance she heard a man advertising his products. Suddenly feeling hungry and thirsty she groped about in her pocket for some loose change to pay for a packet of tuna sandwiches and a can of coke. She paid for these and found a bench. Thankfully she took off her rucsac and laid down her bags. She gobbled down the food she had just bought. Outside the weather had become worse with rain clouds coming desidedly closer. She decided, as it had started to rain to stay in the warmth of the station and ponder over the clue. After ½ an hour of resting she decided to go and find somewhere to stay. Charlotte left the station still finding her bags very heavy, the straps were digging into her shoulders. After about ten minutes of walking she decided too ask someone the way to the Youth Hostel where she was planning to stay a night. Adventusly she came across a girl who looked her own age. Charlotte went up to the girl who was reading a newspaper and asked her the way to the youth hostel. The girl said she was also statying at the youth hostel so charlotte could go back with her. The two of them made their way back too the youth hostel. As they were walking through the streets Charlotte started asking the girl questions like What's your name? Where do you come from? How long are you staying and so on. After about 5 minutes they were great friends each taking it in terns to tell about themselves. After 20 minutes they arrived at the Youth Hostel. Both girls went straight to reception. Charlotte asked the warden if she could stay 1 night at the youth hostel. The warden Mr Sinclair said she could share a dormatry with Katie (her new friend) and some other girls from a school on a visit. The two girls had tea which was Shepards Pie and Jelly. After tea they decided to go on a walk around the walls of york. They two girls walked around going in all the Bars and Gates on the way. Once they had been around they stopped at a supermarket to buy a drink for the evening. They got back to the Youth hostel at 10pm and they went to their dormatries.*

The class were quick to identify the problems and to praise the strengths in the writing. They spent about ten minutes talking about the work in pairs, and a class discussion followed. They all saw that the first part was the best. One comment was: 'the attention to detail is interesting up to the point when she meets the girl, but it becomes boring after that'. They identified the need for direct speech, paragraphs and some exploration of the feelings of the character. They felt they wanted to know more about the friendship between Katie and Charlotte. At this point I intervened as teacher, introducing them to techniques which might improve their writing.

It is interesting to look at Richard and Ian's second draft to see how they took advantage of the discussion on their work:

The atmosphere in York station at the rush hour was electric. People were scurrying here and there boarding and departing Inter-City 125's. A tired looking girl slowly stumbled off the Inter-City train from———. It was Charlotte. Heavily weighed down by rucsacs and bags, she ambled through the station gazing endlessly at the ornamental bridges and carvings in such a modern station. After about five minutes of fighting her way through the crowds she eventually appeared outside the station.

The day was sunny with white wispy clouds in the sky. There was a slight breeze that ruffled Charlotte's hair as she started wondering through the city. As she approached the city walls she caught sight of the Minster, a huge golden building caught in the afternoon sun. Charlotte kept walking and around the next bend she was confronted with the Minster. Awed by the sight, the bags on her shoulders suddenly became lighter and Charlotte felt herself walking faster in the direction of the Minster like it was a magnet and she was caught in the field.

Glancing quickly to the left, Charlotte noticed a bench with a girl of about the same age sitting on it reading the guide book for the Minster.

The girl was quite pretty with long golden hair let loose down her back like a horses main. Her face was brown with the sun and she had a pair of white framed glasses on. Her eyes were big, round and staring, the same colour as chestnuts. Her lips were wide and smiling as Charlotte came near, the sight of a girl of here own age had obviously pleased her. She was sitting rather awkwardly with one leg over the other and she was swinging them around like a branch in the wind.

Charlotte came over and shyly asked the way to the Youth Hostel where she had booked a dormatry for a night. The girl replied, 'I am also staying there so if you want to come back with me you can!' Charlotte as quite taken back in how the girl had looked so friendly a minute ago, she seemed now quite grumpy and unfriendly but Charlotte decided to follow her as the girl slowly got up.

Suddenly, Charlotte started asking the girl who was now grinning again, things like 'Where do you come from?' The girl's replies were short and precise: 'London.'

'Why are you here?'

'I am on holiday.'

'For how long?'

'Until tomorrow.'

This conversation gradually built up and the girls shyness and temper began slowly slipping off her face and two minutes later Charlotte and Katie were deep in conversation about each other. They were talking about exams, how they loved to have finished school and what they were doing at this moment. In no time at all the girls reached the drive was lined with trees that had curled over to form a total archway over the road. Katie and Charlotte started walking up the drive. The sunlight that was filtering through all the trees occasionally struck one of the girls' faces and for a second that girl had to shut one eye because the sun was so bright.

> *Charlotte had just put her things in her room when the dinner bell rang. Katie and Charlotte ran down the stairs and entered a large room with tables and chairs. The room was hot and a slight buzz could be heard from all the people's conversations. Tea was a rather grey looking shepherds pie with a dollop of peas, which was served on and even more boring plastic plate. But never the less the girls were hungry so they had finished within half and hour.*

Apart from the punctuation, the first part is little changed. They discarded the rather pointless sandwich-eating and introduced us to the city of York in a paragraph formed by sentences of varying length, showing their ability to handle syntax of some complexity. They show they can use imagery, too. There is a simile inviting us to picture the Minster as a magnet attracting Charlotte in its field. The metaphorical use of 'caught' enlivens the picture of the Minster: 'a huge golden building caught in the afternoon sun'. To adult readers, this may grate as a cliché, but I believe young people should not be discouraged from using such elaborate imagery. It is essential for them to experiment with literary techniques if they are to develop confidence, and a personal writing style.

Despite her 'golden hair let loose like a horse's mane', the character of Katie is not simply a cliché. She has 'white framed glasses' and is 'sitting rather awkwardly with one leg over the other'. Perhaps the notion that she is swinging them around like a branch in the wind' seems a little off-key, but the experimentation has paid off in the following observation:

> *The sunlight that was filtering through all the trees occasionally struck one of the girls' faces and for a second that girl had to shut one eye because the sun was so bright.*

They had made a great deal more of the youth hostel, omitting the dull details at the reception desk in favour of re-creating the atmosphere of the dining room. To me, there are worlds of difference between:

> *The two girls had tea which was Shepards Pie and Jelly*

and the evocative

> *Tea was a rather grey looking shepherds pie with a dollop of peas.*

As a result of these sessions many pairs made radical changes to their first drafts, and some did a complete re-write. Afterwards, one boy wrote:

> *Two people's thoughts and ideas are different and better than one. Also, if one person wrote a long chapter (which ours was) the person would get bored and the chapter get worse and worse as it got longer and longer ... Sometimes I found it frustrating when my partner was commenting poorly on a bit of the story I thought was good. But I think his moaning was justified because our final chapter, I thought, was quite good.*

When all the drafting and re-writing was done, each pair had to make a fair copy, some choosing to type or word-process their final version. I was impressed with the trouble they took, some spending hours typing their chapter finger by finger at home. I left it up to the pairs to organize a fair division of labour. Some wrote out half the chapter each; others chose to separate the tasks of writing and illustration.

At this stage, I was the only person who had read the novel as a whole. I could not provide them each with a copy, as the duplication costs were prohibitive, so we taped the whole novel in class. The authors of each chapter had to take part in reading it, but I allowed them to recruit others from the class to read the 'parts' of the characters. This process was a long one, as many of the chapters were 3000–4000 words long, but it was essential that they could get a feel of the novel as a whole. They read well and enjoyed listening to each other, particularly good chapters being spontaneously applauded.

Putting the novel together

While the children were writing their chapters, I was busy with a map of the British Isles and a list of their chapter locations. Starting in Charlotte's home town of Bridgwater in Somerset, I made the most plausible route I could out of the place names. Her journey took her down to the West Country, up to Wales, across to East Anglia, by train to London, north to Yorkshire, Cumbria, and finally to Scotland, home of her late aunt Annabel. Once the pairs knew their chapter numbers, they met with those doing the adjacent chapters to ensure continuity. They would give a summary of their chapter, discuss the best way for Charlotte to travel from one location to another and agree on who should be responsible for dealing with that journey. I warned them not to write about the journey itself, unless they had a positive reason for doing so, as I feared the story could become tedious with dull hours spent in bus stations and on railway platforms. Each pair had to entrust the authors of the preceding chapter with their clue which would send Charlotte to the next location. Many groups felt a proprietorial interest in their clues, and through discussion they would approve the means by which the other group would have Charlotte discover it. These discussions took place while the chapters were in progress, so they had an awareness of how Charlotte might be feeling at that particular stage.

The final chapters

By the time they had heard the novel being read, they had developed ideas for the final chapters. Kathy suggested that the clue should lead her to a chest of drawers in the late aunt's bungalow in the Western Isles. Here, instead of finding money, she would find her own face looking back at her in a hand mirror. Thus, Charlotte finds herself enriched, not by money, but by her experiences on the journey. This idea was approved by the class, as was the notion of an enormous party peopled by some of the characters she had met on her way.

To my surprise, the class suggested that *I* write the final chapter. There was justice in this, as over the weeks of work we had all become involved; criticizing and enthusing with a feeling of intimacy born out of the common task. I felt quite nervous at exposing my writing to their scrutiny. Indeed, since finishing my O levels in 1969 I had not attempted any creative writing!

The strength of the finished novel lay in the consistent treatment of the central character, Charlotte, and the fact that she, and the dead aunt, were the only threads which had to run through the whole. Ironically, variety in pace and mood was achieved simply by the fact that the novel was written by so many authors. However, it is true to say that the coherence of the novel was not my main concern. To me it was the *process* which was important. There is a delicate balance to be found between insisting on the polished finished product and treading too heavily on the enthusiasm of the children. What was very clear was the importance of the physical product: the book itself. It meant a great deal to them. They often asked to see it and enjoyed reading each other's chapters. Most of all, they relished the feeling of flicking through a real, weighty book *they* had written.

10 Children as critics

MARY MARTIN

Anyone who has spent time discussing stories with pre-school age children is usually spellbound by their capacity to handle the intricacies of plot and motivation, and often startled by being asked some profound and hitherto unconsidered question. At an early age children's powers to perceive order in a work of literature are already apparent. They crave an understanding of recognizable pattern and quickly dismiss or ignore the clumsiness or artifice of the second-rate. A clarity of mind and readiness to absorb representations of life in the symbolic form of literature are qualities that children bring to their listening to stories in the first instance.

We are now familiar with the notion that the absorption of the echoes of narrative derived from hearing stories read or told is a crucial element in developing literacy in children. If children are encouraged to write their own stories, too, even at an early age, narrative foundations are visible. Here is a 'story' written by my five-year-old daughter:

> LOC LEF AND RIT
> Thee wons wosa rabit
> theat crosd the rod Subody rod ov
> it the sumody got rabi iyis
> in the bisicl

(*Look Left and Right*. There was once a rabbit that crossed the road. Somebody rode over it. That somebody got rabbit ears in their bicycle!)

A second-year class found this story amusing though somewhat gory. I think we can see here the young child's capacity for graphic detail. We also have in it an example of plotting at its simplest in three steps:

- Introduction of character involved in everyday event.
- Disastrous event.
- Comment on consequence.

This follows the basic familiar story formula of beginning, middle and end.

Primary schooling tends to afford children ample opportunity for perfecting this formula. At a later stage in the secondary school pupils, by collaborating with their peers, can be helped to refine their appreciation of good writing and grasp more readily the elements required to produce it themselves. By comparing like with like, children are able to apprehend masterly execution of the structure of narrative in a very precise way. They can be taught to see order first in a literary text, and then be critical of approximations to it in each other's work. The children demonstrate, through close scrutiny of each other's work in a structured procedure, their capacity to be able to disentangle the original from the derivative, and the genuinely felt from the cliché. In an atmosphere which encourages an appetite for lively but ordered expression, the criteria by which children view their own work are refined. Lip-service is not in evidence at all. Praise is given for real achievement in every case. If one starts from the premise that everyone has something valuable to say in capturing his or her view of the world, then it does not take long for the whole range of talent in a class to start revealing itself. Being truthful and clear about what constitutes good writing provides stability and security for pupils to venture further once they recognize the signposts of the terrain.

In essence, I think the strategies I have employed to encourage children to write with some sense of conceptual framework informing their writing, merely build on their natural skill as storytellers and 'critics', but are also grounded in the firm belief that children are capable of the sophistication necessary to create a consciously shaped poetic construct. Although interested in published texts laid before them, they are more fascinated by the written efforts of their own classmates and prepared to collaborate assiduously in putting them under a microscope.

An acquaintance with the writings of Lévi-Strauss[1] has provided me with a means of analysing texts in a way that makes them accessible as models for children's writing. Although some of Strauss's ideas are now discredited by post-structuralist critics and rejected as encouraging too formulaic a view of literature, his attempts to find the skeletal shapes of stories – in particular, myths – are useful instrumental procedures to follow. At any rate it was from this area of criticism that I gleaned some beginnings for this particular method of working with pupils on writing. Jerome Bruner[2] emphasizes the importance of recognizing visible structure in material to maximize learning potential. I am thoroughly convinced by Bruner's oft-quoted hypothesis that 'any subject can be taught effectively in some intellectually honest form to any child at any stage of development'. In my classroom this means that children can be taught to write coherently through being made aware of the structure and relations in a work of fiction and being encouraged to imitate and manipulate these same patterns. Later, the pupils learn to 'criticize' each other's efforts in terms of how successfully they have been able to implement the various devices of the narrative form.

Bruner talks of learning involving these almost simultaneous processes. The first stage, *acquisition of information*, is about understanding the structure of a story, albeit through arbitrary delineation of form – one person's analysis of a story may differ in emphasis from that of another. The second stage Bruner describes as *transformation*, and, in the approach to writing I have outlined, the children would have made their own stories and conformed to or deviated from the original as they chose. The third aspect of learning which continues to gain prominence in modern educational priorities is that of *evaluation*, and this is where children come into their own as critics. Some people may be sceptical about the claims I am making for children's capacity for structured analysis at secondary school level, but I do not think these claims are exaggerated. People may also doubt whether the whole ability range can cope with what amounts to demanding levels of thinking, but my experience has shown that nearly all children can benefit from induction into logical strategies for writing. In fact, I have often been impressed by the way children with weaker literary skills cope with ideas; this capacity that children have to think, create, reflect and analyse is far more developed than many surmise though in some children the potential is unrealized. This is often the fault of low self-esteem, poor teaching and an undemanding and uninviting curriculum. I think that at the heart of my approach to encouraging children to collaborate with each other in the writing process lies a firm belief in their innate intellectual prowess and confidence in their capacity to learn from and encourage each other.

Children's potential for achieving coherence in narrative often lies dormant. I would suggest that, except for those amusing utterances of children that are repeated by delighted parents, much of the shaping and ordering of experience that occurs through exposure to story goes on randomly and unnoticed. By the time children arrive in secondary school they are expert recipients of stories and are very discerning 'critics' of both class texts and their own writing. Insufficiencies in a class reader or intolerance of a classmate's poor-quality writing are made manifest to the teacher by obvious waves of class boredom. Pupils' instinctive judgements are usually quite reliable. (However, this natural capacity for discernment needs to be drawn out.)

When I first started secondary-school teaching I was surprised by the lack of order in pupils' own written narrative and also by the lack of precision in their comments about writing. I decided, therefore, to follow the artist's method of learning to paint by copying Old Masters, and asked my pupils to write their own stories based on the analysis of a story read in class which provided a framework or model for the pupils to follow. Far from this being too prescriptive and therefore restrictive of their imaginations, I found that this method provided them with the support they needed to write in an orderly way, but also offered freedom to explore and interpret ideas as they chose.

As a sixth-former I had studied Elizabethan episodic fiction by writers such as Thomas Deloney[3] (1543–1600) who precedes even Defoe as 'father' of the modern novel. Although these Elizabethan novellas were entertaining, their chief value to me in my subsequent studies of literature lay in their deficiencies which threw into sharper relief the greater novelistic skill displayed in more substantial works. I found that prolonged exposure to limited characterization, episodic 'plots', scant description and superfluous incidents enabled me to appreciate more keenly the skilfully executed features exemplified by better novelists.

The small-scale nature of these works was significant in suggesting a link with children's work, which tends to be on a small scale and is essentially the work of apprentice writers – as the Elizabethans were in terms of the history of the novel. The idea of being able to make comparisons of writings which hold a common framework is crucial to creating the conditions which will allow children to make decisions about the positive and negative elements of their work. For this reason I am very keen on offering children skeletons of stories which derive from an analysis of a story that they have read.

I find that children have good memories for incident in narrative but need to be taught to see the underlying shape of it in its entirety. By outlining an analysis of how a story is organized, it is possible for them to hold the shape in their minds and begin to plan their own with an attempt at overall coherent design instead of a series of additions in the form 'And then ... And then ...'.

Once a plan is taken on board by the children, it is possible to discuss sections of the story with a view to rewriting or being reassured that it is worth continuing with a first draft. When there is some apprehension of a whole form in the background, children are prepared to remake some of the integral elements. Writing becomes therefore a more recognizable craft whereby the honing and polishing of language is readily grasped as a tool of the trade. Let me illustrate the points I've been making with some examples of recent collaborative work by my pupils.

Using a text as model: a collaborative exchange

In presenting Ted Hughes's tiny novel, *The Iron Man*,[4] to a class of first-year pupils, I found that the majority had encountered it in the primary school, enjoyed it, and thought that it was a text for younger readers than themselves. This suited my purpose as I wished to explore it with them with a view to them writing *their own versions* for a real primary audience. This immediately created great enthusiasm for a close reading of the text and overturned their previous scepticism.

Before I supply the framework for *The Iron Man* writing, I should say that I never offer such a framework cold to a class and I do not try to suggest that my analysis of a text is definitive. All the examples I include here are flawed and could be improved upon. The important thing for me is that I have attempted some sort of analysis of a text prior to discussion with a class which informs my questioning of the pupils and enables me to elicit from them their understanding of the patterning of events so that we can make sense of them together. Children are always free to move away from my formal plan and frequently do. Here is my framework for Chapter 1 of *The Iron Man*, followed by a very simple outline of the whole story and an account of the activities which ensued, including contact with the junior class for whom the stories were written and who later responded to my pupils by letter.

The Iron Man: Analysis of Chapter One

INTEREST AROUSED BY INTRODUCTION – 'The Iron Man came to the top of the cliff'... 'taller than a house'... 'head shaped like a dustbin'... 'and the Iron Man stepped forward, off the cliff, into nothingness' – involvement with a striking character in an unusual situation.

CATASTROPHE – 'all the separate pieces' – a concentrated description of physical detail reminding us of the material he is made from.

FIRST WITNESSES – 'Two seagulls' – predators, minor characters introduced offering an expansion of the immediate focus.

REHABILITATION AND ACTION – 'He strode about the beach searching for his lost ear.' Opportunity to create balance in the opening: that which was broken is remade.

NEW ELEMENT – 'He walked towards the *sea*.' Another dimension; alternative landscape or setting.

The Iron Man: Skeleton plan of whole story
1. 'X' Man and disintegration or collapse
2. Remaking
3. 'Man trap'
4. Escape and 'bargain'
5. Danger from another source
6. Challenge
7. Resolution

Having obtained examples from the class of their versions of invented characters, we decided to send these along to a primary school class and ask them to offer their opinions. At the primary school, these stories were received with delight and the children spent some hours reading and discussing their views before writing replies to my pupils. An important factor in generating interest seemed to be the personal element where each child had a particular story to review. The primary teacher and I felt very enthusiastic about the quality of the comments made by his pupils, but at first my pupils were less so. It was clear that my pupils were ready for praise but not for criticism.

An important factor here is whether the critic is known to the writer as, in general, I have found 'criticism' in class by pupils' own peers to be perfectly acceptable to them as long as the comments are justified and not, of course, unkind. I gave my pupils the opportunity to comment to me about their feelings regarding the primary pupils' statements about their work, and this seemed to provide a welcome release valve for them. On reflection many of them agreed that their 'critics' had made valid points. Here follows a model of the collaborative process (Figure 10.1) and two mixed-ability examples of *Iron Man* imitations, written critiques and in the final case the pupil's response to criticism. I should perhaps emphasize that only the opening sections of my pupils' stories were sent to the primary schools, that is Chapter 1 in each case.

Figure 10.1 Model demonstrating stages of criticism inherent in collaborative process between junior and secondary pupils

Secondary pupils are 'critical' readers of *The Iron Man*

↓

They use *The Iron Man* as a framework for their own writing

↓

Junior class are critical readers of older pupils' work

↓

Juniors are critical letter-writers addressing remarks to older pupils

↓

Secondary pupils are recipients of criticism and commentators upon it

THE ICE MAN
The ice man started out of a cup of water in a warehouse. One night the warehouse was robbed and one of the robbers knocked the glass of water in a big empty freezer. The water went in with a splash and the glass broke with a smash and then the alarm went on and they ran off just as the man who owned the warehouse came in and caught the robers. When all this was happening there was something else happening. The water that fell in the freezer went into ice. The ice went into the shape of a man and there was a cracking noise. Crack Crack Crack. The ice man was as big as a very big freezer. Then the freezer went bang! The freezer was in little bits all round the room. He got up and walked out of the warehouse and he was still growing. Then he stopped growing. By this time he was the size of a double decker bus. As he walked along the street his feet made a crunching sound. Crunch Crunch as he walked along. He sat on a lorry. Then he felt a hot wave. He looked around. There was a fire but it did not matter. He just sat thinking. Then he started to go all wet. He was melting. First his left foot started to melt. There were big puddles where he was sitting. When he got up and walked away he was about 15cm tall. He walked away. He stopped melting.
(Paul)

Dear Paul,
I have just read your story about the ice man I thought it was a good storyI injoyed reading it I like the idea at the beginning of the story when the ice man is made from a glass of water. butwhat happend to the robber's. I would like to know what happend to them because you have not told me.
Also the story does not describe what the ice man felt about what was happening to him I like the idea of the ice man growing like a double decker bus and I found the idea of eating icecreams obvious. I wish you had made up his own food.
Joanna

Interestingly, Paul deleted the icecream section in copying this out.

PEGGY THE PEGDOLL
Peggy the Pegdoll peered out of the bag with interest. Her two two blue eyes looked left then right. The old woman had made her with care. She was dressed in red velvet. She had yellow thread for hair and a tiny painted face. The boy scout was carrying her roughly. Curiousity made her want to explore the gutter. What was in that tin-can? Her blue eyes looked around, then hop! She was out of the bag and into the gutter. She took a tiny hop forward. Then another tiny hop ... into nothingness. She went down the drain, with a tiny splash she hit the water. She sank a bit till she bobbed back up again.
Caroline

Dear Caroline,
I have just read your story. I thought it was very good. I liked the descriptions in your story. I also thought there was too much about Peggy. I thought there could have been more characters such as more peg people and insects.
Nicola

Caroline wrote in response to this:

1. *I think that saying that their was too much about Peggy is wrong. Because Peggy is the main character.*
2. *I don't see what other characters I could of put in, and I don't see what insects have got to do with it. Although Peg people was a good idea.*
3. *I like the way Nichola points out the bad bits but also the good bits.*

The benefits of this exercise in collaboration with a real audience were enormous in terms of generating enthusiasm for writing, enabling the children to see purpose in writing and fostering the beginnings of encouraging a climate of constructive criticism.

Dissecting a pupil's work

In this section an illustration of the fruits of children's capacity to 'criticize' specifically the language in their own written work is offered. A group of second-year pupils had written stories about King Arthur and his knights after we had read a variety of examples and discussed the features of Arthurian legends. The following is an example from a pupil whose writing skills were still at a level of simple competence yet whose ideas were strong and merited better treatment:

KING ARTHUR IN TROUBLE
One day Arthur met a knight dressed all in black and the black knight decided that he wanted to fight Arthur so Arthur agreed. They got down off their horses. They started to fight the swords clashed thay were both getting tired Then Arthur wounded the knight in black so Arthur let him escape. he rode off, the black knight shouted, 'we will meet again. After Arthur got back to the castle he told Kay and Ector, about the black knight and all agreed they would look for him.

They had been gone about two months. Then they returd they had seen no sign of the black knight.

Arthur was riding alone in the woods when all of a sudden the knight dressed in black swony down from a tree, He said I told you we would meet again So Arthur pulled out his sword from his scabard and started to fight as they started a load of men surrourded Arthur and tied him up. Then they took him to a secret cave After Merlin got back from a walk he wonderd whereArthur was so he tried to use his magic to find out where he was. After about ten minutes he had a picture in his head that he was in a cave and in trouble Merlin went to find some knight, after Merlin founed some knights they went in seach of Arthur, Then they went in an opening of a cave and Arthur was tied up as they were untieing him, all the others came back and started to fight. In the end the black knight rode away and all the others came back and started to fight. In the end the black knight rode away and all the other people were killed so Arthur and Merlin went back to the castle.

In class, with the writer's permission, we discussed the deficiencies of style and organization of the piece, while applauding the success of the plot and drama elements. Then each member of the class was asked to rewrite a part of the story:

Early one December morning, the sharp, frosty air bit upon Arthur's face. He was out on his horse which was as pure as snow. Far in the distance stood a knight of darkness, his armour a deep black showed his evilness. The Black Knight called out 'I challenge you to fight'. Arthur accepted this challenge and they both dismounted off their horses.

They drew out their swords and moved towards each other. Arthur's eyes showed anger and determination. Their swords clashed and the sun blinded them both as it reflected off their swords.

They were both exhausted and the Black Knight was wounded, so Arthur let him escape. the Black Knight did not turn back, but for once, he shouted, 'We will meet again'.
(Mary)

After Arthur had arrived back in Camelot he told Kay and Ector about the black knight. They all decided to meet at the round table in two months time. So they set off in search of the Black Knight. Two months had passed and Kay and Ector had not arrived back in Camelot. As Arthur got more and more worried he sent Lancelot in search of them. They arrived back in Camelot soon after and told Arthur they had found no sign of him.
(Tom)

After having reflected upon what the Black Knight had said Arthur had gone for a ride to the woods near his home. While he was riding the Black Knight suddenly swung down from a tree.
(Peter)

Merlin had now returned to the castle after his walk and pondered over the whereabouts of Arthur. Being of a superstitious nature, he decided to turn to magic. Ten minutes elapsed and an image had formed in his mind. He sensed that Arthur was in a cave, and in need of great help. Merlin went in search of some knights, and, having found them, diverted the search towards finding Arthur.
(Helen)

They hurried through the woods in search of Arthur. As they were running they saw the opening of a small cave set into the rock. One of the knights saw Arthur struggling inside. They ran in and started to untie him. As they were doing so they heard movement at the entrance to the cave. They all turned round and saw the Black Knight and his men. Merlin and the knights drew their swords. There was a large scuffle in which many of the Black Knight's men were killed. The Black Knight saw that he was losing and hurried off as soon as he could. The rest of his men were killed and Arthur and Merlin rode off through the woods together.
(Frazer)

The original writer's revisions were technically much more accurate, illustrating that he had benefited from the public criticism of his work. He was also flattered by positive comments about his piece and pleased that it could sustain so much scrutiny.

Discussion is at the heart of the enterprises I have been describing, that is, discussion at a level where the pupils 'criticize' authors' novels and each other's writing in a discerning, thorough and perceptive fashion. Sometimes the honesty and accuracy of pupils' comments would not be out of place in a university seminar. The belief of the teacher in the intellectual capacity of young people is essential for the enterprise to work. I cannot stress too much how important it is *to take children seriously as thinkers*, genuinely to esteem their ideas and therefore aim to establish a climate in the classroom where every pupil's offerings and outlook are regarded as valuable and bespeaking the dignity of that person.

However, faith in pupils' potential is not enough. I think it is important to provide pupils with opportunities for growth through discussion by defining parameters and pinpointing features for focus so that listening becomes a structured activity. To help children with this activity, I usually provide them with points for consideration and ask them to jot down short notes as they listen to a classmate's work being read aloud. I find that this helps provide direction for the discussion and facilitates meaningful comparisons between pieces of writing

Some examples of children talking about their writing.

A third-year class had read Michael Baldwin's *Grandad With Snails*[5] and, having discussed with them some features of Baldwin's writing, I asked them to write a chapter which could have been included in the original text. The sort of issues they had to consider before writing were: the kinds of incident that occur in each chapter, the learning experiences of the boy, the use of dialogue and description and how the new chapter would fit in within the context of the book as a whole. Here are some extracts from the pupils' discussion of their chapters. First, Natalie's piece:

Teacher: Would it fit in?
E: It's another Silky adventure so it would.
D: It's written in Baldwin's style.
Teacher: How is it like Baldwin?
N: He comments in it a lot.
Teacher: He comments on the action. Is that different from yours, Natalie? Because, in fact when marking yours I suggested that there was something missing which was really the commentating.
E: It follows on – the chapter before that, Michael was worried that it would get out and it does.
Teacher: So you've got a danger that has actually cropped up as a possibility being realized. So you've got continuity. How important is continuity?
D: Well the chapters fit together and the boy is in all of them.
L: You could take some out and it wouldn't matter.

Next, Ben's chapter:

B: It was something new.
Teacher: Something new in character or activity?
B: A new activity.
T: I think it was good the way he said two shillings and not ten pence.
Teacher: Right, so it kept in period detail.
D: It was exciting.
N: It was good but I don't think it fitted in because he didn't make that many comments.
Teacher: So you didn't have much reflection on what was happening. It was mostly action.
A: There could have been more description.
Teacher: Of what?
C: Of characters.
L: It was a bit predictable – obvious that he was going to win.

130 COLLABORATION AND WRITING

Teacher: Would it have been better if he'd lost?
K: No, but it would have fitted in better if it had been at his school because there's a lot about his school in the book.
H: I think it was written very well. I thought the description of the go-kart race was good.
Teacher: OK. When you say that something is written well what do you actually mean?
H: Trying to write it like the actual writer.
Teacher: What does that mean?
K: There are no bits written for the sake of it – it's all essential.

I hope that these discussion extracts show that the pupils have been able to identify characteristics both in the original Baldwin chapters and also in their own versions. They have shown that they have understood the purpose of individual chapters, whether or not they fitted in with the general context of the story as a whole, and what effect individual elements such as description or the introduction of new characters have. Another time I set up a story writing exercise with a class of 12-year-olds. We agreed on possible key elements which included: deliberate scene setting, family or other problems causing inner conflict for individual, expression of thoughts and feelings, resolution of problem exemplifying a learning situation. While we listened to the stories I asked the class to consider the following features: setting, atmosphere, characterization, use of description, use of dialogue, plot, exploration of thoughts and feelings, use of language and realism. Although this may seem an extensive list, I have found that asking pupils to attend to a range of features in a piece of writing offers enough scope for different individuals to notice different elements.

I think that the following extracts from the children's discussion show that they were greatly helped by being asked to focus on particular elements in the stories and reveal an acute capacity for incisive and relevant comment. The following discussion took place about Stephen's story:

A: Everything happened so quickly. There was no detail. He didn't have nothing in it.
C: I'd like to know why he was in a hotel, who was he after, what was he after and also I don't think it had anything to do with family problems.
D: It didn't show any feelings.
S: Or thoughts.
L: Sounds like Inspector Clouseau.
Teacher: Is that good or bad?
L: Good but it's still confusing. Details like 'oak rafters' were good.
C: I thought it was the average detective story – they always have bugs and people creeping around.
H: There was lots of action but no detail.
A: He didn't build up character.
E: He didn't say where it was set clearly enough.
L: The storyline was not clear.
Stephen: I could have written it more clearly – it was rushed.

The next extract is from our discussion of Paul's story:

Teacher: What do you think about going straight into a story like that?
C: Well, if you dive straight in it means you'll have to catch up with the story, whereas with description first, it might be a little bit boring but it tells you what's going on.
Teacher: What does it do to the pace?
C: It makes it much faster.
E: There wasn't much dialogue in it – there could have been a discussion with the tramp.
Teacher: What made the story true to life?
O: When he described the graffiti and the place as all scraggy and that.
C: I liked the bit about the trains. It showed he'd been researching when he mentioned those stations.
H: It would have been better to describe their home town more so that there was more contrast between Reading and Liverpool. You didn't know what sort of area they came from.
M: He said that they'd survived there for a year and a month but I'd like to have had some sort of comment on how they'd survived. I mean he said they didn't have any money.
Teacher: What about the exploration of feelings in the story?
L: There was an example when he was stuck in the lift with the tramp and felt claustrophobic.
A: His feelings about Liverpool. By the sound of it, he didn't like Liverpool at all.

I hope the preceding sections have demonstrated that it is possible to use children's innate storying capacity, to deconstruct a text to lay bare its foundations in order that these might be used as the basis for their own writing, and that group collaboration and constructive criticism can enable children to perceive honestly the virtues and flaws in their own work. I hope that I have shown that writing and its appraisal are aided by the structured intervention of the teacher. I believe that the processes I have described support Bruner's thesis that 'the heart of the educational process consists of providing aids and dialogues for translating experience into more powerful systems of notation and ordering'.[6] I think that the approaches I have outlined in working with children are concerned with seeking order in writing and fostering skills to encourage its development in the work of young writers.

I should like to conclude by quoting from one of the greatest believers in the powers of imagination to transform perception. Samuel Taylor Coleridge in *Confessions of an Inquiring Spirit* says:

Reflect on the simple fact of the state of a child's mind while with great delight he hears or listens to the story of Jack and the Beanstalk. How could this be if in some sense he did not understand it? Yes, the child does understand each part of it – A, and B, and C; but not ABC = X. He understands it as we all understand our dreams while we are dreaming, each shape and incident or group of shapes and incidents by itself – unconscious of, and therefore unoffended at, the absence of the logical copula or the absurdity of the transitions.[7]

I would like finally to suggest, unlike Coleridge, that the unconscious can be made conscious and that children can be taught to see that ABC = X.

Notes

1. Claude Lévi-Strauss, 'The Structural Study of Myth', *Journal of American Folklore*, vol. 68, no. 270, 1955.
2. Jerome Bruner, *The Process of Education*, Harvard University Press, 1960.
3. Thomas Deloney, 'The Pleasent historie of John Winchomb in his yonger years called Jack of Newbury'. Reprint of 1626 in *Shorter Novels of Thomas Deloney*. Vol. 1, Everyman.
4. Ted Hughes, *The Iron Man*, Faber and Faber, 1968.
5. Michael Baldwin, *Grandad With Snails*, Routledge and Kegan Paul, 1960.
6. Jerome Bruner, *Toward a Theory of Instruction*, Harvard University Press, 1966.
7. Samuel Taylor Coleridge, *Aids to Reflection and the Confessions of an Inquiring Spirit*, Bohn-Stand, 1884.

11 'Hotel Beck'

CATHY POMPE

Working towards child–teacher collaboration

Every piece of work a teacher sets a child is a teacher–child collaboration. When seen and negotiated as such, when teacher and children are aware of the ingredients of good collaboration, the potential and talent locked inside a classroom may be released. This chapter looks at this central relationship, drawing on my experience of a long-term project, stretching over a term and a half.

If they are to work fruitfully, it is the task of collaborators to make their respective perceptions intersect. The process of negotiating and creating this shared ground is in itself a major enterprise.

The project I was involved in was, among other things, an attempt to make more explicit, to myself and to the children, the dynamics of child–teacher collaboration. We made an issue of the processes of negotiation, responsibility, cross-fertilization and collective creation. These issues needed to be brought into the open in order to free ourselves from wariness, misunderstanding and manipulation of each other, and to harness the great wealth and range of talent that was assembled in our still relatively lifeless classroom.

The dilemma

As a teacher I have wanted to foster imagination, resourcefulness and self-motivated learning. I have often felt caught in a basic tension: on the one hand, wishing to respect completely children's ideas and helping them to build upon these; on the other, the need to manipulate, interfere and cut through mediocre and convention-bound trains of thought, the let's-settle-for-the-first-thing-that-comes-to-mind approach. This latter is the sign that someone's thinking has not been sparked and challenged, and it is often the end result when children are given a project and then left entirely to their own resources.

To respect completely children's ideas?

In spreading my own ideas among children, to whom they only partly make sense,

I engage only a fraction of their capabilities: I fail to tap into the energizing, inventive powerhouse of the self-possessed thinker. I am sure most teachers recognize the humbling experience of really 'getting it right' once in a while, when somehow a situation, a stimulus, just the right – for once – words (not too few, not too many) makes prodigies of them all, and every class member produces a personal masterpiece. It is humbling because it reveals, in a glimpse, each child as astonishing and powerful, and shows that untold talents are lying there only intermittently tapped. And why do they remain hidden? The very success of our spectacularly getting it right once in a while lays the responsibility for the acres of rest-of-the-time wastage at our teachers' feet.

Learning to respect and wait upon children's trains of thought is an act of faith and a long-term investment on a teacher's part. It is for me a battle for wisdom, a huge and difficult exercise in patience; it leads to the kind of stillness where finally the scales start to drop from one's eyes.

Teaching mathematics has highlighted powerfully for me what must be the case in all aspects of the curriculum: that the connections between concepts, and between certain words and certain concepts, which I, the teacher, take for granted, only exist in the subjective networks of my own mind and do not make the same, or any, sense to my pupils. Yet we do not find the time to recognize quite how far away from our own modes of thinking lie the places where children can feel enough solid ground under their feet to start thinking creatively for themselves. By jumping conceptual stages, by making them walk precariously on air and juggle with fragments that appear to them unconnected, we rob children of access to their own intellectual and emotional powerhouses.

And so it is a first principle for me that children should take a major part in generating and structuring learning experiences in ways that are meaningful to them. This dictates a whole approach to 'learning to learn', which is not the subject of this chapter. I wish instead to grapple with the other side of the dilemma I stated at the outset: the contrasting and possibly even conflicting onus to create an atmosphere of meaning and excitement, where new stimuli will burst in and unsettle stale or unchallenged outlooks and spark greater awareness.

Cutting through convention-bound trains of thought

There are stages of work and involvement where children – when their well-intentioned meddling muddling teacher is a safe million miles away – will work intently, with the true seriousness of professionals. But there are other emptier, half-realized moments when children are working alone and are not even half aware of the possibilities of a situation. At such times, when I have been in a purist frame of mind, I have avoided offering any assistance for fear of hijacking their enterprise, and have allowed children to founder or 'run dry'.

It is at these times that I see a role for myself in stepping in to celebrate the task, to bring out the 'box of colours', toss out wild possibilities, turn things around and generally clown about in order to break down the blank walls of the humdrum which surround the task in the child's perception.

This is, of course, a knife-edged path: for the teacher trying to inspire is only a hair's breadth away from the danger zones of swamping, theatricality, manipulation, self-indulgence and delusion. However, there are moments where a teacher *can* become an equal partner in a collaboration, and is given an entry into the warm buzzy laughter-laden atmosphere of the peer network. Neither magnanimously effaced (the teacher midwife), nor dominant (the teacher theatrical), the teacher can simply belong and participate. By chipping in, because she has some extra skills or instincts and maybe a wider view, she can help bring the task more easily to fruition. There is an almost tangible chill wafting from the anxiety-born, brain-numbing state children get into when they work with a sense that what they are doing and thinking is not what is really on the menu: so most importantly, because it is *her classroom*, and potentially an alienating place to children, a teacher's honest participation and warm, inviting, accepting presence among them in some way 'switches on the lights' and guarantees the value of the effort, investing it with meaning and status.

At one stage of the project which is the subject of this chapter, the class of eight- to nine-year-olds had to evolve a story which would show something of the workings of a television studio, to be presented at a school assembly. I had stipulated that the assembly should reflect something of the knowledge we had acquired during our media project. 'Hotel Beck' was a detective story we had begun to make up and which we as a class were planning to shoot on video. Now our new story, 'The Making of "Hotel Beck"', itself became a thriller, with the down-at-heel manager of a tacky television company sending his pack of incompetent but stylishly sinister sleuths to spy on the operations of a successful rival TV company responsible for producing the award-winning blockbuster serial 'Hotel Beck'. At one point when the story was still a skin-and-bones affair, I felt that a team of children needed to breathe life and add flavour and character into the setting by writing the story in words.

The team of enthusiasts who volunteered to work on this could not carry out their assignment alone, without the kind of 'celebratory' stepping-in by the teacher which I have just described.

It could be that among themselves the struggles for power or democracy made it impossible for the team to make decisions about which suggestions acquired the status of henceforth becoming part of the story. Too large a group could not negotiate, but a small unit would not represent enough facets of the class to be entrusted with touching up the collective creation: it would be no different from having the *teacher* write the play for the class.

It could be that at eight and nine years of age they were too young to hold the correct delicate balance between rigidly adhering to the essentials of the agreed plot, which could not be departed from, and searching widely and freely for flavour and detail which would enrich the story without swamping it – a complex skill indeed. So I needed to sit in with the group: to keep the play within the bounds of the established plot; to provide a focus and a sanctioning leadership role so that scraps of ideas could be dreamed up and incorporated into the story; but, above all, to make the task comfortable, to bring it to life, to laugh, coax, open windows, give a feeling that anything goes, that the group had the resources to pull something out of it ...

Here is an extract of the text, which does not stand out for its literary value or originality, but which meant a lot to all those involved. It was significant to me, for the joy and fun we had sitting on the carpet writing it, for the rare experience of being part of this vibrant hilarious underworld. Maybe for the children who, unlike their teachers, are much more used to having good times down on the carpet together, it stood out as an experience when a joyful moment of feeling authentic and at ease became the birthplace of ideas and of an effective piece of serious writing. The little scraps of crazy ideas their heads were full of at the time became the opening mood-setting piece of our assembly of the next day. For all of us it was the experience of a brief moment of perfect coming together.

Deep down in a murky unclean warehouse there was a fat old manager sitting in a comfy chair watching TV. His name was Mr Z. The chair had lost all it's bounce through sitting on it all year round and from not cleaning the covers. This grotty old gentleman was the manager of a TV company which didn't seem to get on: the Z Company. It was the worst TV company in the world (and in the whole history of TV making as well). They made programmes like 'the Best Trousers in the World' which was completely boring and went on for hours and hours about trousers and especially flares – and nobody wears flares now ...

The media project

As this book deals with collaborations in writing, I need to state that my choice of a media project reflects the wider growing concern that the concept of writing should not merely apply to the written word, but should embrace 'texts' written in other media. Developing the ability to 'read and write' the audio-visual languages which now dominate society,[1] requires a widening of our notions of literacy.[2] This has not yet been tackled in schools, despite the latent expertise and interest of our media-sophisticated pupils.

Working as an infant teacher taught me the value of the 'enormous' class topic. First, because it provides a common ground, a shared experience within which relationships can grow: the antagonisms, fears and friendships within a class are a critical dynamic that informs the work of every individual. Once the emotional and interactional dimensions of class life become part of the explicit curriculum, these potentially destructive forces can be harnessed and become a major driving force for purposeful work. Second, topic 'immersion', the state of involvement that can be achieved when a rich class topic touches all registers, emotional and intellectual, and connects to wide ranges of experience, often means that great levels of commitment are achieved. Topic work reaches beyond the classroom as the topic workers eat, dream, think, read and talk topic: they start to do overtime, and draw on all the resources which compartmentalized ways of thinking do not dream of making use of. Lastly, topic work provides a context within which the disparate skills and concepts we have the responsibility to develop in schoolchildren become meaningful.

Teaching infants, as I used to, it was a simple matter to become enveloped in the magical make-believe that transforms the classroom into a different time and place. Working with juniors, by contrast, seems to require more credible and realistic contexts for creating the imaginative and committed atmosphere of the class topic. One crucial condition is the existence of real purpose, the perception by children that they work in some sense as professionals, that their labours are not merely exercises to be entombed in workbooks. The 'Media Studies' our class became involved in last year incorporated notions of production and audience which made it very fruitful as a context for 'real' work.

The topic as a whole progressed from the controlled and somewhat manipulative 'teacher in role' input designed to put the topic on the agenda, towards levels of increasing involvement and commitment where control of the project shifted to the children.

Drama as the starting point for topic work

I am deeply indebted to Jonathan Neelands[3] for showing me how improvised drama can become the powerful vehicle and context for any kind of project or class topic. His methods, influenced by the work of Dorothy Heathcote[4] and others, use the teacher working in role to elicit a response, also in role, from the people she is working with. A dramatic situation is created, feelings are stirred. Then in stages, through the skill of the teacher stepping in and out of role, and with the children working to maintain the atmosphere created, the 'play' becomes a serious venture. I have seen Neelands 'pied-piper' people into living through experiences which bring into play all the information, skills, researching and learning which characterize serious topic work. Sessions in role fuel background preparation and research: the serious actor needs to speak with accuracy the language of the parts she is playing and acquire some of the professional knowledge and skills of the role she has taken on. Reading, drawing, writing, investigational work, planning, discussion, model making, experimentation – all these are the stuff that serious classroom work is made of.

I used the Neelands approach to create the initial meaningful context for developing a topic about different communication and mass media, which took up the second half of the school year, and became the spur for much standard classroom work, from handwriting to science, and the impetus for some joyous collaborative creations. The children were second-year juniors in a city-centre school.

One morning in the school hall the children found themselves called upon as employees of the shabby and now almost bankrupt publishing firm 'Pompkin Press'. A high-powered business consultant, Belinda Nash (class teacher in executive garb), had been sent in by the board of directors to investigate goings on at the firm. She spoke sharp words about the low standards and uncompetitive goods marketed by the Press (showing examples). The latest news was that the infamous Pompke, Managing Director, had disappeared abroad with the liquid assets of the company. Belinda Nash explained that she was here to investigate the state of the firm, and decide whether it should be closed down, or relaunched under new management. Employees were asked what jobs they had held, and asked to give their own accounts of prevailing bad practice in the firm. The boldest children led the way, but little by little all the employees (who had not worked with a teacher in role before) identified themselves as financial administrators, printers, illustrators, authors, marketing agents, and so on. Lists of grievances were supplied, ranging from bad pay, outdated machinery, work overload, the shortage of pencil-sharpeners and other hammed-up echoes of real life in the classroom ...

Over the next few sessions in role employees were asked if they felt the firm was worth saving, and for their ideas and requirements for a revamped publishing company. Application forms for a post in the new firm were completed, and employees underwent some formal 'tests' to assess their basic competence for the job. Now employees of the new firm were offered a programme of retraining. Belinda Nash, her mission completed, had left and been replaced by a more homely character, who was in charge of the training programme. The drama took over class life, or rather merged with it. I found the 'training' format particularly useful as it allowed me to conduct some fairly formal class sessions in a rigorous way, in the playful and spoofy context of our negotiated Pompkin-drama.

The media project itself started with a look at *lettering and graphics*. The range of lettering we collected from magazines and newspapers opened our eyes to a whole world of diversity and expertise we had never noticed before. Handwriting was renamed calligraphy and soared in status as a class activity. An English and a Japanese calligrapher led sessions in the classroom, as did a Chinese brush painter. Children bought their own calligraphy pens. Beautiful books were perused and handled with care. The class had been involved in writing books for younger children, alone or in pairs: *presentation, layout, design* and *illustration* had already become a concern. A handful of employees were shown some graphics software and asked to spread their expertise around. I showed children slides of the artist and poet Tom Phillips's book, *A Humument*,[5] which is the reworking of each page of an obscure Victorian novel, *A Human Document*, deleting and stringing together words and letters from the page to create new meanings and a new poem-painting. We, too, sacrificed an old book and created poem-paintings on each page. The qualities and properties of *paper* were also the subject of scientific analysis. The science co-ordinator in the school, announced as a mystery visiting scientist, led a session to launch that line of investigation. A parent who works sub-editing typescripts collected up examples of all stages in the editing and publishing process, and came to talk to and be interviewed by the children. One day there turned up in our classroom a real-life Belinda Nash: Brenda Stone, the publisher of Macmillan children's books. We were starting to get a glimpse of the collaborative and complex nature of the professional world. The editor of a scientific magazine, a parent, brought in large sheets of unused or wasted unfolded printed up sheets for children to fold. We also cut up the columns of writing to use as galleys to arrange and paste up on layout sheets. We visited a local commercial printing firm, and saw the process of four-colour printing, folding and binding, and watched as sets of little exercise books were generously assembled and made up for us to take away. The firm even offered to print a small work of ours at a later date. The children studied the working of school office reproduction equipment, learned to use the Banda copier, which resembles the offset-litho printing process, and from then on took over much of the class Banda sheet production: a child or group would write up and illustrate some item in the project on a Banda master, and make copies for the whole class, and they produced letters for parents and other outsiders. Later on we befriended the grandmother of a child in another class: she had developed an interest in bookbinding while trying to repair damaged books, and she initiated a small group of children into the art: later each child stuck and sewed up the work of the project into a hardback book.

Having looked at historical developments in writing and printing through the BBC television series *Zig-Zag* on 'The Media', our training moved on. We looked at our role as authors, shapers and creators of meanings. Using the same television series programme on journalists, we tackled issues of the 'construction' of texts, writing from a particular standpoint, and writing with a view to captivating an intended audience. A group of teacher trainees worked with us over a period, devising relevant programmes for small groups of children: newspaper front pages, familiar stories written in journalistic style and from contrasting points of view, photo-stories, illustrations, looking at types of mass media, and so on. After a few weeks' retraining a very formal meeting of the 'board of directors' (half a dozen adults dressed up) reviewed the progress of the employees of the new firm.

The publishing firm drama gradually became irrelevant as a feature, a kind of joke, and eventually faded away as the children became more involved in the outcome of the project work as such. Maybe this was because limited energies had left us falling something short of creating a real publishing company with a real budget and marketable output. A related factor certainly must have been that most of the fun and glory, the dressing up and theatricality, had remained the preserve of the adults involved. I had the feeling the children's enjoyment was a shade resentful. Because our energies were not directed that way, the company and its employees did not develop real identities, rituals, or a strict division of roles. It did not matter. The project opened many avenues I was keen for children to get a glimpse of. The Pompkin drama was quietly dropped – it had served its purpose.

A rash of journalism developed: reporters with little note-books scoured the playground for stories in their free time, grievances and traumas made headlines:

SALE SCANDAL
On Friday the 27th there was supposed to be a sale for all the school, only the infants bought everything.

BOY KICKED
Sam in class 3 gets kicked by Nick in class 5. Sam was crying. Teachers were not notified.[6]

The next focus of collective emotional involvement for the class grew out of some writing we had all attempted, read to each other, and then acted out or mimed in groups: the rewriting of *Little Red Riding Hood* in different 'genres', and for different kinds of audiences, from horror story to slapstick, from cosy tale for tiny tots to cool story about sophisticated females... In fairly immediate improvisation sessions, little groups chose a soundtrack from a selection offered, to suit the mood of their piece: quite a lot of drama group work had taken place previously in the year, and some of the performances delighted us a great deal – it was time for the individual and collective talent of the class to find expression in some larger, more meaningful, drama. But how to build it up together?

As a pure demonstration of how easily we could create drama together, we sat in a large circle in the hall, and turned our chairs round and straddled them like horses. There was a hat at the foot of each child, to wear or not to wear, as the mood took him or her. Between us lay the large arena created by the backs of the chairs, an expectant space. To demonstrate instant play-writing, one rule: whatever was said, by anyone with an idea, became an irrefutable ingredient of the story. In a few minutes we had a plot. The teacher runs through the story to confirm the sequence of events, a few minutes later all the required parts are taken on – many children have several. Another few minutes to specify character and mood, and we are ready for the performance. Hats are swopped around as appropriate, a few garments and props are quickly and autocratically bestowed on a few actors (in need of a personal boost and to create a little atmosphere). With the help of a few musical items from our soundtrack menu the teacher sets the mood and pace and cues the players by narrating to the performance, at once leading and following the flow of the improvisation: the story fleshes out and expands in the improvisation. The whole process took place in half an hour, everyone had a part in the creation, anything could have been woven in, anyone's ideas accommodated.

We now set to to evolve in a similar way a drama created by, and featuring, everyone in the class. Our media project had meanwhile moved on to the study of audio-visual media. We were offered the chance to visit a broadcasting television studio, and from then on everything else paled into insignificance: books and the pedestrian printed word were blasted right out of our minds! It was thought we might construct a film out of our drama rather than perform it as a play, and use a video camera, cleverly selecting shots in and around the school to create whatever illusions we would require.

First steps: creating a story

The most crucial moment: small groups convening to work out the setting for a drama with large cast. Now the latent power structures within the class started to show through; as each group put forward its proposal it became clear who had a finger on the pulse, and who in contrast chose a setting with minority appeal. Whose interests would sell to the rest of the group, and whose closed-in private world prevented them from registering the needs of those different from them? We had: a hold-up in a bar; a bank robbery; a king in a zoo; a murder in a hotel; a riding panto; a classroom 'disasters' comedy (where everything goes wrong).

Here is the submission scribbled by one group during that first brainstorm free-for-all:

THE KING IN THE ZOO
One day a king went to the zoo. He liked the animals so much he decided to have a Private Zoo of his own. But he only had three monkeys. Zephir, Arnold, and the last one ...

Expanded later in the classroom, after I had voiced a concern that the format of the story should provide a wide sweep of exciting parts for the range of children in the class, and not just be a one-star show, the story begins:

One day a King went to the zoo. He had not been to the zoo before, and he liked the animals. There were five monkeys, two lions, three parrots and one donkey, and one tortoise who wouldn't pop his head out of his shell. After going to the zoo, the king decided he wanted a Royal Zoo with every animal you could think of in it. The Royal Guards and Soldiers said 'it's not possible and it will cost too much', but the king took no notice and ordered the Animals ...

The sophisticated but painfully shy girl who wrote this incorporated plenty of fine dramatic elements into her long story: comic animal characters, a flawed king, the clattering of disgruntled Royal Guards and Soldiers ... one can share her director's eye. On the other hand the text was very rigidly penned in a written-story form, with every last detail specified: bringing the drama to life for the reader, but hardly the document to appeal to a bunch of classmates with heads full of their own ideas. She had not attempted to package her drama in a form that would sell to the rest of the class, and she probably had not been sufficiently aware that in the prevailing atmosphere of this year, the class would not be wild about the innocent fairy-tale world of the King and his Royal Zoo. It is also significant, I am sure, that this deep-down humorous and thoughtful child does not have a television at home, a parental choice.

By contrast, I have no written record of the idea that gained consensus, only the boiled down words which I jotted down when summarizing for the class all the proposals that had come up:

Hotel
Murderer – loses her knack[7]
Sleuths
Manager

This group concentrated its energy on shaping a flexible proposal, it kept ideas alive and developing: they were helped by the fact that they were a larger group – there will have been, I imagine, more argument and counter-argument, flaws pointed out, rows, victories and defeats ... The contrast between the more isolated child who had to safeguard her ideas by writing them down, with the attendant limitations of that means of communication (teacher-orientated), and these children who were able to take the risk of tossing their ideas around, despite the danger of ending up with nothing, because they knew it was a more powerful way to work, reminds me of the parable of the talents: the fate of the fearful, and the success of the investors.

By contrast again, here is the proposal of another vigorous and larger group of girls, jotted down:

BAR SENE
Group of people in bar
Group of gangsters come in with splurge guns come and attack
take hostiges come back next day take more hostiges
police round up people go to hide out and surround them

The document shows this group to be well aware of the task and challenge: it is a provisional working draft, with its main ideas well condensed, with a clear indication that there is still much to negotiate.

Some of these girls had starred earlier in the year as some delinquent teenage birds propping up the Crow Bar in our anthropomorphic bird documentary/soap opera 'A Day in the Life of Sesame Street'. The realistic set provided then by a child whose parents run a pub ensured that from then on scenes of drunken debauchery were a firm favourite in the range of children's improvised scenarios! My reticence to endorse the production of yet more scenes on the theme of alcohol abuse contributed to the sinking of this bold proposal from a group of budding little feminists, to my great regret: for, like the hotel proposal, it left a lot of space for all kinds of detail and sub-plot. The plot also hints at children's own spoofy strategies for exploring the real world issues that confront them daily in the media.

Now only the hotel setting remained that had the width and flexibility to incorporate, potentially, all the other ideas bubbling up, including the possibilities of a bar scene *and* a hold-up! We welcomed the setting, but provisionally held back as to whether it would be a murder.

Was this proposal, from a group of boys, ideal because they had in mind the needs of the whole class? I doubt it was consciously worked out, but more a matter of flair, habit and dominance, and the ability to echo the prevailing culture of their time. Because they functioned successfully within a large and lively friendship gang, they were open and flexible. Because they were children of their time who watched television a lot, understood and felt comfortable in the world about them, they were able to pick up and play about successfully with the codes and conventions of the dominant media-conveyed culture, their references were understood and shared by everyone else in the class: it was perceived as 'cool' and it created a consensus. The fact that they were boys was a clinching part of this: they felt comfortable and confident reproducing the recognizable stereotypes drawn from a male-figure dominated world of fiction. For a group of girls to become a bunch of gangsters they have either to impersonate men, which they have had a lot less practice doing and are likely to be less convincing at, or else do a send-up and reverse the conventions: the female gangster with 'splurge gun' – still a genre with minority appeal. The whole chain of events derived from growing up with a sense that as men they are due to 'inherit the earth' leads little boys inevitably, in my experience, to breathe more expansively and comfortably, in the classroom, play a shaping role in class 'public affairs', and exert more power in the classroom.

What about the girls? Some of them might huddle in inward-looking girl groups, gaining strength from togetherness and insulating themselves from the damage which boys' views of them may inflict on their self-image, though by defensively refusing to compete they forgo a role in 'public life'. Then there are also the girls who have started to articulate and agitate about the discrepant state of play between the genders, but indignation sells less well than the persuasive power of the confident: overwhelming odds for little women to surmount, though a challenge they can tackle, on their own witty and subversive terms, especially with a good dose of support – to learn to look outwards, consciously study the boys' marketplace, crack it, and stake a claim in it. It is something I told all the individuals who did not enjoy watching popular television programmes and were failing to 'make it' in playground conversation or classroom collective work: don't just watch television because it is fun, watch it in order to crack the codes and discover the world that your colleagues belong to, so that you too have an entry into it, and can secure a platform to put over your own concerns.

The next stages of work involved creating the hotel: in no time, with the help of a few tables, chairs and stage blocks, guests and personnel materialized out of thin air: bellgirls bustled with luggage, French waiters glided around the dining-room and the gaggle of delinquent female teenagers tracked down the bar without delay, where they were served by the fawning and flirtatious boy 'waitresses'. In the Reception the wily rummage-in-dustbin local tramp (permanently drunk) was contriving to elude the burly security guard.

We thrashed out the vital components of the story, drawing together successful elements from the improvisation and the logical constraints of the emerging murder plot. Children wrote and worked on the ideas, and posted information on the classroom walls. In brief, this whodunnit features the unpleasant manager of Sport Hotel Beck who is found murdered. Suspicion rests on his wife, on the employees, on a tramp found lurking in the area, on the guests ... Sleuths and cops look for clues but either fail to find them or pick the wrong ones. However, the trail of clues is to be obvious to the viewer. These consist of items that clearly point to a sweet-looking elderly couple.

Where the children attempted to establish the plot in writing, and in small group work, they easily got lost in a sea of cluttering detail, which choked overall progress. Yet their meandering attempts concealed a highly developed sense of film conventions and genres in the children, and a very precise awareness of what they wanted the story to become, but only managed to articulate publicly and effectively in teacher-supported discussions. Broad and abstract concerns about the overall shape of our detective story ranked high in the minds of the writers, but best came to light when someone was able to sweep up and slot into place the disparate comments and suggestions.

While decisions were negotiated by all, a degree of ownership of the story was retained throughout by some children. One powerful figure in the class was a child whose own experience of staying in an Austrian hotel, at a place actually called 'Hotel Beck', had influenced the group that put forward the murder in a hotel idea. The name of the hotel is itself evidence of this. It was not part of the original proposal, yet it sprung up along the way, seemingly part of the next stage of creation, yet unmistakably a sign that this child's original vision of the story was part of the unquestionable 'givens' of the plot. This is but one instance of the countless influences at work that clog or galvanize the energies of children, often invisible to the teacher removed from the conversations and machinations of the class. Certainly in the class, however, there is always someone who *does* know and notice, and who *will* explain if we as a class find the stillness to listen.

The next phase

While individual or group contributions were the powerful background out of which our story was able to grow, it is clear to me that the only significant forum was the whole-class 'happening'. Writings posted on walls were in a sense lifeless documents, and no small work team could determine what only a teacher-held class event had the sanctioning power to decide. The rows that occurred in the small groups were not so much a question of too many ideas tangling up, but the desperate need to find and establish fair procedures.

The search for rules and for the many and appropriate kinds of fairness was a major concern woven into every strand of the project, and it further points to the way personal and social concerns sit at the centre of the learning process. The teacher was needed at the heart of the collective creative process for that very purpose, as the figure in the only position to uphold certain principles of fairness. Significantly, there were certain children whose involvement in the project went far beyond personal ambition, and whose visibly disinterested contribution healed and nourished others. With the teacher strongly behind them, their status and influence grew: their suggestions created consensus, and children began to entrust them with positions of leadership.

The casting

Casting slips, listing each child's favoured parts, were processed by a small dedicated team, without my intervention. Over a few days they ferried to and fro between the children, shuffling slips, negotiating, questioning and arguing. They were touchingly concerned to accommodate everyone's feelings, and worked extremely hard to resolve conflicts. One of them was Robin (famous in another chapter of this book), a child normally fed up with himself and school, but who became a powerful and tireless ideas man during the project.

While this was going on, some children were scouring the school premises for possible camera shots suitable for the scenes of a hotel drama, and storyboarding them.

When everyone had been found the right part, the children prepared their costumes and props at home. Our hall time improvisations gathered momentum. Successful sketches were 'written' into the story which was sharpening into focus. The callous 'teenagers' terrorized little children at the hotel by telling them murder stories at night. The 'zoologist', who kept ringing up his mother from wherever he was in the world, had long arguments with her from the phone in the hotel bar which the barmaid thought were addressed to her. The 'cook' leered into her mixing bowls looking wild-eyed and wickedly manic.

It was at this point that a teacher who was doing freelance media work for the local authority offered her help. She organized funding for us to spend two separate days with her at an LEA drama centre equipped as a two-camera studio. The children would be in charge of all aspects of the production, from mixing the soundtracks to working the cameras.

The school year was drawing to a close, the school assembly being prepared, and meanwhile our little film had grown into a major venture. The days we were offered at the drama studio fell two days after the performance of our assembly, and 'Hotel Beck' was still only a vague proposition. I offered the children a choice: we could go to the television studio and tidily film our assembly play, 'The Making of "Hotel Beck"', which was licked into shape and ready; or we could enter the unknown realms of 'Hotel Beck' itself, and have a mad rush making a kind of improvised film, unscripted and unrehearsed. The children were unanimous: we had to make the real film of 'Hotel Beck'.

I attribute the decision to two things. 'Hotel Beck' was the children's own creation. After years of creating classroom topics around 'worthwhile' and idealistic subjects, I had finally allowed my class to become immersed in a topic entirely of their own choosing: a murder in a hotel! Because the story truly belonged to them, they showed themselves capable of extraordinary commitment in the days that led up to the making of the film. The second reason reflects the other side of the dilemma I mentioned in the introduction to this chapter, the tension between utter respect for children, and the need to be *lifted out* of convention-bound trains of thought. Our story had become such a powerful world that we shared together, that it had somehow become real. It was real because many strands of our lives had been woven together into it, and it was 'real' because we shared this fantasy together – as if collective imagining had had the power to create another world inside the looking-glass. Even though it did not even properly exist as a story as yet, we had to explore it.

The last days of the project took on the character of a military operation, with great debates to work out the precise character of the film, and activity on all fronts. On the day after our assembly, which was also the last school day before the film was shot, we held a marathon session. I had planned that working out a shooting script needed to happen while we rehearsed. The desks were moved into a great circle for the day, creating an acting space at the centre of the room. The children, who were all seated at their desks, could work, or doodle if they were not involved at any point. In the event we spent the entire day talking. We had to establish what kind of film we wanted, work out the precise sequence of events, and which characters would become suspects... The children were clear that they wanted the film really to work as a thriller ('You know, not with the cops too ... too funny.' 'Sensible like, but not like with loads and thousands of all jokes. Some waiter jokes ... ') The need to establish a psychologically fitting ending was also important, and we spent large parts of the day debating this. The reasons for this seem clear. The film was, first, about themselves, as individuals of the class: we had to find something satisfying that worked for everyone. Then the film was also their statement to the world: they wanted it to stand out from the wash of stereotyped films they watched every day on television. It had to carry their commentary on the conventions, and they were fastidious about the exact shades of meaning they wanted to convey.

In the last few moments of the school day, we made a decision on one of the most delicate issues of the whole project: the choice of a director for the film.

Throughout the year I had tried to encourage individuals and hear tiny voices, but now that the pressure was on us to shoot an unscripted film in two days, it was too late to invest in the unconfident and the hesitant: only those who proved competent to tackle a critical job would be offered it – the harsh laws of the open market. There could only be one, or at most, two directors: the job would take a good while to learn. The director sits in the gallery, the top of a hierarchical structure, creating under great pressure the exact shots which will make up the film, but in fact delegating every actual operation to the various members of the production team, telling sound and vision mixers where and when to fade in or cut between soundtracks and images, relaying by radio concise and detailed instructions to camera operators, and via the floor manager to actors in the studio which cannot in fact be seen from the gallery: a person of vision, a leader, a communicator, a fast thinker. A tall task for any eight- or nine-year-old. In fact one of the lessons of that experience was that most of the children, when given any of the great responsibilities in the production team, rose to it in ways that defied all expectations of them: given time we could have turned out a whole classful of directors.

Time however was in short supply. I agonized over how to make this choice, and despaired that not one girl had had the recklessness to put herself up for the job. It seemed that their very awareness of the importance of the post colluded with their sense of collective responsibility in humbly excluding themselves from the running.

I did not want an autocratic decision to be misinterpreted. I was determined that the class should share in this decision and be clear about the only grounds upon which that choice could be made: the post had to go to the person who would do a good job. Also, the harsh workings of the 'open market' provided the only possible mechanism I could arrive at that would throw up the right person: someone that the class would accept and endorse as a kind of boss. On the last half hour of that eventful Friday, I held auditions. Applicants were asked to direct a scene of their choice: to position and instruct the actors and the two camera operators of their choice. The cameras were cardboard boxes with an eye hole at one end, and a screen shaped opening at the other, enough to frame a shot. Five children tried for the job, two girls in the end, though one lost her nerve and withdrew. It was a perfect situation, for the successful candidate was exceptional: in that audition he handled with natural flair and simplicity the task that the other dear over-thoughtful, indecisive, or over-garrulous candidates were still struggling with, and this was obvious to all.

I asked children to propose candidates they felt they would have confidence in as directors, and to identify their qualities. Here are some unprompted comments about Tom G. We had not previously discussed the personal skills a director would be needing:

Julian: (*proposer*) He made them move into all the right positions, and everything, and he didn't take just like a great time saying 'nnn, go there, go there, go there' finish. He took a long time and selecting where he really really wanted them.
Teacher: A very long time did he take?
Julian: Not a really really long time, but quite a long time.
Teacher: So you thought he was thoughtful? (*many assenting voices*)
Matthew: Not too thoughtful, like mmm 'you go over there, *you* go over *there*, oops you better come back, you go over there ... '
Tom C.: He didn't babble on about exactly where he wanted you, he said it in a gentle way.
Teacher: He spoke simply, that didn't take too long. I thought you were very clear. I think that was that you had a loud voice, that's one advantage.
Emma: He thought quite quickly, and he ...
Matthew: Once he'd actually said suggestions like 'go over there' he didn't say 'actually you can go over there' [i.e. somewhere different]
Teacher: He stuck to what he thought, he was quite firm.
Julius: He didn't order kind of them around.
Teacher: He didn't make them feel small. He wasn't bossy.
Lily: He didn't really move around very much, he just stayed there most of the time.
Teacher: He actually was able to ...
Lily: ... yes to tell them
Teacher: ...what to do without having to walk around?
Lily: Yes.

Again consensus was achieved, and Tom G., entrusted with this high honour, received special training on the Sunday. Also on that Sunday, other children turned up to make props, pools of PVA blood, green soup, and so on; a great pub decor was transferred piecemeal into the classroom. Two children and I selected soundtracks for the different scenes which I then taped onto individual cassettes, ready for the sound-mixing technicians to use.

In two exhilarating days, we made as much of 'Hotel Beck' as we could manage – after editing it ran to 40 minutes! Directors and anyone who had the energy and concentration to help, planned camera positions, and the precise sequence of events. In the morning children sat together on the coach to work out the conversations they would hold in front of the cameras, and in the studio thoughtful stage hands hunted among the carrier bags for somebody's lost moustache . . . Camera crews and other jobs rotated. Children's skills improved dramatically after their first exposure to a task, but we could not always afford the time to let children get beyond their initial stumbling experiences on a new job. Some children did not get the chance to prove what they could do given a little more time, and were unceremoniously removed from their posts if they could not manage. There were a few children who slipped through the net in some way: because scenes were cut or altered their performance was squeezed down, and they probably carry that small sorrow even today.

Perhaps everybody's favourite memory was the filming of the bar scene. After a period during which every stumbling sequence had needed several retakes, actors and production team glided into perfect co-ordination. The scene went on and on, flawlessly, 'barmaids' and tramps performing feats of improvisation, intense concentration maintained in the control room as the director kept track of the screens, and the vision mixer carried out his orders, till we were gradually overcome by laughter.

We were greatly privileged to be given the professional means to make our work come to life in this way. The two days at the television studio will remain a highpoint. The children deserved it in every way, but, like much of the other work and involvement they give us in school, their insights and dreams could easily have evaporated away, and each child left alone with his or her own thoughts. There are other scenes of 'Hotel Beck' we never filmed; they remain half-imagined and half-shared in a kind of twilight zone, still full of fascination. The scenes we managed to make did come into existence. They are a shared memory we all owe to each other, and in which we can all meet again, always.

I will close with an extract from the book of the film, which is in preparation. It is being written in little snatches out of school hours: I left the school I was working at after this project. The offer by the printing firm we visited to produce something for us still holds, so an editorial team met up at the new establishment I am attached to. Concentration was difficult at the end of a week in school, and the intense atmosphere of the classroom was impossible to re-create. Not much got done, but droves of children turned up, to pour out lemonade and draw pictures.

Tom C. wrote this extract: he composed it alone – I wrote it down for him at the session to help keep his ideas alive, and he typed it out at home. He is a child whose part in the film got squeezed, and who did not have any great production jobs. He never mentions it though, unless you bring the subject up, and you realize it is a little painful. I like this piece because it manages to peep round new corners of the magical Hotel Beck. But I like it especially because his lovely ideas reassure me that nobody in the class really got left behind.

On a beautiful mountain above a scenic valley in the Alps, just below sparkling glaciers, there's a grand hotel where very important people can stay (for scientific skiing holidays). But no very important people stay there, mainly because it is too far to walk and the road is usually blocked by an avalanche. If you look inside, it is a damp and dark old hotel, and the nice brown plants are really dead daffodils: there's a broken swing and seventy one acres of slush and mud. The window shutters are a hundred years old, and rotting and falling off. The toilets here only have half a seat and there's only one of them and it doesn't flush. Plus the fact that there isn't any hot water because the gas leaks. But it doesn't matter anyway because there aren't any taps.

Notes

1. Len Masterman, *Teaching the Media*, Comedia, 1985.
2. Cary Bazalgette, 'New kinds of Literacy' in Colin Mills and M. Spencer (eds), *New Directions in Primary Education*, Falmer Press, 1988.
3. Jonathan Neelands, *Making Sense of Drama*, Heinemann, 1984.
4. Dorothy Heathcote, 'Materials for Meaning in Drama', *London Drama*, vol. 6, no. 2, 1981.
5. Tom Phillips, *A Humument*, Thames and Hudson, 1987.
6. Extracts from 'The N.N.N.' (The No-Name Newssheet), a lunchtime production.
7. 'Her' will have been my rephrasing to avoid the assumption that the murderer must be male, but 'loses knack' is likely to have been a child's words.

PART FOUR
A community of writers

12 The school as a community of writers

JENNIE DUNN

It seems to me that good schools are ideal places to encourage young people to write. They provide a supportive and caring community of local people made up of pupils, staff, parents and their families, ancillary support, kitchen staff, caretakers, cleaners, neighbours of the school, tradespeople, local churches and other community establishments. My own school has connections with the local church and has a Home for the Elderly next door, so that the children are involved in activities and projects which put them in touch with a wide variety of people who know and support the school.

There are many ways in which the writing one does with a class can reflect and/or focus on the school as a community. There are many ways in which the school community can be used to stimulate writing. I have picked on several examples which, I hope, will serve to illustrate the points I wish to make about writing and about working together.

Problem post

I would like to map the progress of this idea from its first appearance to the fulfilment it found in the children's writing. It was an idea which grew without the benefit of planning, at least in its early stages. It is, I think, worth noting that many projects undertaken in the classroom can start in an apparently haphazard way and that serendipity is one of the teacher's most useful and rewarding faculties.

The problem post idea was really born seven months before it emerged as a piece of collaborative writing. The caretaker and I decided to smarten up the school Christmas post box and when I showed the shiny, red box to the children in assembly I invited them to begin their Christmas correspondence. That lunchtime the children crowded round the box simply to have a look at it, and, by the following morning, it was overflowing with cards and letters.

The flow of letters continued for ten school days. It seemed that everyone was writing to everyone else in school. It was a pity that all this communicating had to end once Christmas was over, and, much later in the school year I was reminded of the post box.

One morning I took an assembly on 'Problems with Parents'. The idea was to get the children to imagine their roles reversed with those of their parents, to see parents as *their* responsibility. It was lighthearted in tone and dealt with such problems as the mother who had a temper tantrum in Woolworth's or the father who wouldn't eat all his green vegetables. When I asked if there were problems the children could share in the same way that mums and dads shared problems at the school gates, about two hundred hands were simultaneously raised.

When the assembly ended my own class of fourth-year juniors was anxious to continue the discussion. We spent the next 40 minutes talking about parents and, after lunch, the children told me that all the classes had been swopping stories about their problems. I, too, had often been asked what I thought about such matters as the mum who made her daughter eat all her peas or the dad who expected his twin boys to wash up on alternate evenings. I remarked jokily that the children ought to write to magazines for advice about things like this and it was from this remark that the idea really began.

During the afternoon two children approached me with a suggestion. They wanted to set up a team of agony aunts and uncles to help deal with the enquiries they had received from other children in the school. There had been so many questions – at this stage still verbal – from children who considered themselves wronged that some of my class decided to do something about it. Their concern and interest were genuine enough and, on the whole, the problems they had to deal with were to do with such things as clothes, uniform, food, bedtimes and so on.

The following week I introduced the team of agony aunts and uncles – three boys and three girls – to the rest of the school. I told the children that, if they wrote their problem down, the team would try to help them by writing back with advice. I began by designating a section of a noticeboard for problem post and children pinned their letters to the board. However, letters were lost in this way and the team revised their methods of communication and announced that they were going to produce a 'book of problems and their solutions'. This new approach meant that they asked children to write their problems in a large book placed in the entrance hall. The team then wrote their advice straight into the book.

Dear Problem Page,
My mum says I have to eat my vegetables and I hate them. Do you have to eat yours?
From Mark.

Dear Mark,
When we were your age we did not like many vegetables. Our parents tried to make us eat them. We eat them now and we are strong and healthy (as you can see). There is a book in the library which tells you all about healthy eating. If you come on Wednesday we can show it to you.
From The problem page team.
P.S. I'm afraid your mum is right.

The book of problems proved very popular. Dinner supervisors, the school secretary, teachers and visitors – particularly parents – enjoyed jotting down their responses beneath the day's problem page. It soon became obvious, however, that, while this was interesting and acceptable to most children, there were some who preferred their correspondence to remain private. This was when we dusted down the Christmas post box and put it in the entrance hall to receive the letters that were *not* for everyone to see. Some of the letters from this growing batch were from children whose need for advice was quite genuine and more serious. Obviously their problems had not been resolved by discussion with parents. For example, one girl was constantly woken by her much older brother when he came to bed at night. The girl couldn't get back to sleep and became distressed by the situation, as well as tired and irritable the following day. Another child resented his parents accommodating lodgers during the summer months. One child whose father spent a long time away from home had a mother who spent much of each evening on the phone. The child felt lonely and excluded. All these problems required tactful and diplomatic replies. Initially I was unsure how the advisory team would manage to deal with them. I sat with the children sifting through the post and discussing the problems. I watched the group develop good relationships and I was impressed by their kindness and concern.

Dear 'Listeners',
my gerbil has died and I am sad.
From Clare.

Dear Clare,
We are sorry about your little gerbil. We feel sad too. Do you have any pictures of him or her? We would like to see them. Have you told your teacher? Perhaps she would help you to make a book about your pet and that might help you feel better.
From 'The Listeners'.

This project lasted a month, finishing when the agony aunts and uncles left junior school. They had sorted, read, discussed and replied carefully to each letter they had received. They provided their own coloured writing paper and envelopes, designed a logo, gave themselves a name ('The Listeners') and kept folders of past correspondence. They had also written to the Post Office for stickers and advice about letter-writing.

It was fascinating to see how the common goal influenced the quality of their written work. One child used a jumbo typewriter to give her work a more professional look. They helped one another with spelling, grammar, handwriting and punctuation. It was these acts of collaboration and the feeling that their writing was purposeful that brought about this attention to detail; an impulse generated from within the group and not imposed on it. But there was more to it than this improvement in writing skills. The children had listened carefully to one another's views and had taken pains to find the most appropriate word or phrase in response to the needs of the writer. They saw how important it was to capture the exact meaning and make their advice clear and helpful.

This flourishing and fruitful correspondence was undoubtedly worthwhile but it did throw up a number of difficulties which ought to be noted.

The problem post required the commitment and involvement of a supervising member of staff who knew the children well and could tell when it was appropriate to intervene. In order to prevent subversive comments and the bad feelings these may have produced I dealt personally with children who wrote about problems with members of staff. On the two occasions when this arose I spoke to the children involved and was able to resolve the problems quickly and comparatively painlessly.

Another difficulty which such a project may create is the resentment parents could feel over the public airing in school of their perfectly reasonable domestic rules. I recall one rather distressed parent who was concerned that her insistence on early bedtimes might have been considered excessively hard when taken out of context. Because of the organic nature of the project, we had to cope with these problems as they arose. Anyone else contemplating similar work would be well advised to impose some limitations at the outset. It may be helpful to restrict the work to a two-week spell, for example, or to keep it within the bounds of one class so that the teacher is better able to monitor its progress.

Our problem post came to a natural conclusion when the summer term finished. It had started almost by chance, although it is worth noting, I think, that it was given particular impetus in two school assemblies. The assembly provides an excellent opportunity for directing and focusing the attention of the school community. There were, I feel, two especially important aspects of the teacher's role in the project. The first was the recognition of an idea created by the children themselves and a corresponding awareness of its potential. The second was the provision of time and space for that idea to develop.

Radio plays

It was as a direct result of these collaborations involving letter-writing that I became interested in the notion of the support and involvement a group of children could share in a single piece of writing. I decided to draw on drama work I was already engaged in and we began the project by discussing various types of story. Most of the children wanted to work on stories involving suspense and mystery. We discussed the difficulties this might present. How, for example, could we make the suspense in a story vivid enough to leap off the page for a reader? It was at this point that a child suggested we wrote out play scripts and tape-recorded them with sound effects. The class divided quite easily into six self-chosen groups, each with five members.

I wanted to avoid too didactic a role in this project so, during these planning sessions, I spent my time visiting each group and taking notes about the ways they planned to tackle the work. Eventually we decided that the groups should consist of: sound-effects technicians; writers; tape technicians; and typists. All the children were involved in making decisions about all the tasks that made up the project. Once these were decided they then moved on to the actual story and its characters.

Most groups began acting out their stories long before anything was written down, although one group, having efficiently organized its jobs during the first session, started writing immediately. This group's aim was to produce a short story each. They then planned to take the best elements from these stories and start again. This democratic approach, in fact, made the writing process complicated and I had to work quite closely with them to help with the periods of frustration and slow progress.

The most successful collaborations in this project were those which had no more than three named writers in the group. It was interesting to see how respect and tolerance developed between these writers. Some of the writing happened quite spontaneously and yet the children set themselves high standards – only the best was good enough. It is worth pausing to note that, in this project at least, the democratic ideal of collaborative writing – six writers making six contributions which had to be fairly merged – produced comparatively laboured results. Truly collaborative writing cannot be imposed. It is an organic process which grows at the same pace as the trust and understanding which develop between a group of writers.

An interesting development in one particular group was the writing of character descriptions *before* a plot was hatched. Each child wrote a full description of the character he or she wanted to play in the taped version and then read it out to the group. In twos they wrote a play around these six characters before taking elements from each of the three plays to produce a script which they all more or less agreed on. Finally they acted out the script, each child playing his or her own character again. This was a fairly time-consuming exercise but also a fascinating one.

Each play lasted about ten minutes and the children learned how much writing, thinking, planning, taping and sheer hard work goes into such an apparently short time. There were, of course, problems. Any creative enterprise on this scale in a classroom is bound to create problems. For example, some of the children found it difficult to work together closely. Sometimes the sound-effects technicians became annoyed when the writers decided to scrap a good effect because they had changed their minds about a scene. One boy spent some time trying to get other groups to include a meal scene in their plays because he'd gone to great lengths to record the sounds of his family at the breakfast table. Problems like these, however, can be beneficial to a project. Their solution can – and did – lead to some quite creative decision-making.

Other problems need careful and sensitive handling by the teacher who must be aware of group tensions. Everyone has a contribution to make and this contribution should be properly valued. At the end of the writing and recording we all listened to the plays, discussed them and considered what we had learned. The comments were revealing:

You wouldn't think that was about 16 hours' work, would you?

I feel quite proud because I couldn't write this stuff on my own.

You get fed up with other people's stupid mistakes, though – especially spelling.

I'm good at ideas and he's good at writing down right.

Laura made me think about my characters so that they were real to me.

No one makes you do it. You just want to because the group's worked so hard.

It's better writing in a group because you're all in it. You all help each other – that's what I like best.

It's what I liked best, too. Many children in the class with spelling and handwriting difficulties and problems of organizing their thoughts were freed from these limitations and became much less tense. This helped them to think more creatively. Those children who were competent and imaginative writers were encouraged to experiment and to allow their work to be modified and developed – even improved – by others. In all cases the collaboration encouraged communication in a fresh and challenging way. Participants felt themselves to be involved in and responsible for the work they were doing.

When the project was finished the children wrote about the experience:

It was good fun working in a group to produce a play for radio. Different people did different things. Ben and Edward wrote down the script and Hettie and me helped with just about everything. All of us spoke.

It was very different working in a group. It took a long time ... because we had to talk about what we were going to write. We had to sort out who would do what.

It was hard writing the play because we could never agree what to write. Peter wanted everyone killed. The bit I enjoyed was playing the part of the murderer.

Infant–junior collaborations

Working with infants is good because you get ideas off them and they get ideas off you.

The way me and two infants wrote was like this. One infant thought of part of the story then the other thought of the other part. Altogether I enjoyed myself.

The success of the play script collaborations set me thinking about other situations which might foster similar attitudes. I had been most encouraged by the growing confidence of hitherto diffident writers so I looked for opportunities to develop such confidence in other groups of children.

I set up an experiment in which, for an hour a week, each member of my class worked with one or two six-year-olds. My pupils acted as scribes/teachers for the younger children for writing activities varying from instructions for playing games to fiction.

Again, this idea began with a small group of children working together and later developed into a larger project involving 60 children. The initial stimulus for the writing was a scene created by using Play People characters. I chose this stimulus because I had often observed the infants in the playground. Small plastic figures seemed to provide them with endless ideas for imaginative play and I wanted to arouse and extend this imagination to use within the classroom. My own class of fourth-year juniors enjoyed setting up the situations – rescuing a cat from a tree; two people on sledges in deep snow (expanded polystyrene chips); workers digging a hole in the road; knights on horseback getting ready to joust... The older children had thought hard about what they were doing and had tried to make the static scenes as active as possible. I took time to prepare the older children for this writing session, reminding them that younger children would need longer to organize and articulate their ideas. I also reminded them of their own skills and of those of the six-year-olds and impressed upon them that they all had an important role in this session.

When the infants arrived in the classroom (many of them holding the hand of the older child) they were excited to see the little scenes we had created. Some were a little shy at first but soon most of them were involved in telling stories to their junior partners.

To begin with the older children joined in with the play activities but they soon realized that no writing was being attempted. They therefore began to intervene more, suggesting that the children set down their stories, so, in this halting and rather reluctant fashion, the writing started.

The most successful work was achieved by those children who spent the most time talking their stories through. Many of the children who seemed to have written particularly imaginatively were also those who had been encouraged to draw their characters before attempting any writing. Duncan, aged five, after drawing, composed the following:

This is Bill. He is a baker. He bakes French bread and quite a lot of buns and not many loaves. When he makes doughnuts he eats most of them. One day he used the wrong recipe for doughnuts. He tasted them. They were HORRIBLE! He gave them to his cat, but first he put cat food inside them instead of jam. He put cat biscuits on them instead of sugar. When the cat tasted them he thought they were DELICIOUS!

This particular collaboration was especially successful. As Duncan related his story he moved Bill around the desktop, enacting the bun-making and the doughnut-eating. He was engrossed in the task of creating his story while his scribe wrote down his words.

Sarah was given two Play People figures, a girl and a boy. This is her story:

Charlie is 5 and Louise is 7. It is Wednesday lunchtime when Louise and Charlie go to the teacher and say that their mummy is at the school gate and we have to go for lunch at home and the teacher says yes. So they go home and they get some food but they run away. They ran away to a den they had made. Meanwhile at school the teacher was doing the register. She called out Charlie's name but he was not there. The teacher called out Louise's name but she was not there.

This collaboration enabled Sarah to draw on her wide vocabulary. She is a child who enjoys talking but is reluctant to commit much to paper. She really enjoyed working this way, pausing with her chin on her arm as she thought and said 'meanwhile'. She was daring to use story language once she was freed from having to labour over the written word. Eventually, in an hour's session, Sarah produced two closely written pages of story. Her scribe had worked very hard to get it all down!

This highlights a problem for the older children. In this particular example, Debbie (the scribe) found it hard to keep up with Sarah's flow of words, whereas, in other cases, the older children became restless when their infant storytellers had difficulty finding enough to say. One particular junior boy helped a hesitant infant by drawing pictures of the story and asking 'What happens in the next picture?' 'What do you want to happen now?' He was a patient and sensitive boy and yet, when I joined him to see how he was coping with the situation, he stopped talking and only continued his teaching when I had moved on to the next group of children. He was not aware of his skill as a teacher and, despite my acknowledgement of their role, some of the older children were reluctant to continue their teaching when I was with them.

Another child, a boy who was especially good with young children, was paired with a girl who had difficulty in concentrating. She only wanted to play with her toys and offered no story at all. Jonathan (her scribe) found a very effective way of eliciting responses from Jeanette. He drew lines on her blank sheet of paper and asked Jeanette to say something for each line. He began: 'What is your animal called?' Jeanette replied, 'It's called Jenny and it's a baby tiger.' Jonathan wrote:

There once was a cub called Jenny.

He read this back to Jeanette and asked her where the cub lived. 'This is for the next line now', he told her. Jeanette replied 'And it lived in America.' She was beginning to make her own story. Jonathan wrote:

And it lived in America.

He read both sentences to Jeanette. She was encouraged and went on to say more. The story finished like this:

She ate meat and lived in a cave, but she had a tummy ache and started crying. She was sad.

Jeanette was very pleased with these sentences and carefully illustrated her work and, with Jonathan's help, she read them back to her friend.

Bonnie, a positive, cheerful junior girl also overcame problems with her infant, Emily. The story involved a rhinoceros and Emily was struggling to find something to say. Bonnie decided to write a poem and asked Emily to join in. This was the end result:

Tall thick tusk, painted at the end.
His skin like armour,
All floppy like a baggy jumper.
He has small stubby ears,
Like a hunter's horn.
He runs like a baby that has just
Learned to walk.
    Emily and Bonnie

This was a delightful collaboration with both children suggesting ideas and helping each other to think of ways of describing the animal.

All the junior children had gained insights into teaching, established good relationships with younger children and become more sympathetic towards me immediately after the collaborations! They had gained understanding of the teacher's role. They were also more confident about their own work, because the collaborations highlighted for them the skills they had developed during their time at primary school.

Poetry

This collaboration involved junior children of seven and eleven years old. I had read 'I am not yet born' by Louis Macneice to a group of top juniors. It is a difficult poem and I had prepared them carefully for it. After discussion, I asked them to write poems about their own birth. This was Noah's poem:

I am not yet born,
It's very cosy here inside.
Suddenly a whirlpool forms
The whirlpool is sucking, sucking me,
Down into the outside world
I'm trying not to fall,
It's too strong,
I can't hold on!
There's a light ahead and it's getting bigger,
Sucking me through
Suddenly, I find myself being cuddled by loving arms.
Now I have all the time I like
To scream away the pain of birth.

And this one, Bradley's:

> *Oh well. Come on. I'm ready.*
> *Going down the birth aisle.*
> *Slow and steady.*
> *Soft and cosy*
> *Do not leave me*
> *When I get out*
> *Will my eyes deceive me?*
> *Will I be deaf, dumb or blind*
> *My future mum . . .*
> *Will she be kind?*

Sam wrote the following:

> *I AM NOT YET BORN*
> *I'm packing my case, socks, pants, T-shirts*
> *Jumpers, shoes, scarf and coat.*
> *I'm at birth station and the*
> *Baby-is-born express train is pulling*
> *Up at the platform.*
> *Phew! I'm on the train*
> *Reading the newspaper*
> *We are in a long tunnel*
> *We've stopped at a station*
> *Lots of people are getting on*
> *We've started.*
> *Hey! It's getting cramped in here.*
> *Oh! my shoulders are getting crushed together.*
> *Ouch! This hurts a lot.*
> *I feel like I'm in a can of beans.*
> *We've come out of the tunnel now.*
> *Blimey! It's bright!*
> *We've stopped and I'm getting out.*
> *Help! There's an earthquake.*
> *I'm getting flung about the place.*
> *I'm breathing at last.*
> *I think I'll stay with mum*
> *For a while.*

The poems were very lively, vigorous and mostly optimistic. I wanted the work to have a wider audience than children in their own classroom so I asked the authors to read their poems to a group of first-year juniors. They also enjoyed them and, stimulated by the writing of the older children, they wrote poems of their own. This was Michael's:

I am not born yet,
I wonder what awaits me.
I wish I knew whether I should go or stay
I think I will go.
No-one has ever stayed.
They have all journeyed in hope of a better world.
I am not one for gambling but I think I will –
This time.

And Francesca wrote:

Here I am all alone
I am not born yet.
It's nice and cosy here,
Except for all the darkness
It's like floating around
In the sky and being an astronaut.
All the warmness. It is so cosy.

Most of the poems by the seven-year-olds were spontaneous and did not rely upon phrases or images borrowed from the fourth-year poems. I read the younger children's work to the top juniors. They too, enjoyed hearing the poems, but were especially pleased to know that their own work had stimulated others to write.

Conclusion

These are only a few of the many ways of helping children to become writers. Collaborative writing, of course, aims at more than this. It is as much to do with helping children work with and tolerate others as it is to do with improving writing skills.

It is by no means the *only* way to approach writing. It is not even the best way. Collaborative writing can be an inhibiting and frustrating experience for the child who is fired with ideas and enthusiasm and must restrict himself or herself to the seemingly pedestrian plans of others. It can, however, provide certain opportunities which would, without a collaborative approach, remain unexplored. It releases children from some of the restraints which can be a burden to them; it teaches them how to co-operate. In some cases the shared experience of working together strikes sparks which create new ideas: ideas which are not the result of one person's deliberation but the result of the collaboration and which would not have come into existence without it.

There are, perhaps, three main points in connection with this work which are worth further reflection. First, a teacher needs to develop an awareness of the working of the community, both the community of the classroom and the wider community of the school it inhabits. Communities, like individuals, have their peculiarities and their needs and have to be approached with sensitivity and care. Second, a teacher should allow enough time for ideas to develop. If an idea is pushed before it has picked up its own impetus it can be greeted with a less than enthusiastic response. Third, a teacher should keep an open mind about the work she wants to do and the direction it should take. Consider the children as partners in the process, with their own wishes and their own contributions to make. In this way the teaching, as well as the writing, becomes truly collaborative.

13 Talking and writing with parents and grandparents

GABRIELLE CLIFF HODGES

> Writing an autobiography is like trying to jump on your own shadow.
> Terry Eagleton[1]

When children are writing about their parents and grandparents they are not just writing part of someone else's biography but their own autobiography as well. There is no doubt that this is where much of the satisfaction they gain from talking with their parents and grandparents about the past lies. The more they find out about their ancestry the more it redefines, however minutely, their perception of themselves within their own families and within society. The fact that they are writing biography and autobiography at the same time poses some interesting problems for them. It results in a strange blending of styles, narrative with transactional, personal with impersonal; of moods and tenses, active with passive, past with present. The process of moving from seeing their parents or grandparents as people to seeing them transformed into texts involves a significant detachment, one which 11–13-year-olds find, not surprisingly, difficult to sustain, and so more often than not they write themselves back into the text. 'The past', says Neil Ascherson, 'is not recoverable like some diamond brooch from the Titanic, partly because it is alive within us.'[2]

What I shall be describing in this chapter is a number of occasions when I have asked secondary pupils to work with their parents and grandparents. I shall also be looking at some of the writing that emerged, mostly by the children but also by the adults, with its curious mixture of detached reporting and personal warmth. I hope to convey my feeling that this kind of collaboration is of value not just to the children but to the adults as well.

> *I am going to interview my nan (Mum's mum) tonight and find out all different things... My nan will enjoy the interview as she likes going back in the past. I know this because often when we talk the past always crops up ... My nan lives on her own and is always glad of some company. Usually when I go to see her I can never find anything to talk about.*

For the children it is an opportunity to hear about family history and then retell it for others to share.

I think it is a good idea to interview old people because most of them like telling stories and just generally talking about old times.

And, as Isaac Bashevis Singer has said: 'Those who don't tell stories and don't hear stories live only for [the] moment, and that isn't enough.'[3]

I am interviewing my Grandad ... it will take me quite a while because he loves telling stories and will ramble on a bit.

I think it is worthwhile to do an interview because if my Nan gets older and loses her memory a bit she will have all good and bad times on a bit of paper.

For the parents and grandparents it provides an opportunity to re-create their past for someone whose past it also is. We all have stories to tell, we all need people to listen.

Basically the collaborations have involved the pupils in interviewing an older relative either about their lives in general or about a particular aspect of them, for example, childhood, schooling, the war. Their findings have then been written up partly for the interviewees to read, partly for the rest of the class. Sometimes the interviews have resulted in the adults doing some of the writing; mostly, however, the interviews have been conversational. Nevertheless, there have been occasions when the adults have been specifically asked to write.

The pupils with whom I worked on these collaborations were mixed-ability groups. Two first-year groups interviewed their parents about what life was like when they were 11, or about important childhood memories, some second-years interviewed grandparents, while third-year groups worked with parents and grandparents to gather background information and to ask for written contributions to their autobiographies. In all cases the collaborations arose out of what we were working on at the time rather than being isolated activities but there were a number of specific things which I hoped would come out of them: I wanted the children to begin to understand that everyone has a story to tell and that ordinary everyday experiences can be dignified, shaped and preserved by being written down; I wanted them to be reminded how much there is to be learnt from encouraging older people to speak about themselves and I hoped that the people with whom they collaborated would later be important readers of that writing. In addition, I thought that their writing might develop because they were committed to their subject matter, although this did not necessarily appear to happen, as I shall show later.

Furthermore, I am aware of how seldom, compared with primary schoolteachers, we in the secondary schools make use of the pupils' parents and families either as resources for learning or as working partners. I think we sometimes underestimate how close the children still are to their relatives despite their obvious inclinations at this age towards greater independence and individuality. I had certainly underestimated how much willing co-operation the pupils would encounter. Many of them obviously come from families where family history is often talked about but they still seemed to unearth new information and anecdotes. The fact that they were initiating the discussions for a particular purpose perhaps made a difference here. It did, anyway, for a few whose experience hitherto of talking with grandparents about the past seems to have been akin to that of the wedding guest with the Ancient Mariner!

First-years talking with their parents

Twice recently I have suggested to first-year classes that they might like to interview their parents in order to find out more about the past. On both occasions the idea was greeted with eagerness and they set about their task energetically.

With one class the idea had arisen as a result of reading *Gaffer Samson's Luck* by Jill Paton Walsh,[4] a novel set in our area, on the edge of the Fens. After a homework during which they investigated accents and dialects from other regions, wherever possible by questioning their parents, it seemed that there were plenty more aspects of their parents' early lives waiting to be tapped, and further more detailed interviewing ensued. The children's brief was to find out what life was like for their parents when they were 11 or 12. Narrowing it down to a particular age would, I thought, provide a helpful framework within which they could work.

A shared list of questions was drawn up before the interviewing took place and we discussed the importance of picking an appropriate time for conducting the interview to ensure the best possible results. (Several later reported sitting their parents down and making them cups of tea before beginning; one or two who tried asking questions over breakfast decided to start the interviews again later!) The parents were very co-operative, not just agreeing to be interviewed but also looking out mementoes for their children to bring to school. These, together with all the historical details and anecdotes they had collected, were the subject of many rich conversations in the classroom.

We had agreed early on that they would write up their findings in booklet form so that they could easily be taken home and read by the interviewees themselves and passed round. Encouraged by the children's enjoyment of their material I looked forward to some high-quality writing. Several other factors contributed to my optimism. One was knowing that there would be other audiences for their work than just myself; another was that most of the class had opted to produce their booklets in pairs or in groups and, by their own admission, consultation with one another was giving them more ideas. They added that it was more interesting because sharing ideas gave you other people's points of view and, furthermore, partners could stop you making mistakes if they noticed them.

What became apparent, however, as they embarked upon their booklets, was that it was proving hard for most of them to get started. The swopping of anecdotes and comparison of information never ceased and I thought perhaps that it was the need for quiet that was the answer. But when I insisted on silence for writing one afternoon, a pupil protested afterwards that 'it's spooky and you feel secluded if you can hear the birds singing'.

Looking again I began to feel that one of the main difficulties for them seemed to be the business of transferring a series of questions and answers and a collection of miscellaneous anecdotes into some sort of shaped text. At the age of 11 or 12 the majority of children probably still write best when they are writing in the personal, narrative mode and many will not have consolidated the kind of technical control necessary to handle the amount of material that children in the first-year class were working with. Conventions like paragraphing or the use of the passive voice rather than the active may not yet be firmly established in their repertoire, thus narrowing the choice of organizational methods available to them. Scarcity of good models of non-fiction writing for pupils of this age is a contributory factor. It also seems to be a question of finding a framework. Some, like Tony, stuck to the original question and answer framework, as can be seen from this extract from his piece, which he called 'My Mum At My Age':

I interviewed my mum about the things she had, did and liked. She went to a convent in Scotland. It was very strict. Her best friend was Alison, her boyfriend was Michael. The Move was her favourite pop group, untill the Beatles came about. Her favourite colour was blue. Monopoly was her favourite board game. Like James out of Gaffer Samson's Luck *my mum liked biking for relaxation.*

What Tony has done here is simply to present a list of the answers his mother gave to his questions although even this proved to be quite an effort as he writes laboriously and frequently misspells words. The final line, however, is completely different from the rest. This piece of information about cycling provides him with a point of comparison with his class reader, moves him away from the mere reporting of facts and results in a sentence with a noticeably more complex structure.

Sean is another pupil who struggles with technical aspects of his writing. He is sometimes reluctant to write and did not, therefore, at the time of interviewing, write down very much of the material he gathered. Subsequently he seemed less hidebound by the question and answer format than Tony. He also has a good memory and an ear for the sounds of language, both of which he brought to bear on his piece. He decided to collect information not just from his parents but from one set of grandparents as well. What this enabled him to do was to divide his writing into four parts, one about each of the adults, and then to refer from one to another as necessary. The first section of 'When They Were Young' is about his mother. Then comes the second section about his father:

My dad went to the same school as my mum and did not like school either . . . he lived near the coman like my mum and he said most of the kids in his street did not have any pants to wear and just wore trousers. He was always romeing about in the woods where now there is houses and factories. He did not have a TV and his dad did not have to go to war because he was an electrishion and had to keep the country going. My dad just cort the end of rashioning.

Sean's piece, which tends towards a narrative style, is stopped from becoming wholly so by the insertion of references to the other sections within it: 'My mum told me she went to a school near St. Neots coman ... [My dad] lived near the coman like my mum ...' and references to the present day: 'the woods where now there is houses and factories'. It is balanced throughout between a personal, an informative and a narrative style. It was beginning to be clear to me that interest in the subject matter was not, on its own, necessarily helping very much towards the quality of writing. What was also required was a clear framework to place it in. Sean here is constructing his own: it is made from the four members of the family and from past and present time-scales.

What were emerging, then, were pieces of writing which reflected the fragmentary nature of the evidence the children collected and which were, therefore, though delightful to read, proving difficult to shape into a fully coherent form. Because of the highly personal connection of the writers with their subjects there was an understandable unwillingness, even an inability, to distance themselves very much from the people about whom they were writing and so there was also a strongly personal flavour to all the pieces. Above all, however, there was still a definite sense of the children being in control of their material, because they were the custodians of their parents' and grandparents' memories and reflections. Their unique position is nicely illustrated by Samantha, who included some old photographs in her booklet, one of which was of her parents on their wedding day. It is entitled 'Another Wedding Photo' and shows her parents standing alone in the sunshine on a lawn smiling happily. Samantha has written beside it:

My mum is laughing because it was windy and the best man is kneeling behind her holding down the dress.

The second occasion recently when I asked a first-year class to interview their parents was after we had discussed the character of Bill Sparrow in Philippa Pearce's *The Battle of Bubble and Squeak*[5] and his memories of keeping white mice when he was a child. Bearing in mind the difficulties that had arisen previously from pupils trying to make use of quantities of varied material, I suggested that this time they might simply ask their parents about one aspect of their childhood, something that had been important to them such as keeping a pet, going to school, being naughty. Instead of a series of interview questions they therefore focused on a single topic and their rough notes this time were more like a first draft of their final piece than a questionnaire or discrete bits of information. I also spent more time on this occasion discussing how to make use of the narrative mode as a framework to retell what their parents had said and how they could make use of paragraphs to help them organize their material.

Once again the parents were extremely co-operative and the children returned with some fascinating family histories. Their writing, I think, reflects above all the close attention with which they have listened to their parents' stories and tried to reproduce them in the spirit in which they were told. Focusing on one particular aspect seems to have helped with the organization of the material as a selection of opening lines suggests:

When dad was eleven in 1946 things were a lot different to what they are now.

When my mum was eleven (like me) she went up to the High School for girls in Wolverhampton.

My Dad enjoyed his childhood and it looked as if he got up to some mischief.

From these fairly generalized opening statements they move into more particular detail. Their writing shows a wide range of control, the weaker pupils still struggling slightly with how to present the information they have collected, the middle of the range harnessing the narrative role quite successfully, and the most able making full use of their ability to write fluently.

Elizabeth, a very competent writer, said she was going to write up her piece, 'School in 1955', in the form of a diary so all the anecdotes she had gathered from her mother were drawn together within the framework of one single fictitious day. It works well. The other interesting thing about it is how much of her mother's storytelling voice is reflected in Elizabeth's writing. When asked about how she got her information Elizabeth said she had asked her mother about it one morning after her father had gone to work and she had got into her mother's bed for a bit. She proceeded to imitate her mother telling her about her schooldays and she emphasized how good her mother was at doing all the accompanying actions and sound effects for her stories, as can be imagined from the following extract:

Soon they heard Mrs. Benton coming. A whisper went through the class as they heard her striding down the corridor. When she entered everyone stopped fidgeting and looked up. Mrs. Benton was built like a man. Her silvery blonde hair pulled back into a tight bun and her stocky shoulders stuck out like a rugby player's. The teacher came in and started writing on the blackboard. John Parker was whispering to his friend Ben Matthews. Mrs. Benton turned around and saw him talking. Quietly she picked up her blackboard duster and threw it at John's head 'WOOMPH' it flew through the air and hit John's head. The teacher should have been a javelin thrower for she was a perfect shot. 'Ow' cried John but he knew what he had to do, he picked up the duster and took it to the teacher who hit him. He came back to the carpet and sat down.

Elizabeth's piece is also notable for the distance she succeeds in placing between herself and her subject matter. Making it into a story rather than just making use of a narrative style has resulted in her writing herself right out of the piece. Others, like Megan, place themselves more prominently alongside the parents about whom they are writing:

When dad was eleven he never really got into any big trouble, well that's what he said.

She reports the sorts of thing he did get up to and what punishments he subsequently received:

When he did these naughty but stupid things he got some horrible punishments like the cane to the bottom, writing lines ... when he was naughty at home he had punishments like a clout round the ear ... or the one we all hate – tidying up his bedroom. (Poor Dad.)

Although many of the children have to struggle hard to overcome difficulties of style and organization there is no doubt in my mind that it is well worth the effort. First, the collaboration between the parents and the children is immensely valuable, as the quality of the classroom conversations afterwards makes quite clear. Second, if the material is transformed from the oral to the written then something that is precious to each child is made concrete, and personal experience (which is also their own history) is dignified by being made permanent.

As teachers we can suggest opportunities for collaboration and appropriate frameworks which will help children to shape their material. This should leave them free to write as fluently as possible, moving easily between narrative and informative styles or shifting from the personal to the impersonal as and when they need to do so. If successful they will see their relationships with their parents and grandparents reflected in their writing and the information they have collected will have been preserved.

A final point worth making here is how this work was received by their parents when it was finished. Many of the children admit that they usually prefer not to show their parents the stories they have written because, they say, the only comments their parents make are about spelling, punctuation, handwriting, and so on. So if they want to share them with their parents they read them out loud to them instead!

When their parents were themselves the subject of their writing things were apparently rather different. The writing provided more than the usual amount of amusement, enjoyment and interest. One boy said that his mother had taken his booklet to work and shown it to people there as well. The collaboration comes full circle when it is read by the adult and thus seems rounded in shape and satisfyingly complete.

Second-years writing about their grandparents

The writing that second-years have done about their grandparents compares interestingly with the first-years' writing. They were asked to write about their grandparents as heroes or heroines for a Book Week publication we were producing on that theme. We read 'The Topiary Garden' from Janni Howker's short-story collection, *The Badger on the Barge*[6] and discussed the idea that everyone has a story to tell but might not do so unless the opportunity arises. We also read a poem about a woman who dies in a geriatric home without anyone apparently realizing that her brain is as fresh and clear-thinking as ever, despite all the evidence to the contrary. The pupils were moved by the poem and it lent a determination to their efforts to find out what they could about their grandparents' lives.

Because they were writing about their grandparents as heroes and heroines, the war was what tended, inevitably, to dominate the conversations and many remarkable incidents were reported.

My Grandad didn't mind talking ... so it was quite easy. He liked telling me about it. I'm sure it made him feel quite proud.

Having this sort of focus for the piece of writing they were going to do helped the children to shape their descriptions into very readable thumb-nail sketches. Unlike the first-years, they had relatively little material to sift through and were, therefore, better able to organize it. Being several months older, many of them had begun to show a greater command of their written style. Their writing was also permeated by a tremendous sense of pride in their grandparents' exploits, a reflection of the pride their grandparents felt in relating their stories.

What emerges from the writing is an affection which is special to the relationship between the writers and their heroes and heroines, enhanced, perhaps, by the knowledge that the work would almost certainly be read by the grandparents when it was finished. There began to be a sense in which this writing was not such a solitary activity as usual, but instead it was almost as if there was an arm round the child as he or she wrote, affording a similar feeling of warmth and security to that experienced by the child who reads a story with an interested and caring adult in the early years.

Here, for example, is Richard's short piece:

In the Second World War my Grandad got caught by the Germans and was locked in a room in the German prison. There was a window in this room. He managed to force this window open and jump out. Outside there were two motorbikes. He jumped on one and drove off. My Nana got a telegram saying he should have been awarded some sort of medal. So my Grandad, to me, is a great hero.

He is staying at my house at the moment, and I take my Nana and Grandad a cup of tea every morning, and every morning they say, 'That saved my life. We will tip you at the end of the week.' I do a lot of sports like football and rowing and they praise me for everything I do.

Once Richard has told his grandparents' story he seems unwilling to remain distant from them any longer and so, as with many other pieces of writing like this, there is a transition from past to present, from subject to writer and it is here that the characteristic warmth of the writing seems to lie.

Here is Jenny on 'Pépé and his Adventures':

Pépé is my grandfather. He is ninety two coming on ninety three. When we see him he always talks about the war and when the Germans invaded France. He is French and at the time lived in Paris. He used to make me laugh and still does! One of his fabulous stories is about food-snatching. The Germans used to take the French people's food. At night he and his good mates went risking their lives to get food which the Germans had put in their huge lorries. There were German guards but they managed to creep in. They stole the food which the Germans had taken and took it home to feed the starving people of Paris.

Her piece has a useful introduction to her grandfather which manages to convey a little bit about his past, about how old he is now and about her relationship with him. Her second paragraph in which she distances herself from him a bit in order to tell his story still, nevertheless, reflects her personal feelings towards him as her hero, for example in the words 'his fabulous stories' and 'his good mates'.

Steve's piece, entitled 'The Wartime Farmer', seems to reflect a joint pride – his and his grandfather's – that is obvious not so much in his choice of words as in his grandfather's (and subsequently his) selection of information:

In the Second World War my grandfather was a farmer. He had to work from around 4.30 a.m. to around 9 p.m. every day. He had to supply people all round with wheat, barley, oats and rice. If there was a German plane flying above he would get his shotgun out and shoot at it. The place he worked at was called West Farm in which he kept German prisoners to help him do the work. The prisoners he had were very lucky because he treated them properly and he was friendly with them and he didn't overwork them. That is why many people from Germany stayed in England.

Today he never stands still for more than ten minutes. He always finds some work to do despite having a tumour removed from his brain and having asthma.

At the beginning of this chapter it was suggested that one of the prime reasons for encouraging these kinds of collaboration was the importance of writing down and cherishing ordinary people's experiences. That, I feel, is particularly exemplified in the following two pieces both of which touch on the less obvious but important heroism of the grandmothers, something less frequently mentioned in the history books:

My Gran told me about my Grandad because when the Second World War broke out he volunteered. He trained for two weeks then got sent to France. My Gran said that it was horrible lying in bed at night and thinking what was happening to him.

My heroine, Grandma, is a kind and generous seventy two year old and my hero, Grandpop, who I am told was very funny, is dead.

In the war my Grandpop was the owner of a Post Office and he was in the Fire Brigade. I think he used to drive the fire engine, and save people, of course. My Grandma worked in the Post Office with a friend. She had a lot to think about at that time because she had to deliver the mail as well as working behind the counter.

Every time Grandpop went out she never knew what time he would come back or if he would come back again ...

These pieces, I think, reflect the very close, personal nature of the collaborations, the fine dividing lines between the adults' and the children's particular contributions, the need to be distant tugged at by the desire to be close.

One girl's contribution demonstrates graphically the duet-like nature of the work. Her grandmother typed her a letter because they were unable to meet and talk. Beccy then cut the letter up and interspersed it with linking pieces of her own. The grandmother actually doing some of the writing herself suggests yet another way in which the collaboration can be carried out and the extent to which adults are prepared to play an active part in their children and grandchildren's work. That is what the final section of this chapter is about.

Third-years writing their autobiographies

One of the activities that mixed-ability pupils in the third year particularly seem to enjoy is writing their autobiographies. They are at a stage of development which David Jackson has described as one of 'expanding perspectives'.[7] As they write about their early lives, first experiences of school, the transition to secondary school, they are able to be more detached than hitherto. For the most part, however, they willingly undertake the research which has to be done in order to write sections on family history, to draw up family trees or to gather anecdotes about their own early years.

Once it was clear how readily parents and grandparents contributed to the project I suggested that some of them might be asked to do a piece of writing themselves, for example a brief bit 'About the Author' to go on the back cover when the finished autobiographies were made into booklets. I was not prepared, though, for some of the writing that resulted. I had not expected to find myself so deeply moved by some of the adults' contributions which ranged from mini-biographies to humorous character sketches and even poems.

Lisa's autobiography, which she called 'So Far So Good', was vividly written and beautifully illustrated with drawings and photographs. Her title page read:

SO FAR SO GOOD
written by Lisa 13³/₄
I dedicate So Far So Good *to the almost stranger who donated blood to me for my transfusion who saved my life. Also to my beloved family who I love dearly.*

And on the inside of the back cover was this:

> LISA
> 'So Far So Good'
> A comment by her loving father.
>
> So Far So Good, by Lisa, about Lisa, is Lisa personified. Quietly and steadfastly she planned what she wanted to do – and got on with it.
>
> Night after night, searching through the family files and photograph albums, quizzing each member of the family until the very few gaps in her quite amazing memory enabled her to complete her story.
>
> The result, a beautiful piece of work created with thoughtfulness, love and care – filled with nothing but good and happy memories and positive thoughts – THIS IS LISA. SO GOOD – SO FAR!

Rebecca's autobiography is another which is enormously enjoyable to read – funny, sensitive and beautifully presented. These were the sorts of comment I was able to make when I finally read it through at the end of term. Somehow, though, her parents were able to go much further in their two written contributions:

> Rebecca has been no trouble since she was born. She was a very good baby and has grown up to be a caring and understanding young person. As a child she was quite late in getting her teeth, walking and talking. As for the last one we couldn't keep her quiet now even if we wanted to! ... Rebecca gets on well with all people – young and old alike, and will help anyone whenever she can. She is a very generous young person with her time, which to everyone is precious ...
>
> Rebecca also has a very keen sense of humour and ... never fails to create a laugh sometime during the day ... In summary she is a pleasure to have around.

This year's batch of autobiographies contains several wonderful contributions from grandparents, like this one from Tracey's autobiography, 'I Bet You Didn't Know':

> To and about a growing up young Lady. As her natural Grandfather, what can I say? Firstly she is beautiful in the eye of every beholder, ancestrally, a mixture of Latin and English blood because over fifty four years ago I met and married her Grandmother, a lovely local girl I met whilst serving in Malta G.C. Since then we are proud to be Gt. Grandparents, to date the number being 16. They are all lovely, both girls and boys, and Tracey is one of them, lovely, lively, clever, ambitious and delightful.
> Grandad S.

Many of the others were equally affectionate, including one from a grandfather who, sadly, died before his granddaughter's booklet was complete. Her autobiography is dedicated to him.

The pupils often read out loud to one another their 'About the Author' sections and reading something out loud is a fairly sure sign with third-years that they are proud of it. Inevitably, though, if it is something personal they find it easier to joke about it at the same time in case they should appear to care too much! One afternoon I heard David reading out what his mother had written for him and the other three at his table were listening intently:

> David enters his teenage years reflecting on his past successes. Winner of a bodybuilding contest for under 3 year olds, well travelled having holidayed in Spain, Majorca, Ibiza and Butlins Skegness and fresh from a successful business career in the Newspaper Industry (Paper Boy).
>
> He enters the next phase of his life with good looks inherited from his father, ambitions, a sense of humour, and the ability to control his future with good sense and dignity.
>
> A fine young man destined for greatness, but then I'm biased, I'm his mother.

There was a pause as he finished reading. The others seemed impressed. Then one of the girls laughed and said: 'How much did you pay her to write that, then?'

These extracts bring me back to where I started with the idea that biographies and autobiographies in any one family are inextricably linked and, therefore, often difficult to write, but I believe they have importance for adults and children alike and that we should go on looking for ways to encourage them. At a recent third-year parents' evening a number of people particularly mentioned how much their children had enjoyed writing their autobiographies and it appeared that pleasure and pride in them had been felt all round. I also received a letter from the grandmother of one of the pupils including a few comments about the piece of writing she had done for her granddaughter. What she had written for Joanne's booklet, 'Jo ... The Story So Far', was:

> Joanne, my grandaughter, was born on August 23rd 1974 at 9.20 p.m. on Friday evening, her twin sister, Rebecca, arriving just 10 minutes earlier. Their grandfather and I were very excited because they were our first grandchildren ... Joanne is now beginning to study in earnest because she is hoping to become a nurse and her grandad and I sincerely hope her dreams are realised. We are sure that she will be a lovely nurse, very caring. Joanne has lots of interests, including music and like her family enjoys the countryside, wildlife and reptiles. Joanne is a level-headed girl and will be a useful and reliable member of the community.
>
> May I add a footnote? Joanne is a member of a very close-knit family where we are very conscious of each others needs and where we share each others joys and sorrows. Truly Joanne is a family person.

In her letter to me she said:

> I felt very privileged to be asked to contribute to Joanne's project.
>
> It was a very easy task. We are a very close-knitted family and I love my family very much.

To record family history and express personal affection in writing is to create something particularly precious. Unembodied thoughts, as Osip Mandelstam says, return 'to the palace of shadows'[8] but what is written down can be shared, reflected upon, returned to again and again and, above all, preserved. As this kind of activity in school generates so much warm feeling round the children and as they so obviously enjoy working with adults in this way, it seems to me that it is an eminently worthwhile thing to do.

Notes

1. Terry Eagleton, 'Autobiography', talk given at Avon Association for the Teaching of English Annual Conference, 1987.
2. Neil Ascherson, Why heritage is right-wing, *The Observer*, November 8th 1987.
3. Isaac Bashevis Singer, *Naftali the Storyteller and His Horse Sus and Other Stories*, Oxford University Press, 1977, quoted by M. Benton and G. Fox, *Teaching Literature Nine to Fourteen*, Oxford University Press, 1985.
4. Jill Paton Walsh, *Gaffer Samson's Luck*, Viking Kestrel, 1985.
5. Philippa Pearce, *The Battle of Bubble and Squeak*, Deutsch, 1978.
6. Janni Howker, *The Badger on the Barge and Other Stories*, J. Macrae, 1984.
7. David Jackson, *Continuity in Secondary English*, Methuen, 1982.
8. Osip Mandelstam, *Selected Poems of Osip Mandelstam*, Oxford University Press, 1973.

14 Stories and remembering

MARY HILTON

> ... as beings endowed with memory, we cannot have a perception of the present that is not strongly influenced by a version of the past – some sort of version – which we have internalised in the course of growing up, and articulated in our adult lives ...
>
> P. J. Rogers[1]

> The culture of the past is not only the memory of mankind, but our own buried life ... study of it leads to a recognition scene, a discovery in which we see, not our past lives, but the total cultural form of our present life.
>
> Northrop Frye[2]

When Morag Styles entered my classroom for her last visit of the term, even she, who had been helping my class with our topic and very involved in its development, was startled by the amazing amount and variety of coloured paper we were spreading everywhere ... Above the hubbub I brought her up to date. We were creating marketplace collages. We had already made a graveyard mural and some crucifix designs after visiting a church. We were doing a project I called 'History Around Us'. What really struck her was the fact that the project seemed to have turned many of the seven-year-olds prematurely grey ... I assured her that it was only talcum powder, that that morning we had performed a play for assembly about ourselves as old people remembering ...

Inside this seeming chaos that my class and I had created was, I hoped, a developing sense of the past, cherished and remembered. The shape the topic was beginning to form had a central idea, that historical time is in an important sense an imaginative extension of memory.

Some of the most exciting recent history projects in primary schools have been oral history ones. Children have gone out into the community around them and talked to older people and have built up a picture of the past of their own locality using memory, photographs and memorabilia. These children have developed the key historical concept of continuity and change with the living testimony and artefacts of their own communities as evidence. I wanted to try this work but also to extend it. Because the children were so young I felt we had to go beyond living testimony further back in time to stories and old myths, to explore how history is built up from a vast range of voices and interpretations through the ages. This would give me more flexibility in tuning the topic work to the children's own writing voices. For I was anxious that the children should learn history through the process of writing it.

I feel that *writing* history is the best way to be actively involved in building up an understanding of the past. Recent research has shown that through writing children form and develop, as well as articulate, latent understanding. And after all, the professional historian's task is to capture the complexity and uniqueness of past events in prose. For me this means that children, however young, should be encouraged to develop their own writing voice and to approach historical ideas and evidence in their own creative autonomous way. Central to this is the respecting of their own memories.

If we can shape our own experiences of time past, we have made a most important step in historical understanding, because history is largely vicarious experience. As Kitson Clark[3] has pointed out, the actions of past people, their words and to an extent the influences behind them can be researched and described, but what went on in their minds can only be understood by imagination and intuition. When, through writing of our own past experiences we make sense of the actions of our own past selves in our own historical context, then we have reached an early and vital stage in developing a rational curiosity about the evidence of other past beings. Historical evidence is, after all, quite different from evidence in other disciplines: the meaning of a document or the significance of an action to those who participate in it has no parallel in other evidential problems, to those in, say, natural science. Historical evidence must make a cohesive whole with our own sense of the human condition – it must make human sense.

It was a series of collaborations – with Morag, then with a teacher colleague, and then finally with an old friend who was willing to collaborate with the children – that enabled my class of first-year juniors to explore memory. And it was through these collaborations within the work on our 'History Around Us' topic that I began to see that a feeling for time past is built up through their own preferred form of written expression – narrative.

The teaching aim I had set myself for the term was to try to encourage my seven-year-olds to develop a strong sense of themselves in history. To develop a feeling for the past as a sort of miasma which is involved in everything we do, rather than something concrete which can be totally understood. I wanted first to take a patch of space – that is, the locality – rather than one of time and begin to build up a sense of time past within it. Second, I wanted to study, or at least listen in to, the way the children reacted to this idea. I wanted to know how much they knew about their environment in this historical sense and whether they linked historical time with themselves and the recent past. I wanted to use story, oral tradition, the landscape, museums and artefacts, the familiar locality and places beyond it. This was my scheme of work:

SCHEME OF WORK

The idea this term is to deepen the children's sense of historical time and place by looking at our environment, both natural and human-made aspects of it. We will be considering England, East Anglia, Ely, Cambridge and our own school locality. We will be using a variety of stimuli and will include, I hope, several field trips. Although I don't want to settle firmly into a 'patch' of time, for our patch is our locality, I aim to build up bit by bit a rough picture of the medieval world in this region – with the undrained Fens, the rivers as communication links, the villages with their parish churches and the monastery and cathedral at Ely.

Family History
Oral History
Talking to Older People

Work on Churches,
Markets, Villages,
Cathedrals and
Monasteries.
Transactional Writing
Using Reference Material

History of the School and
Rampkin Road Area. The recent
Fire at the School.
Considering Firsthand
Evidence. Finding Clues
to the Past

HISTORY

AROUND US ...

Listening to stories
of British History:
William I, Hereward the
Wake,
Thomas à Becket,
Macbeth
Considering Motives and
Context

Recording and Re-enacting
Writing and Drama
Using Maps, Pictures and
Timelines

Field Trips
Looking at Landscape, Buildings, Natural Flora
Considering Roads and Rivers

Because this was my third term with them I felt I had got to know the children in my class well enough to run the work in a loose and somewhat impressionistic way, taking leads from them whenever possible. Most members of my class were secure individuals, eager to learn and to express themselves, with at least one adult at home giving support and encouragement. All of them lived on the surrounding council estate. There was a range of abilities but, more importantly, a wider range of characters and approaches in the class: divergent and convergent thinkers, dreamers, humorists, arguers and artists. The only common characteristic that stood out, in fact I still wonder if they were not all fanatical in that respect, is that they all *loved* stories. I know all seven-year-olds are supposed to like stories but I had never experienced such a constant powerful appetite in a group. During the previous term I had tentatively started a topic on Greek mythology. Then I felt we had experienced a deep intensity of interest as the children had been fascinated and caught in the spell cast by the ancient stories of gods and heroes. The only worry I had carried with me throughout that term was the children's lack of interest in whether any of it had been *true*. They seemed to sidestep my promptings about the details of real life in ancient Greece, unless of course the 'details' were structural matters in the stories of the heroes. For these details within the stories they had shown a consistent, academic, almost pedantic interest.

What I had witnessed was in fact a valuable part of the process of learning. Margaret Donaldson writes of the 'primitive matrix'[4] in which young children's thinking is embedded. She shows that even pre-school children can remember and reason well about the events in the stories they hear. But when their thinking is prised out of this matrix, beyond the bounds of immediate human sense – that is, 'formal' or rather 'disembedded' thinking – educational failure is often produced. Logical reasoning and information which is out of understandable context can become impossibly difficult. However, *story* like *play* enables children to make sense of the world by extending their imaginative and intuitive grasp. Stories provide children with a kaleidoscope of shifting motives and contexts from which to develop their powers of reasoning. And, as Robert Leeson writes: 'It teaches as it pleases, it extends as it relaxes ... Time, repetition, tradition make the lesson as natural as breathing.'[5] I was to rediscover how factual evidence and logical reasoning have to be sensitively incorporated into children's imaginative world to enrich rather than to deny this inner 'primitive' state. That real objectivity is a final natural outcome of balanced imaginative nourishment.

To introduce the children to the new topic, I felt I had to set the scene by talking to them about the study of history and asking them what they knew already. As a class they were extremely hazy about the idea and very wary. When I pressed them some of them said that the project on Greek myths was history but ... didn't it have to be true? Some of my class had done a project on the Romans the year before and one of them called out that this had been history. They all cheered up and began to talk to each other about having been to Castle Rising and other school trips in the past. Because I knew of their love of a story I pointed out that Britain was an island and that when the Romans had gone away England had been invaded several times. I quickly followed this up with the story of William the Conqueror and the Battle of Hastings. I showed them a map of England with the Norman Baronies marked in colour and I asked them to think how the Saxons must have felt when they lost their king and had been conquered. It was nearly lunchtime and the children became restless. In the afternoon they were still rather excited and rolling words like 'conquer', 'Norman' and 'William the first' around. They didn't seem to have any inclination to take it seriously. I began to realize the extent of the problems. How on earth was I going to make the topic stick and how was I going to get them involved in the disciplines of study?

I discussed this problem with Morag. She had already offered to take some of the children individually and gently probe them about what they already knew about the past, and about the work in hand as the term progressed. We were both curious to listen in to the way they constructed a sense of 'place' and a sense of 'time past'. That first afternoon she talked to Dominic, Terence (two of my four top infants) and Shinaz whose first language is Urdu.

At this stage all three of them were very vague about the significance of her questions. Shinaz was totally silent. When asked about their own houses on the estate they answered in monosyllables ... They were not sure how old ... Dominic thought Christ College might be old ... His mother worked there ... It was different because 'it had bedrooms for students'. Terence very hesitantly mentioned a church in the centre of town. What Morag and I were struck by was how their discourse and their appreciation of factual evidence became more sophisticated and assured once involved in narrative. They were all eager to tell her the story of William and Harold.

Morag (*after hearing this story*): What would they have in those days ... Would they have books ... ?
Dominic: Yes, because they wrote the Domesday Book because ... er ... Duke, King William sent all his men around Great Britain ... and they made a list ... all the men, all the animals, villages ... made the Domesday Book.
Morag: So would there be a lot of books then?
Dominic: I don't know.
Morag: Would there be as many books then as now?
Dominic: I don't know.

Once Dominic was outside the story he lost his bearings. Here is another example of how he only gathered factual material together within the coherence of a story:

Dominic (*after telling the story of the Battle of Hastings*): So at Christmas William was crowned king.
Morag: Where is Hastings?
Dominic: I don't know.
Morag: Is it in France or in Britain or somewhere else in the world?
Dominic: Oh in Britain. I think we've got a map with it on.

Because I was anxious not to become too involved with a 'history book' view of history I decided that it was essential to get the children out into the environment as soon as possible. I wanted to see whether they brought their predilection for narrative to concrete experiences. We walked down to the eighteenth-century parish church of St Andrews Chesterton (much restored) and spent the morning in the graveyard and church. We scraped away moss and lichen from headstones and noted dates and inscriptions. We sketched and copied fixtures and furnishings. In the afternoon we created our own graveyard mural in the classroom. Later Morag had a chance to interview three more of the children about this work.

This time the children seemed more aware of the significance of her questions. They could all see that the graveyard was 'old' and could tell us something about the past. They were still a little hazy about *what* it could tell us. One of the more imaginative children, Yvonne, simply invented her own highly embroidered version... keeping Morag fascinated by rich tales of 'Ancient Briton' headstones and Saxon graves. She even went so far as to introduce a few famous people:

Yvonne: There was one there for Florence Nightingale.
Morag: Uhuh... How long ago did Florence Nightingale live?
Yvonne: I can't remember.
Morag: As long ago as the Romans?
Yvonne: No I don't think so. It was just after the Angles had left... She was an Angle.
Morag: She was an Angle... Right... OK.

It was obvious to us both that Yvonne's rag bag of 'facts' was out of sequence and without the conceptual anchor of story actually impeded her understanding. For as soon as Morag asked her about the story of William the Conqueror she became accurate, cogent and displayed a knowledge of context.

Yvonne: ... and how Harold had broken his promise he would never take the throne of England over the bones of the saints... um... We decided that he lost the war between them because he knew he had broken a promise between them because they were really strong Christians then...

Morag and I also noticed how the children would cling tenaciously to their own interest in the details of a story, however irrelevant or far-fetched they might seem to adults. After Morag had asked Tessa some searching and sensitive questions about the history of the child's family and about the building of the housing around the school she asked her:

Morag: Is there anything else you would like to tell me about the past or ask me about history? Or anything you don't understand?
Tessa: Yes, There's one thing... about when... I mean there's a bit about Harold. He was waiting for the battle when every night he saw this thing in the sky that meant bad luck. He didn't actually know what it was... I can't remember what it was called but it had the head of a lady I think and the tail of a fish?

A week later we went on another trip. This time I took the class to the Fitzwilliam Museum to see the Greek and Roman collections, and on to the Cambridge marketplace to observe living history. We followed this up with some work from books on shopping in the past and how towns grew up around markets. We looked at maps of Cambridge and coloured in the river. We then traced the rivers on a huge three-dimensional map of Britain which clearly showed the Fens, Ely and East Anglia as low-lying country. Eventually we made a model of the Isle of Ely and we went to Wicken Fen and travelled into Ely by river. We discussed rivers and roads as communication links. The children were becoming more curious and I felt the project was beginning to form a shape in their minds.

However, their writing showed certain definite characteristics that were impossible to change; that is, they showed a general and deep distaste for any sort of transactional writing. Wherever we went, whatever we did and whatever concrete evidence and experiences I could provide them with they resisted the idea of recording them as straightforward factual reporting. In brief, they turned everything into narrative. But not exciting deeply-felt story, rather a low-level flat sequence of events. Within this form they were trapped: on the one hand, by certain features they knew they had to mention – for example when we went to the graveyard they knew they had to mention the tombstones – and, on the other hand, by some of the more clumsy conventions of story as they perceived it ... 'after breakfast it was time for school. After register we chose partners. I chose ...' Although the project appeared to be going well in some respects, the children's written response was in this grey monotone.

> Nature, not art, makes us all story tellers. Daily and nightly we devise fictions and chronicles, calling some of them daydreams or dreams, some of them nightmares, some of them truths, records, reports and plans. Some of them we call, or refuse to call, lies. Narrative imagination is a common human possession ...[6]

By half-way through the term I felt I could no longer set the natural narrative approach of the class to one side. In my anxiety to provide the children with concrete experiences that were directly related to their immediate environment, to show them bits and pieces of evidence of the past, I was ignoring the way they made sense of this material. I had to revise my own view of the way we learn history. I had in fact been playing devil's advocate, for it had struck me before that Piaget's developmental stages as setting the limits of children's thinking were too narrow.

If we accept with Barbara Hardy that we are all natural storytellers and listeners it is not surprising that narrative is the first stage of sustained written expression that young children produce. When they first come to school children can *tell* stories and have therefore already internalized most of the formal conventions that make a story cohere – a beginning and an end in time, a point, and closure. Andrew Wilkinson writes:

> Because life is chronological – events happen in time – then to relate what happens comes naturally. Quite young children can recount events in the order in which they happened. But what a 'story' requires is some sort of coherence, some logic of connection between the parts, some subordination or exclusion of less significant detail. And when the story is written the requirements become more rigorous.[7]

He, like me, had found that seven-year-olds frequently used narrative for writing tasks for which he considered it inappropriate – objective reporting and analytical argument. He goes on to provide an answer for this: 'the sheer mechanics of writing' and the lack of knowledge about the conventions of writing where the reader is only given partial information: 'a person speaking can often assume a good deal – his words are *context bound* ... a person writing ... must normally assume much less'. Things like where and why, reasons and explanations we expect to be 'woven into the texture of the writing ... In the writing of young children much of this information is often missing ... Basically the written style of most seven year olds is a spoken style.'[8]

While this is true, what I believe must be appreciated is that the way children write is not simply clumsiness with conventions but, like anyone's writing, *is a mirror of their understanding*. What had happened with my class was that I had mistakenly attempted to cut them off from the natural logic and coherence of their own narrative voice. Instead of drawing out the connections they themselves made inside their story of the trip to the market, I was trying to tell them significant points, to tell them to consider the form of the marketplace and its connections with communication links such as roads and rivers. But they had no natural form of written expression to create an inner map to make that sort of information cohere. Clearly children cannot be *prised* out of the 'primitive matrix'. When my class told me they 'liked the stories best', I began to see that it was only through story that historical information and experience made sense and were remembered.

Although this powerful link between narrative and understanding has been pointed out before, for example by Rosen,[9] there have been good reasons for history teachers to set these thoughts aside. Here is an example of what I was taught:

> With the coming of Queen Victoria to the throne in 1837, a new era opened in Britain. The crown acquired an honoured respect which had been sadly lacking for a long time. The Queen's example of domestic happiness was an inspiration to all, and due to pioneering inventiveness and hard work the country grew in prosperity.[10]

The book from which this extract is taken consists of 86 chapters, 61 of which are titled with the name of a famous person, usually a king or queen. Although it and many like it are based on stories, here I feel is history of the worst kind, really more a dangerous mythology. Whether one believes it or not, there is very little a modern child can relate to, or get any purchase on. Apart from all the amazing gaps in its substance, the rhetoric alone, with its high moral tone, is totally unbelievable to the modern post-war child. But although slightly more up to date in this respect, many of the modern story-type textbooks have a more fundamental problem.

The problem with these texts is the heroic aspect of their narrative approach to the past. If to have history stories with any real bite it is necessary to have great individuals, then we are stuck with a view of the past that devalues the experiences of ordinary people. The subordination or exclusion of less significant detail requires suppression of the lives of the majority of people. On the other hand, history is a vast series of stories and much of its fascination is lost if that aspect is neglected. However, this does not mean that we have to teach a grand narrative in the old style of, say, *A Pageant of History*.[11] History in the primary school can be built up from narrative fragments of all kinds to form a more dynamic base from which to view the past, preparing children with interpretative skills to use as they gather more evidence. Recent disillusionment with scientific methodology does not mean that we have to return to what Lawrence Stone[12] calls 'a paper-chase of ideas back through the ages'. He writes: 'One of the most striking recent changes in the content of history has been a quite sudden growth of interest in feelings, emotions, behaviour patterns, values, and states of mind.'

I was lucky enough to collaborate on this matter with another teacher on the staff, someone who had a wide knowledge of the children and had worked many times before on social history. She pointed out that children will readily identify with their own selves projected into a past time which has become tangible to them by environmental work and through artefacts, the 'what you would be wearing, seeing in your home, what you would be using for tasks' aspects. She offered to tell some real tales, based on the mass of things she knew about the history of the school, our street and, most importantly, the great school fire, five years before.

She came into the classroom and talked to the children about these matters, bringing with her old maps and photographs. Later she walked with the children around the school pointing out clues to its past in its physical fabric. Later on again in the term she told them about the fire that had devastated the school five years before and showed them the school photograph album with pictures of the debris and the building of the new school. While I pinned the pictures and maps on the wall the children listened fascinated. But what I felt was happening was not a growing concern with the physical evidence – the children did not spend much time looking and considering (although they did want to see with their own eyes) – rather, what was taking place was their increasing involvement with the ancient spell of story. The patchy bits and pieces of evidence with which they were somewhat off-hand at first were beginning to fit into a whole – but not a pictorial whole, more a *literary* one. What they remembered from her talking (she is a good teller of tales) was the way she put it together, her intonations, her selection and suppression of detail, her beginnings and ends in time, her points and closures. To put it another way, they were applying their own internal conventions to the stuff in hand. When I talked to them later they were very excited. They retold the story, lingering over details. Several of them claimed to remember the fire as though they had been there (they had in fact been two years old at the time and tucked up in bed). The story was amended this way and that: 'everything went black', 'the hamster died in the cage', 'people came to help clean up ... I was there'. They were not learning the 'facts' of the past; they were appreciating and teaching themselves about *the way it is told*. Thus it was the possibilities for self-expression at the interface between historical evidence and their own literary imaginations that interested them. The possibility of linking themselves into this story made it all the more powerful.

Eventually, through collaboration with an old friend, I found a way of developing this story-writing aspect of the work. But before then I had to consider in depth how next to develop the ideas.

Bit by bit I felt the children were beginning to get interested in the topic work generally and to get 'hooked' on the idea of time past. What I now wanted to draw out and emphasize was how time past must be valued and cherished by individual people. I felt we were ready to experience this in the people close to us. History at its deepest level is one of the ways in which we make sense of our experiences by enabling us to put our lives and experiences into a context and to tell our own story. Having worked at heightening this awareness, the time had come to work on memory. We were ready to hear how people older than us, who were close to us, remembered and shaped experiences and told us of events from time past.

It was our turn to produce a class assembly. I talked to the children about oral history and asked them to go home and question their parents about the things they remembered in their childhoods, particularly their schools and schooldays when they were about seven. Like many oral history projects it triggered off an exciting amount of interest and support. The children arrived at school every morning for the next week waving pieces of paper with interesting stories and details of school life by parents and grandparents. Occasionally a photograph or a piece of work was included. Some of the parents wrote several pages. We read all these out and had some lively discussions, but again what I felt and observed was that what interested the children the most was not the *facts* of the cases, school was not so very different then after all, it was rather the particular way that the different people expressed themselves. It was the way small incidents and peculiarities were shaped and described that made living testimony interesting. As Val Moore[13] also noted: 'Little details which capture the imagination are more real than facts and figures and the official version of history, it seems.'

Using these pieces of paper as a model we talked about the sorts of thing we might remember when we were old. The children were very funny and ironic and soon developed the knack of seeing themselves in this perspective. It was easy to form their comments into a play:

> I'll remember that we always tell jokes on the way to swimming on Mondays.
>
> I'll remember that your jokes aren't very funny ...
>
> We'll remember that Labour won the election ... [It was on the eve of the General Election – how wrong this memory idea turned out.]
>
> We'll remember that 1987 was the year the adventure playground was finished.
>
> It'll look pretty tatty in 60 years' time ... we'd better mention that.
>
> I know we could have old Mrs Hilton ... Gee you'll be old by then!

The play, which consisted of the whole class now grey and lame hobbling into the stage for a class reunion 60 years on and 'remembering' 1987, was a success. Old Mrs Hilton was brought forth out of retirement (she had shrunk considerably over the years) and the climax came with the elderly headteacher who had also shrunk to less than half his previous size, hobbling on to play a tune as the old head one last time. This was fun and the ideas had flowed easily for the children had been working from a creative model – the shape and expression of their own parents and grandparents' reminiscences.

At last I began to see a way forward with their writing that would be cutting *with* the grain of their conceptual approach rather than across it. I could see that it was now vital to give them a chance to write narrative prose, the form they naturally understood and yet to use an accurate historical context so that they might use their new inner historical vocabulary – when and why things had happened. This was a culmination of the topic because, having talked and written about and re-created bits and pieces of the past and heard how a feeling of time is constructed, what they were now going to do was to put themselves in it. I do not mean that I was going to ask them to be, say, one of William the First's Norman barons building a new castle and to write about it. I don't think they could have projected themselves into a contrived fictional historical situation of that sort – the sheer amount of information the children would have needed for that and also the experience of narrative conventions of that order were beyond most of them at their young age. What I needed was an older person who could talk about his or her own childhood in such a way that it would open up a special dialogue with the children. I needed someone who was skilled enough to shape their own experiences in the twilight zone between speech and written story so that the writing conventions would be close to the children's own. This would give them a working model to draw out their stories from their own memory store and to set their inner feelings into a context. The person needed, too, to be able to tell his or her stories in a small way but with a sense of historical importance so that the children would be encouraged to order their own experiences in the same way. I found someone who had worked with children for many years, a retired primary schoolteacher.

I went to her house and asked her to talk into a tape-recorder, to reminisce, to talk about events in her past, particularly when she was about seven. Her knowledge of children had given her the knack of making each small story interesting and closed and complete in itself, and yet with underlying concept of 'continuity and change' always present. At the end of a few of the stories of her childhood she invited the children to write to her about similar and different things that had happened to them.

I was amazed at the enthusiasm with which the children took to this work. When I asked them who wanted to write back they all put up their hands. They seemed to have been almost bottled up over the weeks of historical investigation and my friend had at last given them the chance to write their own 'history' from memory. During the first two terms with them I had often asked them to write about themselves and their experiences and I had often given them headings and ideas, but now they had a more developed sense of time cherished as stories and memorabilia, and they had a working creative model that was in line with their own writing 'voice'. Somehow the history work had also given a boost to their own self-consequence. It had enabled them to see themselves as actors on the stage of history. This was the final process in which they could write about themselves as people with a rich store of memories that were worth recording and that other people outside the classroom wanted to hear about.

As she had promised, my friend Miss White wrote back to every single child who had written to her. On receiving a letter the child would sit down and immediately write again. I felt excited that we had broken the mould of monologue. What we had now was a *dialogue* between people who both had rich and important memories. Another fascinating feature of the work was how the children nearly all abandoned the more pedestrian conventions that they had been stuck with – 'I got up in the morning and I had cornflakes for breakfast' – *and* because there was a dialogue they came straight to the heart of the matter as they do in speech.

When I heard you on the tape I thought the first thing I would like to ask you is Did you have playtimes?

Schools have changed alot since you went to school Miss White, we do not have forms like you used to have. In the morning we sit on the carpet for register.

I would like to tell you a story about when my shoe was stuck on the roof.

With the new historical perspective the children appeared to craft their writing more effectively and they opened and closed their stories in time more artistically:

I have always remembered Mondays better than other days ...

A few days and weeks ago I was sitting in a building site ...

When I was in the Infants we used to play with tyres. This was quite a long time ago ...

We ran home. I got told off for being late for dinner ... [This was ironic for Saul had been very naughty.]

I hid the broken one at dinner time because at our school if you were naughty you would be sent by the wall.

Miss White encouraged them to come to terms with some quite traumatic experiences by pointing out to them how we moved on in time and that we grew and developed. 'I am sure you would never want to do that again' was one of her refrains. 'I am sure that most unusual thing would never happen again.' She helped them with context by describing her home and school (she was born in Yorkshire and is now over 80). She told them of school life, its work, injustices, joys and punishments, underlining the fact for them that, although the parameters change, there is a unity in human experience. They replied with:

> *When I fell off the infant climbing frame the headmaster took me to his office and layed me down on the poorly bed and he called my mum and she came straight away and took me home.*
>
> *I have a comic called Beano and that does not say that if you rub orange peel on your hand it will break the cane. We do not have canes anymore.*
> *P.S. Your writing is very nice for 79.*

Even my poorest writers struggled to present their experiences in context:

> *I got 2 pages of sums wrong. It was not fair I was in class 4* at the time *and I was only 5* at the time *and I had to stand in the corner* [emphasis added].

My more able writers, such as quiet little Kathy, could achieve remarkable expression of anxiety with comic irony:

> *My story isn't quite about getting told off, but I thought I would! Well, on mondays we had choir. Now one day I was late. I didn't hear the choir whistle, and Miss Field noticed that I wasn't there, because she couldn't hear me playing the recorder. When I came she looked at me. When choir ended, my friend Paul told me that Miss Field wanted to see me in her room after break. With that my relief that choir was over diappeared completely – I even wished we could do it over again a thousand times! Break ended in five minutes, and I began to feel worried. I went to her room. It took a long time to make her notice that I was there. Then she saw me. But of course she only wanted to know why I had been late.*

As a result of this collaboration (which could have gone on and on as both parties were willing, but the term brought it to a close), and the strength of the writing that it produced, I feel strongly that teaching history to young children is indeed a matter of bringing factual 'concrete' material and experiences into their lives – and then marrying that work to the children's own writing voice. For the way they write is a mirror of the inner map and hangs together in the same way. It would therefore be an over-simplification to say the children in my class liked stories: they loved stories because they hung all their experiences together with story. They made sense of the present and the past with story. They were story-listeners and could come to historical understanding through storytelling. Again and again, when they were asked factual questions, they responded by detailed reference to the coherence and logic of a story. 'How do we know?' 'What happened and when?' 'Why did it happen?' The answers to these historical questions, requiring them to use historical ideas and evidence, grew out of the children's intuitive understanding and love of narrative. This collaboration, following on from the work on history, gave the children a chance to project themselves as writers into their own memory of time past – the first historical context – and showed how skilled they were at constructing the earliest and most important form of historical narrative.

Notes

1. P. J. Rogers in A. K. Dickinson, P. J. Lee and P. J. Rogers, *Learning History*, Heinemann, 1984.
2. Northrop Frye, quoted in Paul Fussel, *The Great War and Modern Memory*, Oxford University Press, 1975.
3. G. Kitson Clark, *The Critical Historian*, Heinemann, 1967.
4. Margaret Donaldson, *Children's Minds*, Collins, 1978.
5. Robert Leeson, *Reading and Righting*, 1985.
6. Barbara Hardy, *Tellers and Listeners: the Narrative Imagination*, University of London/Athlone Press, 1980.
7. Andrew Wilkinson, *Assessing Language Development*, Oxford University Press, 1980.
8. Ibid.
9. Harold Rosen, *Stories and Meanings*, NATE (no date).
10. R. Purton *et al.*, *A Pageant of History*, Collins, 1968.
11. Ibid.
12. Lawrence Stone, *The Past and the Present*, Routledge & Kegan Paul, 1981.
13. Val Moore, quoted in Sally Purkis, 'Personalizing the past: oral history in schools', in T. Booth, T. Potts and W. Swann, *Preventing Difficulties in Learning Curricula for All*, Basil Blackwell, 1987.

PART FIVE
Endpiece

15 Teachers as collaborators

MORAG STYLES

Of all the unusual and exciting collaborations we engaged in, perhaps the most rewarding was within our own group – the exchange of views and experience between teachers from different phases of education was often heady. Under normal circumstances teachers tend to mix with others from the same school, subject area or particular age group. We spanned pupils from six to 18 and found the cross-fertilization rich. In this final chapter I want to unpick several different strands of our collaboration: to give proper weight and value to classroom research by teachers; to look closely at aspects of teachers (and trainers and inspectors) working together; to find out what the teachers had to say about collaborating on this project; and finally, what we found out about the writing process, learning and, indeed, ourselves from contributing to this book, the major whole-group experience of the project.

The last collaboration of all was my invitation to Eve Bearne of the National Writing Project to describe her impressions of our project. Eve wrote as follows:

> All my experience so far, working with teacher colleagues and student teachers, has led me to believe that there is an alchemy which operates when teachers get together to discuss classroom practice. Dialogues with colleagues offer opportunities for stepping outside the close confines of the individual classroom. By making explicit the ways in which learning is organised teachers are able to examine what they want to achieve. Work with children in collaborative settings demonstrates the power of talk to move ideas further; this is equally true of teachers. Similarly, there is the point about ownership of learning. Previous models of inservice have tended to be based on the idea that some people have expertise which they can tell other people about and so make things better. This is, of course, partly true, but it does rather suggest a 'top down' approach, even a kind of medical image of a doctor handing out medicine to make things better! I've recently been saying to people that my view of inservice is not 'doing things to teachers' but rather 'teachers doing things'.
>
> All the points we would want to make about effective learning in the classroom hold true for teachers developing their own practice. There needs to be some purpose or motivation, some relevance in the task, opportunities for sharing ideas, exchanging opinions and choosing areas of investigation, frameworks which will extend and challenge, advice from more practised people, status given to individual

experience, the chance to explain and justify beliefs and scope to experiment, revise and change. All of these depend upon an environment which will support and stimulate ideas. I think that this brief description applies both to the best of classroom practice and the best in teacher research. We can only theorise from a base of experience; what is needed is an opportunity to keep revisiting our own learning so as to place new experiences beside more established ideas. Meetings between teachers offer such opportunities. They need, of course, to be facilitated and structured, which is why a college of education or local authority advisers are essential to a continuing programme of teacher investigations. This moves collaboration up another notch. It has to be built into some kind of broader framework of education if it is to become an established way of working and so actually change classrooms for the better.

The history of teacher education and inservice which has often been built on the transmission model has to be unlearned, in the same way that children have to unlearn ideas about surface feature correctness being the most important thing about a piece of writing. When traditional methods are removed there is often a sense of anxiety. In children it is a fear that they are at fault if their spellings aren't right first time. For teachers, in my experience, there is a sense that they want someone else, an 'authority' on education, to tell them what to do – until, by getting together with colleagues and by having a framework which will enable them to investigate their own classroom concerns, they begin to see that they do have something valuable to contribute.

I am also convinced that there is a sort of 'cycle' in teachers developing themselves professionally. It begins with an idea about teaching/learning which the teacher wants to pursue – it may be a worry or a dissatisfaction, or just something new which has occurred from reading, talking or hearing someone else's ideas. After a period of looking at the classroom anew in the light of this and getting together with colleagues in order to make explicit the area of investigation, there is, I feel, a need (not necessarily felt by the teacher her/himself) to make sense of the new experiences, activities or investigations by writing about them or presenting them to colleagues in a more formal setting. This helps to clarify all sorts of half formed thoughts and gives the spur to taking the work further. What I'm trying to say is that just talking with colleagues, stimulating and comforting as it may be, is not enough; there needs to be some kind of structure which will require a more consciously explicit examination of the issues raised in conversations. This takes us back to a facilitating agency like higher education or the framework offered in a local authority. Publishing, either by running sessions for colleagues or by printed dissemination of ideas, plays a crucial role in helping teachers to theorise their own practice.

So that *your* collaboration with colleagues operates on several levels:

- [look] at children collaborating in the classroom;
- [work] with other teachers to examine practice;
- [join] with a teacher educator within an institution;
- [talk] to others like John Richmond, Myra Barrs or me who are from other places;
- [publish] ideas jointly;
- and so [share] ideas with a much wider audience ...

Teachers learning together as a group

It was beneficial, in the first instance, purely to meet regularly to discuss writing. With our varying backgrounds, new ideas and fresh perspectives were constantly thrown up, different types of classroom practice identified, practice pulled apart, comparisons made. It felt good to be able to discuss issues relating to writing with a sympathetic audience who understood all the trials and pleasures of the job.

Although we ended up with two people in their first year of teaching when the project began, the rest of the group were very experienced and we were all of a similar age (35–40 or so). Perhaps this was one reason why the group gelled so well. We included Scale 1 teachers (now an outdated term), Heads of English, eventually an Inspector for English and all the range in between, but there were *no* status distinctions. We had made a pact to collaborate, we all respected each other's strengths so, perhaps, this made us a fairly ideal group for commenting constructively on each other's work. Nobody pulled rank, nobody attempted to dominate discussions.

Our meetings certainly raised the intellectual level of our daily professional pursuits. Ideas buzzed back and forth, lively suggestions were taken up, inspirational practice was presented as a matter of course. Our work was subject to scrutiny by the group: no one would get away with sloppy thinking. Our teaching sharpened up, depth was added to our planning, and rigorous analysis of our endeavours became the norm. Busy, already well-read teachers eagerly snatched up new texts on their particular areas of interest. Perhaps most importantly, some of us reinterpreted our role in the classroom as facilitators and collaborators with young writers. We were more keen than ever to talk to our pupils about writing and to *listen* to their replies.

Recent and relevant school experience – a college lecturer collaborates with a teacher

When my turn came round (fortuitously while the project was running) to go into school for 'recent and relevant' classroom experience, I automatically looked to work with a member of the group. I was lucky to be able to collaborate closely with a colleague on what turned out to be a Shakespeare Project for top juniors. Although I did most of the research, lesson preparation and teaching, I discussed most ideas with Gareth Davies beforehand, and we scrutinized successes and failures afterwards. We spent a lot of time talking about the responses of individual children, a great bonus for us and them. Gareth often came up with new ideas, cautioned restraint on some of my wilder plans, but gave me the space to try hunches and develop the project as I wished. We probably both worked harder than we have ever done before – having two people in the classroom didn't feel like a luxury at all.[1] My mistakes and shortcomings were very evident to Gareth as, indeed, were his to me. Neither of us felt threatened or worried by the fact that our deficiencies as well as our qualities as teachers were spotlighted for the other. We supported, encouraged and learned from each other all the time.

If opportunities could be made for teachers, tutors, advisers, inspectors and HMI to become involved in non-hierarchical classroom collaborations, perhaps we would all understand each other better.

Collaborating with teachers in their classrooms

Kate Oswald and I had enough freedom in our timetables to visit most of the teachers in their classrooms and to work alongside them on one or more occasions during the project. It was a great pleasure to collaborate with group members, meet their pupils at last and become actively involved in their 're-search'. We did as we were invited – sometimes it was to teach, freeing the teacher to observe; other times we interviewed pupils or took notes on a particular collaboration. We always discussed the enterprise fully afterwards. What follows is a summary of the benefits of these exchanges as outlined by the teachers.

- They enjoyed shared teaching (none of the group was currently team teaching).
- It felt good to be able to discuss individual children with someone else really concerned with their progress. Teachers get very involved with their pupils and there are not always many others keen to know the details of Valerie or Sam's latest piece of work or behaviour, if colleagues are not sympathetic. (In my experience, partners get very bored with this type of conversation!)
- Outside interest in their pupils' work raised its status and encouraged teachers to take their pupils' writing more seriously.
- Positive feedback helped teachers explore the success of the particular venture with which they had been engaged. All too often, on their own, they reflected gloomily on what went wrong. (This tends to be the case more often with very committed teachers with high expectations – they are over-critical of themselves.)

If one thinks of teacher appraisal for a moment, the current models on offer favour a 'bottom-up' or 'top-down' approach. Ours was more of a sideways-on approach – mutual appraisal of action research along 'teacher self-evaluation' lines. Certainly we were forced to examine our practice and share the results with the rest of the group. Nobody's confidence was destroyed, nobody felt threatened, but it did help us improve as teachers particularly in understanding better how our pupils learned. Perhaps at a time when teacher-appraisal is a hot issue, there is something to be learned from our experience.

Collaborating on *Collaboration and Writing*

'It's hard to be a teacher and a writer', said a member of the group. 'And an editor', I thought. I have, of course, since sworn that I will never again edit a book with a lot of different contributors! One has to learn how to coax, bully, encourage; be honest, tactful, tough, patient and to know which stance is right at any given time. If I had not been determined to produce this book, it would never have been written. All the contributors were solid, reliable folk with an investment in the project, so why was it so difficult to get the promised work? The simple reason was that writing is very hard work and each person found the task gruelling. Some found it impossible to clear the time necessary for writing. Others were tempted to go down new, exciting roads – much more fun than trying to make their work with children intelligible to a reader. Everyone was surprised at the ordeal of writing and these were enthusiastic teachers of writing! Everyone at some point lacked confidence in their writing. All are very glad they did it. So what have we learned about the process of writing from our experiences on this book?

Contributors' comments

> I couldn't write for a long time – I was more interested in doing the work with the children than in getting down thoughts about it. It began to come together in my mind at odd moments during the day and especially when the term was over and I was mentally reviewing my work with the children.
>
> The first stage was seeing if I really had something worth saying – acres of doubt – writing fragments at different times – working backwards, forwards ...
>
> It's quite hard to finish the work, though. The more you add to it or redraft it the more there seems to say!
>
> I was reading on the train when I suddenly felt I could write my chapter. I wanted to begin before I got to Liverpool Street and jotted down notes on scrap paper. I was afraid I'd lose my ideas and clarity of thought. I felt very clear headed and positive.
>
> Once under pressure I felt the ideas and the language flowed quicker than I could write. I enjoyed myself immensely.
>
> I reached a point where I felt I had learnt as much as I was going to learn. Redrafting then became painful. In fact I was wrong – I continued to learn more from what I had already written.
>
> I had to talk things out first with close friends.
>
> Trying to write keeps one at the frontier of the process – helps one understand all writers.
>
> Writing is about ultimate fulfilment, because there are few thrills in the short term ...

So much about the writing process here, and yet nothing new. Of course not – but the writers had to find out for themselves the nature of writing. It is quite another thing to know that it is difficult because you had read it and observed pupils as they struggled. Our insights can be summarized as follows:

On teachers	On pupils
We found out a lot of things about writing by writing ourselves.	Teachers do not only provide good models for writing by working alongside their pupils, they learn more about writing themselves.
Effective writing does not always happen when you want it to.	Can we be more sensitive to the difficulties faced by young writers?
On the other hand, the pressure of approaching deadlines can be a great spur.	Sometimes requiring assignments at a set time can jolt the writer into action – the point is flexibility.
When the writing flows it can give great satisfaction to the writer.	By means of help with handwriting fluency, use of word processor, being given meaningful writing tasks (sometimes pupil-generated) the child is more likely to experience writing 'flow' (when the writing almost writes itself) and learn about the pleasures of writing.
Writing for a real audience is more meaningful and demanding than exercise writing.	We need to be aware of the demands of writing for a real readership.
We learn as we write.	Can we share this knowledge with our pupils? Once again, we return to John Richmond's point about writing as a 'unique road to understanding'.
Planning – organization before writing can aid clarity.	Do we spend enough time teaching our pupils the tools of planning?
Redrafting was the hardest part of writing.	Most of us are now convinced of the advantages of pupils' redrafting their writing, but we ought to be aware how hard it is for them and use this strategy sparingly. (Some teachers ask pupils to redraft everything.)
Everybody's timetable for writing was unique.	How can we run flexible classrooms so that we make allowances for each individual unique 'timetable' for writing?
Adult writers can be very uncertain of the value of their own writing.	Young writers can be very uncertain of the value of their own writing.

Beginnings and endings can be tricky, making yourself start, knowing when you've finished.	Beginnings and endings can be tricky, making yourself start, knowing when you've finished.
Keeping a notebook handy for good ideas is useful. They can strike at the oddest moments. Recognizing an odd line of argument can happen falling asleep, riding a bike, in a train …	Encourage pupils to carry a writer's notebook!
Teachers are pleased when their writing is typed neatly, it looks better, reads better.	Pupils are pleased when their writing is typed neatly, it looks better, reads better.
Writing is hard! There is little enjoyment in the process, but tremendous satisfaction from doing it.	Reinforce our pupils' knowledge of writing for a real reason – communicating with others and understanding things better ourselves.
Writers need praise and encouragement.	Pupils need praise and encouragement from teachers for their writing.
Talking, before writing, helped in composition.	Talking, before writing, helped in composition.
When the writing is hardest, we often learn most.	We could explain to our pupils that we learn by grappling with ideas and struggling to provide coherence in written language.

We also learned, of course, about the satisfactions of writing. Communication is at the heart of much writing and contributors gained reassurance from positive comments by other members of the group.

Sometimes we asked ourselves why we had chosen to put ourselves through the painful process of writing for an outside readership. Some of the answers are obvious – but perhaps the most significant was that our project now had not only a goal but an end product. Teaching is relentless, it never really ends. And you rarely see the fruits of your work. You have to trust that all the effort has been worthwhile. At least in this book we could attempt to capture little patches of our enterprise, thread them together in a motley tapestry for others to share.

At the heart of the National Writing Project has been the practice of teachers working together to learn about writing. To quote Eve Bearne:

> With the imminent dissolution of the National Writing Project in its original form I'm very cheered that groups such as yours are working in a way which parallels the working groups of the National Writing Project. All of these initiatives are giving a

model for teacher-led investigations which supports the kind of inservice structure which now operates. School based inservice is already benefiting from people's experience of 'becoming their own experts'. And, neatly, it all boils down to collaborative practices. I'm hearing more and more as I trip around England and Wales that teachers want to establish their own groups and, cheeringly, the question I get asked most nowadays is not so much 'how can I do it on a busy day?' but 'how can I encourage my children to collaborate?'

Our final collaboration is with our readers. We hope that by writing this book we can tempt other teachers to form their own groups and find out for themselves the benefits of supporting each other and working together on a collaborative enterprise.

Notes

1. For a fuller account of this project, see M. Styles, '"Pyramus Loves Thisbe" – a Shakespeare Project in the Primary School' in *Cambridge Journal of Education*, vol. 18, no. 1, Lent 1988.

Bibliography

The bibliography that follows reflects the background reading about writing which underpinned our 'research'. It was compiled by Frances D. Findlay.

Adams, A. (ed.), *New Directions in English Teaching*, Falmer Press, 1982.
Armstrong, M., *Closely Observed Children*, Writers and Readers/Chameleon, 1980.
Barrs, M., *et al.*, *What's Going On?*, Boynton-Cook, 1982.
Barrs, M., *et al.*, *The Primary Language Record*, ILEA, 1988.
Beard, R., *Children's Writing in the Primary School*, Hodder and Stoughton, 1984.
Britton, J., *The Development of Writing Abilities (11–18)*, Macmillan, 1975.
Burgess, C., *et al.*, *Understanding Children Writing*, Penguin, 1973.
Clay, M., *What Did I Write? Beginning Writing Behaviour*, Heinemann, 1975.
Cowie, H., *The Development of Children's Imaginative Writing*, Croom Helm, 1984.
Dixon, A., 'Story Boxes', *Cambridge Journal of Education*, vol. 17, no. 3, 1987.
Dixon, J., *Growth Through English* (2nd edn), Oxford, 1969.
Dixon, J. (ed.), *Proposals for Coursework*, NATE, 1986.
Dixon, J., and Masterson, P., *Making a Start: English Coursework*, NATE, 1987.
Dixon, J., and Stratta, L., *Achievements in Writing at 16+*, University of Birmingham, 1982.
Dixon, J., and Stratta, L., *Writing Beyond Narrative*, Canadian Council of Teachers of English, distributed by NATE, 1986.
Dunn, J., Styles, M., and Warburton, N., *In Tune with Yourself*, Cambridge University Press, 1987.
Goelman, H., *et al.*, *Awakening to Literacy*, Heinemann, 1984.
Graves, D., *Writing: Teachers and Children at Work*, Heinemann, 1983.
Graves, D., *A Researcher Learns to Write*, Heinemann, 1986.
Hackman, S., *Responding to Writing*, NATE, 1987.
Hadley, E., *English in the Middle Years*, Edward Arnold, 1983.
Hall, N., *The Emergence of Literacy*, Hodder and Stoughton, 1987.
Harris, J., and Williamson, J., *Reading Children's Writing*, Allen & Unwin, 1987.
Harrison, B., *Learning Through Writing*, NFER/Nelson, 1983.
Hoffman, M., *Reading, Writing and Relevance*, Hodder and Stoughton, 1970.
Holbrook, D., *Children's Writing*, Cambridge University Press, 1967.
Holdaway, D., *Foundations of Literacy*, Ashton Scholastic, 1979.

Horner, S. (ed.), *Best Laid Plans*, Longman for the Schools Council/NATE, 1983.
Hughes, T., *Poetry in the Making*, Faber, 1967.
ILEA, *The English Curriculum: Writing*, Materials for Discussion (no date).
Jackson, D., *Continuity in English Teaching*, Methuen, 1982.
Jones, A., and Mulford, J. (eds), *Children Using Language*, Oxford, 1971.
Knott, R., *The English Department in a Changing World*, Open University Press, 1985.
Kress, G., *Learning to Write*, Routledge and Kegan Paul, 1982.
Lightfoot, M. (ed.), *The Name for Teaching is Learning*, Methuen, 1988.
Marshall, S., *Experiment in Education*, Cambridge University Press, 1963.
Martin, N., *Mostly About Writing*, Boynton-Cook, 1983.
Martin, N., et al., *Writing and Learning across the Curriculum 11–16*, Ward Lock, 1976.
Medway, P., *Finding a Language*, Writers and Readers/Chameleon, 1980.
Meek, M., et al., *Achieving Literacy*, Routledge, 1983.
Meek, M., et al. (eds), *Changing English: Essays for Harold Rosen*, Heinemann, 1984
Meek, M., and Mills, C. (eds), *Language and Literacy in the Primary School*, Falmer Press, 1988.
Murray, D., *Learning by Teaching*, Boynton-Cook, 1982.
Minns, H., et al., *English 3*, Ward Lock, 1981.
Moffet, J., *Teaching and Universe of Discourse*, Houghton Mifflin, 1968.
Pearce, J., *The Heart of English*, Oxford University Press, 1985.
Perara, K., *Children's Writing and Reading – Analysing Classroom Language*, Basil Blackwell, 1984.
Protherough, R., *Encouraging Writing*, Methuen, 1983.
Raban, B. (ed.), *Practical Ways to Teach Writing*, Ward Lock, 1985.
Robinson, B., *Microcomputers and the Language Arts*, Open University Press, 1985.
Rosen, C., and Rosen, H., *Language of Primary School Children*, Penguin, 1975.
Rosen, H., *Stories and Meanings*, NATE (no date).
Smith, F., *Writing and the Writer*, Heinemann, 1982.
Smith, F., *Essays into Literacy*, Heinemann, 1983.
Steedman, C., *The Tidy House*, Virago, 1983.
Stibbs, A., *Assessing Children's Language*, Ward Lock/NATE, 1979.
Tizard, B., and Hughes, M., *Young Children Learning*, Collins/Fontana, 1984.
Torbe, M., *Language Policies in Action*, Ward Lock, 1980.
Watson, K., *English Teaching in Perspective*, Open University Press, 1987.
Wells, G. (ed.), *Language Through Interaction*, Cambridge University Press, 1981.
Wells, G., *The Meaning Makers*, Hodder and Stoughton, 1986.
Wilkinson, A., *Assessing Language Development*, Oxford University Press, 1980.
Wilkinson, A., *The Quality of Writing*, Open University Press, 1986.
Wilkinson, A. (ed.), *The Writing of Writing*, Open University Press, 1986.

Articles, journals, pamphlets

Centre for Language in Primary Education (CLPE)/ILEA, 'Writing and the Developing Child', *Language Matters*, 1–2, 1983.
'Shared writing', *Language Matters*, 1–2, 1985.
Cleveland English Curriculum Paper 1, *Draft Writing in English* (no date), Committee on Primary Education.
Scottish Committee on Language Arts in Primary Schools, *Hand in Your Writing* (1982). Responding to *To Children's Writing* (1986), *Mr Togs the Tailor – A Context for Writing* (1982), *Foundations of Writing* (1986).

S. Horner, *All in a Week's Work*, Report of First Stage of Sheffield Writing at Transition Project SCDC for National Writing Project, 1986.

National Writing Project, seven Occasional Papers:
1. Margaret Wallen, *A Writing Community*
2. Sue Horner, *Thinking, Learning, Writing*
3. Liz Vicary, *Writing and Work*
4. Georgina Herring, *The Bookmaking Project*
5. Pam Czerniewska, *Objectives for Language Learning*
6. Pam Czerniewska et al., *Writing Development – The Early Years*
7. Sue Horner et al., *Writing and Liaison*

National Writing Project, *About Writing* (newsletter).

Perera, K., *Understanding Language*, National Association of Advisers in English/NATE, 1987.

Smith, F., *Collaboration in the Classroom*, Reading and Language Information Centre, Reading University, 1984.

Smith, F., *Joining the Literacy Club*, Reading and Language Information Centre, Reading University, 1984.

Author index

Adams, Anthony, viii–xi, 43, 53
Ascherson, Neil, 165, 177
Asimov, Isaac, 77, 78

Baldwin, Michael, 129, 130, 132
Barrs, Myra, 2, 11, 15, 30, 32, 36, 41
Bazalgette, Cary, 136, 149
Bearne, Eve, x, 4, 5, 195, 196, 201, 202
Blanchard John, 43, 44, 53
Booth, Tony, 191
Britton, James, 60, 78
Brown, Nick, 42–53, 57–62
Bruner, Jerome, 121, 132
Bullock, Alan, 87, 89

Chambers, Aidan, 71, 78
Chater, Pauline, 42, 53
Chatwin, Bruce, 49, 50
Cliff Hodges, Gabrielle, 70–3, 165–77
Coleridge, Samuel T., 131, 132
Creasey, Martin, 86, 89

Davies, Gareth, 16–29, 93–105, 197
Dean, Joan, 87, 89
Defoe, Daniel, 122
Dixon, Annabelle, 35, 41
Donaldson, Margaret, 181, 191
Dunn, Jennie, 9, 10, 12, 13–15, 153–64

Eagleton, Terry, 165, 177

Frank, Ann, 29
Findlay, Frances, 79–89, 203
Frye, Northrop, 178, 191

Garner, Alan, 10

Graves, Donald, 40, 41

Harding, D. W., 73, 78
Hardy, Barbara, 184, 191
Harpin, William, 37, 41
Harrison, Gregory, 36, 41
Heathcote, Dorothy, 137, 149
Herbert, James, 49
Hilton, Mary, 57, 60–2, 178–91
Horner, Sue, 79, 89
Howker, Janni, 172, 177
Hughes, Monica, 26, 29
Hughes, Ted, 25, 29, 123, 124, 132

Jackson, David, 174, 177

Kemp, Gene, 45, 48
Kitson, Clark G., 179, 191
Knott, Richard, 79, 89

Leeson, Robert, 181, 191
Lessing, Doris, 15
Levi-Strauss, Claude, 121, 132
Lewis, C. S., 10
Little, Joan, 26

MacNeice, Louis, 161
Mandelstam, Osip, 176, 177
Marland, Michael, 87, 89
Martin, Mary, 120–32
Masterman, Len, 136, 149
Meek, Margaret, 15, 78
Miller, George, 3, 6
Moore, Val, 187, 191
Murray, Donald, 37, 40, 41

O'Brien, Robert, 45, 48
Oswald, Kate, 1, 198

Pearce, Philippa, 169, 177
Phillips, Tom, 138
Piaget, Jean, 184
Pompe, Cathy, 62–9, 73–8, 133–49
Purkis, Sally, 191

Richards, Colin, 89
Richmond, John, 2, 3, 4, 17, 196
Rogers, J., 178
Rosen, Harold, 185, 191
Rosen, Michael, 23

Shakespeare, William, 197, 202
Singer, Isaac Bashevis, 166, 177
Smith, Frank, 2, 3, 6, 94, 102, 105
Somerville, David, 30–41

Southon, Jo, 62, 63, 66, 67, 68, 69, 106–19
Stanier, Tom, 77, 78
Stone, Brenda, 138
Stone, Lawrence, 191
Styles, Morag, 1–6, 9–13, 22, 37–9, 57–62, 178, 181–3, 195–202

Thornton, Geoffrey, 43, 53
Tolkien, J. R. R., 10, 13

Walsh, Brian, 86, 89
Wells, Gordon, 1, 6
Wilder, Laura Ingalls, 77, 78
Wilkinson, Andrew, 17, 29, 184, 191
Wright, Peter, 49

Young, Helen, 34, 41